Stoicism

Ancient Philosophies

This series provides fresh and engaging new introductions to the major schools of philosophy of antiquity. Designed for students of philosophy and classics, the books offer clear and rigorous presentation of core ideas and lay the foundation for a thorough understanding of their subjects. Primary texts are handled in translation and the readers are provided with useful glossaries, chronologies and guides to the primary source material.

Published

The Ancient Commentators
on Plato and Aristotle
Miira Tuominen

Ancient Scepticism
Harald Thorsrud

Cynics
William Desmond

Epicureanism
Tim O'Keefe

Neoplatonism
Pauliina Remes

Plato
Andrew S. Mason

Presocratics
James Warren

Stoicism
John Sellars

Forthcoming

Classical Islamic Philosophy
Deborah Black

Confucianism
Paul R. Goldin

Indian Buddhist Philosophy
Amber Carpenter

Stoicism

John Sellars

Routledge
Taylor & Francis Group

LONDON AND NEW YORK

First published 2006 by Acumen

Published 2014 by Routledge
2 Park Square, Milton Park, Abingdon, Oxon OX14 4RN
711 Third Avenue, New York, NY 10017, USA

*Routledge is an imprint of the Taylor & Francis Group,
an informa business*

Notices
Practitioners and researchers must always rely on
their own experience and knowledge in evaluating
and using any information, methods, compounds, or
experiments described herein. In using such
information or methods they should be mindful of
their own safety and the safety of others, including
parties for whom they have a professional responsibility.

To the fullest extent of the law, neither the Publisher
nor the authors, contributors, or editors, assume any
liability for any injury and/or damage to persons or
property as a matter of products liability, negligence
or otherwise, or from any use or operation of any
methods, products, instructions, or ideas contained in
the material herein.

ISBN: 978-1-84465-052-1 (hardcover)
ISBN: 978-1-84465-053-8 (paperback)

British Library Cataloguing-in-Publication Data
A catalogue record for this book is available
from the British Library.

Designed and typeset in Minion.

Dedicated to the memory of Gloria Walker, a true Stoic

Contents

Preface

Stoicism was one of the most influential schools of philosophy in antiquity and its influence has persisted to the present day. Originating in Athens around 300 BCE, it proved especially popular in the Roman world, while more recently it has influenced thinkers as diverse as Montaigne, Kant, Nietzsche and Deleuze. Stoicism offers a distinctive and challenging view of both the world as a whole and the individual human being. It conceives the world materialistically and deterministically as a unified whole, of which we are all parts. It presents the human being as a thoroughly rational animal, for whom violent emotions are actually the product of errors in reasoning. In the popular imagination it is now mainly associated with the ideas of emotionless calm and heroic endurance in the face of adversity. As we shall see, like so many popular images this one is based on an element of truth combined with an unhappy distortion.

The aim of this volume is to offer an introduction to Stoic philosophy for readers new to Stoicism and it does not assume any knowledge of either ancient philosophy or philosophy in general. It should be of use to students of philosophy, students of classics and other interested general readers. As well as outlining the central philosophical ideas of Stoicism, one of its aims is to introduce the reader to the different ancient authors and sources that they will encounter when exploring Stoicism. The range of sources that are drawn on in the reconstruction of Stoic philosophy can be bewildering for the unsuspecting beginner. This, in part, reflects the fact that the works of the early Stoics are almost completely lost, save for fragments reported by others and summaries of their ideas by, often hostile, critics. Works by later Stoics writing in the Roman period – the most famous being Seneca and Marcus Aurelius – do survive, but these have often been deprecated as unoriginal and limited to practical ethics. In this introduction I shall pay equal attention to what we know about the early Stoics and the surviving texts associated with the later Stoics.

Chapter 1 offers an introduction to the ancient Stoics themselves, their works and other ancient authors who report material about ancient Stoic philosophy. Chapter 2 considers how the Stoics themselves conceived philosophy and how they structured their own philosophical system. Chapters 3, 4 and 5 offer accounts of Stoic philosophical doctrines arranged according to the Stoic division of philosophical discourse into three parts: logic, physics and ethics. Chapter 6 offers a brief sketch of the later impact of Stoicism on Western philosophy. At the end of the volume there is a detailed guide to further reading.

It goes without saying that in an introduction of this sort some topics have been omitted and others dealt with only briefly. It has not been possible to discuss competing interpretations of some points, and the treatments here will inevitably appear somewhat superficial to those already well acquainted with the ancient sources and scholarly literature. I do not claim that the interpretations that I offer here are definitive and part of the reason for supplying a fairly detailed guide to further reading is to encourage readers to explore other accounts of Stoic philosophy for themselves. If readers are suitably inspired to delve further into the subject then this volume will have served its purpose well.

This volume was written during the tenure of a Junior Research Fellowship at Wolfson College, Oxford, and I should like to record my thanks to the President and the Fellows for welcoming me into their community. Much of the preparatory work coincided with my delivery of lectures on Hellenistic philosophy at King's College

London in 2004–5, and I should like to acknowledge my co-lecturers on that course: M. M. McCabe, Verity Harte and Peter Gallagher. I should also like to thank Steven Gerrard at Acumen for all his work on my behalf, as well as three anonymous readers who supplied detailed and constructive comments on an earlier draft. Kate Williams has been an excellent copy-editor. As ever, I would not have completed this volume at all without the support of Dawn.

John Sellars

Sources and abbreviations

The following texts are the principal ancient sources for Stoicism, although naturally the list is by no means exhaustive. It also serves as a guide to the abbreviations used in this volume. Full bibliographic details of the editions used may be found in the Guide to Further Reading. A complete list of texts cited in this volume may be found in the Index of Passages.

Aetius
> *De Placitis Reliquiae*, in H. Diels, ed., *Doxographi Graeci* (Berlin: de Gruyter, [1879] 1965)

Alexander of Aphrodisias
> *in Top.* = *in Topica* (*Commentary on Aristotle's Topics*)
> *Mixt.* = *De Mixtione* (*On Mixture*)

Arius Didymus
> *Epitome of Stoic Ethics*, cited by the paragraph sections of Stobaeus, *Anthology*, bk 2 ch. 7, printed in Pomeroy's edition and in Inwood and Gerson's *Hellenistic Philosophy*.

Aulus Gellius
> *NA* = *Noctes Atticae* (*Attic Nights*)

Calcidius
> *in Tim.* = *in Timaeus* (*Commentary on Plato's Timaeus*)

Cicero
>   *Acad.* = *Academica* (*Academics*)
>   *Div.* = *De Divinatione* (*On Divination*)
>   *Fat.* = *De Fato* (*On Fate*)
>   *Fin.* = *De Finibus* (*On Ends*)
>   *ND* = *De Natura Deorum* (*On the Nature of the Gods*)
>   *Parad.* = *Paradoxa Stoicorum* (*Paradoxes of the Stoics*)
>   *Tusc.* = *Tusculanae Disputationes* (*Tusculan Disputations*)

Cleomedes
>   *Cael.* = *Caelestia* (*The Heavens*)

Diogenes Laertius
>   DL = Diogenes Laertius, *Lives and Opinions of the Philosophers*

Epictetus
>   *Diss.* = *Dissertationes* (*Discourses*)
>   *Ench.* = *Enchiridion* (*Handbook*)

Galen
>   *PHP* = *De Platicis Hippocratis et Platonis* (*On the Doctrines of Hippocrates and Plato*)

Hierocles
>   *El. Eth.* = *Elementa Ethica* (*Elements of Ethics*)

Marcus Aurelius
>   *Med.* = *Meditations*

Musonius Rufus
>   *Diss.* = *Dissertationum a Lucio Digestarum Reliquiae* (*Remains of Discourses Reported by Lucius*)

Plutarch
>   *Mor.* = *Moralia* (*Moral Essays*), two of which are cited separately:
>   *Com. Not.* = *De Communibus Notitiis* (*Against the Stoics on Common Conceptions*)
>   *St. Rep.* = *De Stoicorum Repugnantiis* (*On Stoic Self-Contradictions*)

Seneca
>   *Const.* = *De Constantia Sapientis* (*On the Constancy of the Sage*)
>   *Ep.* = *Epistulae* (*Letters*)

Ira = *De Ira* (*On Anger*)
Ot. = *De Otio* (*On Leisure*)
Prov. = *De Providentia* (*On Providence*)

Sextus Empiricus
   Adv. Math. = *Adversus Mathematicos* (*Against the Professors*)
   Pyrr. Hyp. = *Pyrrhoniae Hypotyposes* (*Outlines of Pyrrhonism*)

Simplicius
   in Cael. = *in De Caelo* (*Commentary on Aristotle's On the Heavens*)
   in Cat. = *in Categorias* (*Commentary on Aristotle's Categories*)
   in Phys. = *in Physica* (*Commentary on Aristotle's Physics*)

Stobaeus
   Anthologium, ed. C. Wachsmuth and O. Hense (Berlin: Weidmann,
      1884–1912)

Syrianus
   in Metaph. = *in Metaphysica* (*Commentary on Aristotle's Metaphysics*)

Two abbreviations have been used for the two most useful anthologies of translations for Stoicism:

IG   B. Inwood & L. P. Gerson, *Hellenistic Philosophy: Introductory
        Readings*, 2nd edn (Indianapolis, IN: Hackett, 1997)
LS   A. A. Long & D. N. Sedley, *The Hellenistic Philosophers* (Cam-
        bridge: Cambridge University Press, 1987)

Note also one abbreviation that has been used in the References and Guide to
Further Reading:

ANRW *Aufstieg und Niedergang der Römischen Welt*, ed. W. Haase &
        H. Temporini (Berlin: de Gruyter, 1972–)

Chronology

Inevitably, some of these dates are only approximate; in many cases I have relied on the dates suggested in the *Oxford Classical Dictionary*.

BCE

300	Zeno of Citium begins teaching at the Painted Stoa in Athens.
262	Death of Zeno; Cleanthes becomes the second head of the Stoa.
232	Chrysippus becomes the third head of the Stoa after the death of Cleanthes.
207/205	Chrysippus dies and Zeno of Tarsus becomes the head of the Stoa.
155	Diogenes of Babylon (Zeno's successor) introduces the Romans to Stoicism during the famous visit of the embassy of Athenian philosophers to Rome.
152	Antipater succeeds Diogenes as the head of the Stoa.
128	Panaetius becomes the head of the Stoa, succeeding Antipater.
110	Panaetius dies and the headship of the Stoa passes jointly to Mnesarchus and Dardanus.
78	Cicero attends Posidonius' lectures in Rhodes.
51	Death of Posidonius.
46	Suicide of Cato the Younger.

| 45 | Cicero writes a series of important philosophical works (that now constitute our earliest surviving record of Stoic philosophy). |
| 4/1 | Seneca is born in Corduba (modern Cordoba) in southern Spain. |

CE

41	Seneca is exiled to Corsica by Claudius for alleged adultery.
49	Seneca is recalled from exile (a period during which he composed the earliest of his surviving works).
50	Cornutus begins lecturing in Rome around this time; his pupils include Lucan and Persius.
65	Seneca commits suicide under orders from Nero.
66	Musonius Rufus is banished by Nero to the desolate island of Gyaros.
71	The Emperor Vespasian banishes the philosophers from Rome, but exempts Musonius Rufus.
95	The Emperor Domitian banishes the philosophers from Rome, including Epictetus; Epictetus relocates to Nicopolis in Western Greece.
96–116	Plutarch composes his polemics against the Stoics during this period.
108	Arrian attends and records the lectures of Epictetus some time around this date.
120	Hierocles is active around this time.
130	Death of Epictetus around this time.
161	Marcus Aurelius becomes Emperor.
162–76	Galen composes *On the Doctrines of Hippocrates and Plato*, preserving important material by Chrysippus and Posidonius on psychology.
176	Marcus Aurelius founds four chairs of philosophy in Athens, including one in Stoic philosophy and one in Peripatetic philosophy (later held by Alexander of Aphrodisias).
180	Death of Marcus Aurelius.
200	Stoicism is still considered important at this date, as witnessed by the polemics of Alexander of Aphrodisias and Sextus Empiricus, both composed around this time.

ONE

Introduction

What is Stoicism?

"Stoicism" is a word with which we are all familiar; the *Oxford English Dictionary* cites austerity, repression of feeling and fortitude as characteristics of a Stoical attitude towards life. This popular image of Stoicism has developed over the past four or five centuries as readers have encountered descriptions of ancient Stoic philosophy by Classical authors such as Cicero, Seneca and Plutarch. Like so many other popular conceptions, it contains an element of truth but, as we shall see, it hardly tells us the whole truth.

In antiquity "Stoicism" referred to a philosophical school founded by Zeno of Citium around 300 BCE. This school met informally at the Painted Stoa, a covered colonnade on the northern edge of the Agora (marketplace) in Athens, and this is how the "Stoics" gained their name. This was a period of intense philosophical activity in Athens; Plato's Academy and Aristotle's Lyceum were still strong, while Zeno's contemporary Epicurus was setting up his own school just outside the city walls. Other philosophers inspired by the example of Socrates – by this time dead for around a hundred years – also flourished, notably the Cynics. Like the Cynics – and in contrast to those in the Academy, Lyceum and Epicurean Garden – the Stoics did not possess any formal school property, instead meeting at a public location right in the heart of the city. Zeno attracted a large audience and after his death his pupil Cleanthes continued the tradition. Cleanthes was himself succeeded by Chrysippus, who is traditionally held to have been the most important of the early Stoics.

The tradition of teaching at the Painted Stoa probably continued until some point in the first century BCE. By this time, Rome had become the most important cultural and political force in the ancient world. The Romans found many Stoic ideas congenial and Stoicism flourished within the Romanized world. In the first century BCE Cicero presented to the Latin-speaking world a number of important summaries of Stoic philosophy. Stoics abounded in Rome during the first century CE, from Seneca, Lucan and Persius to Musonius Rufus and Epictetus. The second century saw the culmination of the Roman appropriation of Stoicism in the Emperor Marcus Aurelius, who expounded his own brand of Stoicism in his *Meditations*.

As we can see, Stoicism appealed to individuals from a wide range of geographical origins and social backgrounds: from Diogenes of Babylon in the East to Seneca from southern Spain in the West; from the ex-slave Epictetus to the Emperor Marcus Aurelius; from Near-Eastern immigrants in Athens to members of the Imperial court in Rome. What was it that attracted such a diverse body of admirers?

Perhaps the first thing to note is that, as the popular image of Stoicism captures, Stoic philosophy is not merely a series of philosophical claims about the nature of the world or what we can know or what is right or wrong; it is above all an attitude or way of life. Stoicism does involve complex philosophical theories in ontology (theory of what exists), epistemology (theory of knowledge) and ethics, but these theories are situated within a very particular conception of what philosophy is. Following Socrates, the Stoics present philosophy as primarily concerned with how one should live. The Stoics were not unique in this, however, and the same applies to the ancient Epicureans and Cynics among others. So how did the Stoic way of life differ from those proposed by the other ancient philosophical schools? Here we come to the theories of ontology, epistemology and ethics – theories that look similar in form to those propounded by modern philosophers – for the Stoic attitude or way of life is built on these theoretical claims. We shall of course examine the central tenets of the Stoic philosophical system in some detail in the chapters that follow, but in brief the Stoics proposed a materialist ontology in which God permeates the entire cosmos as a material force. They claimed that virtue alone is sufficient for happiness and that external goods and circumstances are irrelevant (or at least nowhere near as important as most people tend to assume). They argued that our emotions are merely the product of mistaken judgements and can be eradicated by a form of cognitive psychotherapy. They brought these various doctrines together in the image of the ideal Stoic sage who would be perfectly rational, emotionless, indifferent to his or her circumstances and, infamously, happy even when being tortured on the rack.

Although Stoicism had declined in influence by the beginning of the third century CE, its philosophical impact did not end then. Despite the loss of nearly all of the texts of the founding Athenian Stoics, the school continued to influence later philosophers, first via the readily available Latin texts of Cicero and Seneca during the Middle Ages and Renaissance, and later via collections of the fragments of the early Stoics gathered from a wide variety of ancient authors who quoted their now lost works or reported their views. Stoicism proved especially influential during the sixteenth and seventeenth centuries, and formed one of a number of influences that contributed to the important developments in philosophy during that period. Thinkers ranging from Erasmus, Calvin and Montaigne, to Descartes, Pascal, Malebranche and Leibniz were all well versed in Stoic ideas. Debates during the period concerning the nature of the self, the power of human reason, fate and free will, and the emotions often made reference to Stoicism. This later influence of Stoicism has continued right up to the present day, and the most striking recent example can be found in the later works of Michel Foucault and his analyses of the "care of the self" and "technologies of the self". Thus Stoicism was not only one of the most popular schools of philosophy in antiquity but has also remained a constant presence throughout the history of Western philosophy.

The task of unpacking Stoicism as a philosophy is complex for a number of reasons. Most of the early texts have been lost. We therefore have to rely on later reports made by authors who are often hostile towards Stoicism and sometimes writing in a quite different intellectual climate. The Stoic texts that we do have are late, and it is sometimes difficult to determine how accurately they reflect earlier Stoic orthodoxy and how much they embody later developments. All of this can make the task bewildering for those new to the subject. The remainder of this opening chapter is designed to assist those new to the subject by introducing the principal figures in the history of Stoicism as well as a number of other ancient authors that anyone approaching Stoicism for the first time is likely to encounter. It concludes with some thoughts about why so many of the early Stoic texts have been lost, thoughts that although speculative form a helpful way into the subject matter of Chapter 2. Some readers may prefer to start Chapter 2 now, referring back to the contextual information in this chapter as and when it becomes necessary.

The early Stoics

Zeno

Zeno, the founder of Stoicism, was born in the 330s BCE in the town of Citium in Cyprus. According to ancient biographical tradition, Zeno travelled to Athens in his early twenties and on his arrival visited a bookstall where he found a copy of Xenophon's *Memorabilia of Socrates*. While looking through this book Zeno asked the bookseller if or where men like Socrates could be found; at just that moment the Cynic Crates was walking past and the bookseller said to Zeno "follow that man" (DL 7.2–3). So Zeno's philosophical education began – with the Cynics.

The Cynics were famous for advocating a life in accordance with nature, in opposition to a life shaped by local customs and conventions. They claimed that whatever is according to nature is necessary, while those things according to convention are merely arbitrary. Cynicism argues that one should focus all one's attention on getting those necessary things that are according to nature (food, water, basic shelter and clothing), and pay no regard whatsoever to the unnecessary and arbitrary rules, regulations and assumptions of the particular culture in which one happens to find oneself. As we shall see, the idea of "living in accordance with nature" was one Cynic idea that the Stoics adopted and developed.

Zeno had no desire to become an orthodox Cynic, however, and was keen to explore the other philosophical discussions taking place in Athens at that time. He is reported to have studied with the philosopher Polemo, the then head of Plato's Academy, with whom he no doubt had the opportunity to study Plato's philosophy in detail. He is also reported to have studied with the philosopher Stilpo, a member of the Megarian school famous for its contributions to logic, who in his ethics was sympathetic towards the Cynics. Stilpo's blend of Cynic ethics with Megarian logic paved the way for a similar blend by Zeno that would later develop into Stoicism.

After this long and eclectic philosophical education Zeno eventually began teaching himself, some time around 300 BCE. Rather than attempt to set up any formal school, Zeno would meet with those who wanted to listen in one of the covered colonnades or Stoa that bordered the Athenian Agora. His preferred spot was the Painted Stoa on the north side of the Agora. While his followers were sometimes known as "Zenonians", they soon came to be known as those who met at the Painted Stoa: "Stoics".

It is common for scholars to analyse what we know of Zeno's teachings by comparing it with what we know about the doctrines of his various educators. Although this approach can be helpful it sometimes has the unfortunate consequence of presenting Zeno as a sort of intellectual magpie, gathering ideas from here and there without much creative input of his own. While Zeno was no doubt influenced by the various teachers with whom he studied, we should not discount his own philosophical contribution to the foundation of Stoicism, nor limit it merely to a creative synthesis of other people's doctrines. With only fragmentary remains of his works it is difficult to assess properly his own contribution, but from the evidence that does survive it seems clear that the foundations of the central doctrines of Stoicism in logic, physics and ethics were indeed laid down by the school's founder.

The most important of Zeno's known works is his *Republic*. This work of utopian politics was highly controversial in antiquity, both among hostile critics and later apologetic Stoics. The surviving fragments show that it advocated the abolition of the law courts, currency, marriage and traditional education. We are told that it was an early work by Zeno, written when he was still under the influence of his Cynic mentor Crates (DL 7.4). However, this may have been a later apologetic Stoic move, designed to distance the mature Zeno from the *Republic*'s scandalous contents (we shall look at Zeno's *Republic* in more detail in Chapter 5). The titles of some of Zeno's other known works reflect central themes in Stoic philosophy, such as *On Living According to Nature* and *On the Emotions* (DL 7.4).

Zeno's pupils included Persaeus, Herillus, Dionysius, Sphaerus, Aristo and Cleanthes. The last two of these proved to be the most significant.

Aristo

Zeno's pupil Aristo of Chios focused his attention on ethics, paying little attention to logic or physics (see DL 7.160). He is perhaps most famous for having rejected the addition to Stoic ethics of the idea that some external objects, known as "indifferents", might be preferable to others; for instance that wealth might be preferable to poverty even though both are strictly speaking "indifferent" (on this see Chapter 5). Thus he wanted to hold on to a more austere and Cynic outlook, one that has been traced back to Socrates (see Long 1988). In the long run he lost the argument, and the concepts of "preferred" and "non-preferred" indifferents became standard items in Stoic ethics. This no doubt contributed to Stoicism's wider appeal, especially later when it was introduced to a Roman audience, and so Aristo's defeat was probably in Stoicism's best interests. However, his uncompromising heterodox position went down well with the wider public of his day, and his lectures are reported to have been especially popular (DL 7.161).

Cleanthes

Cleanthes, like Zeno before him and many later Stoics after, came to Athens from the East, in his case from Assos in Turkey. He studied with Zeno and succeeded him as head of the school, in around 263 BCE. His principal claim to fame is as the author of the earliest extended Stoic text to survive (although it is hardly very long). This is the *Hymn to Zeus* and is preserved in an anthology of material compiled centuries later by John Stobaeus. The *Hymn* (translated in LS 54 I and IG II-21) is decidedly religious in tone (as the title would suggest) and so it sits somewhat oddly with what else we know of early Stoic physics. Indeed, Diogenes Laertius reports that Cleanthes had little aptitude for physics (DL 7.170), although he is reported to have written two volumes on Zeno's physics and four volumes on Heraclitus. Traditional accounts of Stoic physics often cite Heraclitus as a formative influence, and it may have been via Cleanthes' work on him that Heraclitus made his mark on the development of Stoic doctrine.

Chrysippus

The third head of the Stoa in Athens after Zeno and Cleanthes was Chrysippus, from Soli, a town in Cilicia, in Asia Minor. He succeeded Cleanthes as head of the school around 232 BCE and died at the age of 73, some time around 205 BCE. Chrysippus' importance for the development of Stoic philosophy is summed up in an oft-quoted phrase from Diogenes Laertius: "If there had been no Chrysippus, there would have been no Stoa" (DL 7.183). He was especially important for the continuation of the Stoa owing to his replies to attacks by sceptical Academic philosophers such as Arcesilaus (see Gould 1970: 9). He is probably the most important of the early Stoics and arguably the most important Stoic philosopher of all. His most significant contribution to the development of Stoicism lay in bringing together the ideas of his predecessors, adding his own original material and setting out a highly systematic philosophical system that would become the basis for a Stoic orthodoxy. It is, for instance, only looking back after Chrysippus that we can judge Aristo as heterodox; before Chrysippus matters were not so settled.

He was probably most famous in antiquity for his skills as a logician, but also praised for his abilities in all parts of philosophy. He is reported to have written some 705 books, and there exists a substantial catalogue of his book titles. All that survive, however, are fragments quoted by later authors, especially Plutarch and Galen, both of whom wrote works attacking Chrysippus. There are now some further remains that have been discovered among the papyrus rolls unearthed at Herculaneum, such as parts of his works *On Providence* and *Logical Questions*. It is conceivable that there might be other works by Chrysippus among the charred rolls that have been recovered, awaiting decipherment (see Gigante 1995: 3).

The next head of the Stoa after Chrysippus was Zeno of Tarsus. His successor was Diogenes of Babylon. Diogenes was one of three Athenian philosophers who went on an embassy to Rome in 155 BCE, an important event in the introduction of Greek philosophy to the Roman world.

The middle Stoa

The figures that we have met thus far are traditionally known as "early" Stoics. After the early Stoics come the "middle" Stoics. The validity of this division has been called into question by some scholars, and they may well be right to do so (see e.g. Sedley 2003), but nevertheless the distinction is fairly well established. One of the supposed characteristics of the middle Stoa that marks it off from the early Stoa is an increasing eclecticism, with Stoics drawing on philosophical material from some of the other ancient schools. With these figures, then, we have to ask to what extent a philosopher can deviate from the teaching of the early Stoa and turn to other philosophical traditions on certain topics while still remaining a Stoic in any meaningful sense.

Perhaps the first Stoic after Chrysippus with whom the question of orthodoxy arises is Antipater of Tarsus, who succeeded Diogenes of Babylon as head of the school. Antipater tried to highlight the common ground between Stoicism and Platonism. But the issue of eclecticism and orthodoxy rises to the fore when turning to Antipater's pupil, Panaetius of Rhodes.

Panaetius

Panaetius was born in Rhodes around 185 BCE. He studied first in Pergamum and later in Athens, under the Stoics Diogenes of Babylon and Antipater of Tarsus. He later spent time in Rome, in the circle of people surrounding the famous Roman general Scipio Africanus. He became head of the Stoa in 128 BCE, succeeding Antipater. He died some time around 110 BCE. Panaetius' later significance is due in no small part to his influence on Cicero, who drew extensively on Panaetius' now lost *On Appropriate Actions* (*Peri Kathēkonta*) when writing his own highly influential *On Duties* (*De Officiis*).

It is reported that Panaetius admired both Plato and Aristotle. Although he remained faithful to much of Stoic doctrine (enough to be able to remain head of the Stoa), there were some points on which he deviated. He rejected the Stoic doctrine of the periodic destruction of the world, instead affirming its eternity (see DL 7.142). He may be seen to water down Stoic ethics somewhat by denying that virtue is sufficient on its own for happiness (suggesting that material goods are also required; see DL 7.128), and for shifting the focus of attention from the ideal of the sage to the average person in the street (see e.g. Seneca, *Ep.* 116.5).

Yet despite his heterodoxy on these points and his reported admiration for Plato, he remained faithful to Stoic orthodoxy in denying the Platonic doctrine of the immortality of the soul (see Cicero, *Tusc.* 1.79). It should also be noted that some of his "heterodox" opinions had already been adopted by some of his Stoic predecessors; Diogenes of Babylon, for example, had already rejected the periodic destruction of the world, so on this Panaetius was simply following the lead of one of his Stoic teachers.

Posidonius

Posidonius was born in Apamea in Syria some time around 135 BCE. He studied in Athens with Panaetius (when Panaetius died in 110 BCE, Posidonius would have been around 25 years old). Rather than remain in Athens he moved to Rhodes and this is where he taught philosophy. This may have been because the headship at the Stoic school in Athens had passed to Mnesarchus and Dardanus jointly after Panaetius' death. While based at Rhodes, Posidonius made a number of trips around the Mediterranean, gathering scientific and cultural observations much in the spirit of Aristotle. His most famous pupil was probably Cicero. Posidonius died around 51 BCE, at that point in his eighties. Above all, Posidonius was a polymath, contributing not only to Stoic philosophy but also to history, geography, astronomy, meteorology, biology and anthropology.

Traditionally it has been claimed that Posidonius' most famous and most striking deviation from Stoic orthodoxy was in psychology. According to the testimony of Galen, whereas earlier Stoics such as Chrysippus adopted a monistic psychology (in which reason and emotion were not separated into distinct faculties), Posidonius followed Plato in proposing a tripartite psychology, dividing the soul into the faculties of reason, emotion and desire. Galen took great delight in highlighting this contradiction within the Stoic tradition in his treatise *On the Doctrines of Hippocrates and Plato*. However, recent scholarship has argued that the distance between Posidonius and Chrysippus may not be as great as Galen claims (see e.g. Cooper 1999).

Panaetius and Posidonius deviated from some of the doctrines of the early Stoics. But this should not necessarily be seen as a shortcoming. If they had unthinkingly accepted everything that had been taught in the Stoa previously, then they would have been closer to being religious disciples than philosophers. It seems clear that Cleanthes and Chrysippus were no blind followers of Zeno either, but rather expanded and developed his foundations in ways that reflected their own philosophical tendencies, each making their own individual contribution to the development of Stoic philosophy. Stoics after Chrysippus found a well-developed systematic philosophy. If we assume that these post-Chrysippean Stoics were indeed philosophers rather than devotees of Chrysippus' every word, then we should of course expect some deviation from his doctrines. If Panaetius and Posidonius deserve the title "philosopher" at all, then we would expect them to come to their own philosophical conclusions and to disagree with previous Stoics from time to time. There is nothing inconsistent with doing this while at the same time affirming Stoic philosophy as the philosophical school to which one has most intellectual sympathy. Indeed, if this were not the case then the whole notion of a philosophical school or tradition would run the risk of becoming a contradiction in terms.

It should also be noted that although both Panaetius and Posidonius display admiration towards Plato and Aristotle, this may be less a reflection of personal eclecticism on their part and more a reflection of the wider changing philosophical climate of the period. Whereas the earliest Stoics may have been keen to assert their philosophical independence *vis-à-vis* Plato, by the end of the second century BCE Plato may have been seen as a source out of which Stoicism grew rather than as a philosophical adversary. This period also saw a renewed interest in the philosophy of Aristotle; he was increasingly perceived as a philosopher of pre-eminent stature rather than simply the head of a competing school. As such, any aspiring philosopher would have to appreciate his thought.

Late Stoic authors

Stoicism in the first two centuries CE has a quite different character than Stoicism in the first three centuries BCE. The reason for this is simply that for the Stoics of this later period we have complete texts that we can read, rather than having to rely on quotations preserved by other, often hostile, authors and second-hand reports of their ideas. There have been scholarly debates on the question of the extent to which Stoic philosophy develops in this period. On the traditional view, the late Stoics lose interest in technical subjects such as logic and physics, and focus all of their attention on practical ethics. However, this impression may simply reflect the nature of the texts that have come down to us rather than any substantive shift in philosophical concerns. The best-known late Stoic authors are Seneca, Epictetus and Marcus Aurelius, but we shall also consider lesser figures such as Cornutus and Musonius Rufus, as well as Hierocles and Cleomedes.

Seneca

Seneca is the first Stoic for whom we have considerable literary remains; indeed his corpus is the largest collection of surviving texts for any Stoic. When we bear in mind that the next largest corpus of works, those of Epictetus, was probably written by his pupil Arrian, and that Marcus Aurelius' *Meditations* have a somewhat peculiar character that make them a quite different sort of text, then Seneca's philosophical works take on an additional importance. If we want to read a Stoic author directly then we must turn to Seneca as by far the most important Stoic author whose works survive.

Unfortunately Seneca's reputation has suffered. On the one hand he has been charged throughout the ages with hypocrisy, stemming from the apparent incongruity between his high-minded moral precepts and some of the details of his life (including his role as tutor to the tyrannical Emperor Nero). On the other hand his moral writings have often been sidelined in the study of ancient philosophy (although this is now changing), as they do not reach the same heights of theoretical rigour that we find in Plato or Aristotle. He has also been accused of eclecticism (see Rist 1989), with the implication that he may not even be a good source for information about orthodox Stoicism. But it would be a mistake to judge Seneca only in terms of how faithful he remains to the teaching of the early Stoics. One should also bear in mind that historically Seneca has been a key source for later generations of readers and has thus been a central figure in shaping the image of Stoicism in the West. In part this was owing to the existence of a series of letters between Seneca and St Paul that were taken to be genuine (although now are dismissed as a forgery), and so Church Fathers, medieval readers and Renaissance humanists all approached Seneca as a pagan philosopher whose works were in sympathy (or at least not in direct conflict) with Christianity.

Seneca's surviving philosophical works include an important series of *Moral Letters* (*Epistulae Morales*), addressed to Lucilius, dealing with a wide range of philosophical topics, and a series of *Dialogues* (*Dialogi*). The *Dialogues* are in fact closer to essays in their literary form. They are: *On Providence* (*De Providentia*), *On the Constancy of the Sage* (*De Constantia Sapientis*), *On Anger* (*De Ira*), *To Marcia on Consolation* (*Consolatio ad Marciam*), *On the Happy Life* (*De Vita Beata*), *On Leisure* (*De Otio*), *On Tranquillity of the Soul* (*De Tranquillitate Animi*), *On the Shortness of Life* (*De Brevitate Vitae*), *To Polybius on Consolation* (*Consolatio ad Polybium*) and *To Helvia his Mother on Consolation* (*Consolatio ad Helviam Matrem*). In addition to these, there are also two longer prose works dealing with ethical themes within the context of political leadership, *On Benefits* (*De Beneficiis*) and *On Mercy* (*De Clementia*). There also survives a study of questions in physics and meteorology, the *Natural Questions* (*Naturales Quaestiones*).

Beyond these prose works Seneca produced a series of tragedies that have proved highly influential on later literature, the contents of which have been taken by some to reflect his philosophy (see Rosenmeyer 1989). He also composed a satire on the deification of the Emperor Claudius, entitled *Pumpkinification* (*Apocolocyntosis*).

Cornutus

Lucius Annaeus Cornutus had some connection with Seneca, possibly once being his or his family's slave. Born around 20 CE, he began teaching philosophy and rhetoric in Rome at around 50 CE. His pupils included the famous poets Lucan (Seneca's nephew) and Persius, whose *Satires* he is said to have edited after the latter's death.

Like so many of the Roman Stoics of this period, he was exiled at one point, and it is unclear if he was ever able to return to Rome.

Cornutus is best known now as the author of the *Introduction to Greek Theology* (*Theologiae Graecae Compendium*), an allegorical account of traditional Greek mythology. He also produced a work (now lost) on Aristotle's logic and its interpretation by an earlier Stoic called Athenodorus.

Musonius Rufus

Musonius Rufus was an Etruscan and was probably born just before 30 CE. As a member of the equestrian order he was of a high social rank, and his life as a teacher of Stoic philosophy during a volatile political period was marked by banishment and exile on a number of occasions. He was exiled to Syria for two years by Nero, and on his return was later banished to an isolated island. When Vespasian banished the philosophers from Rome in 71 CE Musonius was not forced to leave, but was exiled by the same emperor at a later date for some unknown reason. When he was in Rome he taught philosophy, and it was here that Epictetus must have attended his lectures. Although we do not have a precise date for his death, it is thought that he died before 100 CE. Material about his life can be found in the works of Tacitus and Philostratus.

The literary evidence for Musonius falls into two groups: first a series of lectures preserved by Stobaeus that are probably notes taken from lectures by one of his students (called Lucius); secondly a collection of short anecdotes and sayings gathered from the works of Stobaeus, Epictetus, Aulus Gellius and others. It seems that all of these testimonies derive from Musonius' oral teaching rather than any formal written works that he chose to publish. Like Socrates before him and Epictetus after, it appears that Musonius chose not to write.

Although there are some interesting philosophical topics developed in the relatively short texts that survive, including an important discussion of gender egalitarianism, Musonius' real significance is as a teacher. His most famous pupil is Epictetus, and without more information about Musonius it is difficult to say precisely to what extent the influence of Musonius' ideas and methods shaped the philosophy of Epictetus. Beyond Epictetus, Musonius' pupils included the orator Dio Chrysostom and the Stoic Euphrates of Tyre. His reputation was considerable in antiquity, and modern scholars have dubbed him the "Roman Socrates". His status as a Stoic sage (although perhaps not in the technical sense) combined with his influence as the teacher of Epictetus, Euphrates, Dio and others have led some to suggest that his significance was so great that he should be treated as the third founder of Stoicism, after Zeno and Chrysippus (Arnold 1911: 117). The contents of the meagre literary remains that survive may make some sceptical of such a grand claim, but nevertheless it is clear that Musonius enjoyed a high reputation in antiquity for his wisdom. Through his influence on Epictetus, and the latter's influence on Marcus Aurelius, Musonius in effect stands at the beginning of a new Stoic dynasty that shaped the Stoic tradition in the first two centuries CE.

Epictetus

By far the most important Stoic philosopher to appear in the wake of Musonius is Epictetus. Born some time around 50 CE in Asia Minor, he began life as a slave and came into the service of a high-ranking Roman, Epaphroditus, secretary to the Emperors Nero and Domitian. Epictetus would no doubt have been in the centre of Rome and had some experience of the Imperial court. While a slave in Rome he was permitted to attend the lectures of Musonius Rufus, and later he was granted his freedom. It seems reasonable to suppose that Epictetus began his own teaching career in Rome, perhaps as Musonius' protégé. He did not remain in Rome for long, however; in 95 CE Domitian banished all philosophers from Italy, just one act in a wider reign of persecution against his critics. Like Musonius before him, Epictetus was forced to flee. He moved to Nicopolis on the western coast of Greece, and it was here that he set up the school where the lectures that have come down to us were presumably delivered. He died some time around 130 CE. It appears that many important figures, including the Emperor Hadrian, came to visit him at Nicopolis, presumably owing to his growing reputation (there exists a dialogue between Epictetus and Hadrian which, alas, is no doubt spurious).

Two texts have come down to us associated with Epictetus: the *Discourses* (*Dissertationes*) and the *Handbook* (*Enchiridion*). One thing that immediately stands out in these works is Epictetus' admiration for Socrates, the ultimate philosophical role model. And like Socrates, so far as we are aware, Epictetus wrote nothing for wider publication. So the texts that we have are not by Epictetus himself (although there has been some scholarly disagreement; see Dobbin 1998: xx–xxiii), but are generally held to be reports of Epictetus' lectures made by one of his pupils. The pupil in question is Arrian, also well known for his history of Alexander the Great's campaigns. In a prefatory letter to the *Discourses* Arrian claims that what he has written is to the best of his ability and memory a word-for-word account of what he heard in Epictetus' classroom. Hence he apologises for their slightly rough style. Indeed, the *Discourses* are quite different in style compared with Arrian's other works, written in a less literary and more common language (the *koinē* or "common" Greek of the New Testament). Although we have no reason to doubt Arrian's sincerity on this point, it is of course inevitable that what he has preserved for us is only a partial and perspectival account of both what Epictetus actually thought and what went on in his lectures.

There now exist four books of *Discourses*. Later ancient sources mention works of Epictetus in both eight and twelve books, and Aulus Gellius preserves a fragment from Book 5 of the *Discourses*, so no doubt what we have is not even all of Arrian's inevitably subjective account. The *Handbook* was also compiled by Arrian, according to the testimony of the Neoplatonist Simplicius in his commentary on it. It is in effect an epitome of the *Discourses*, a distillation of their key themes. Here, Arrian's judgement and selection are obviously central in shaping the character and contents of the work (consider the dramatically different results that might be produced if a number of people were asked to select key passages from Aristotle's

Nicomachean Ethics). Nevertheless the result is a powerful summary of Stoic practical philosophy, and the opening chapter perfectly captures the essence of Epictetus' philosophy as we know it: "Of things, some are up to us, and some are not up to us. Up to us are opinion, impulse, desire, aversion and, in a word, all our actions. Not up to us are our body, possessions, reputations, offices and, in a word, all that are not our actions" (*Ench.* 1.1).

The key to happiness, Epictetus suggests, is continually to analyse our experience of the world in terms of this division between what is "up to us" (*eph' hēmin*) and "not up to us" (*ouk eph' hēmin*). Almost all human misery, he argues, is the product of people not understanding the nature and significance of this division, of assuming that they have control of things that in fact they do not, of grounding their happiness on external things "not up to us" and so making it highly vulnerable to the vicissitudes of fortune. Instead, we should ground our happiness on those things that are "up to us", on those things that can never be taken away from us. If we do that, our happiness will be literally invulnerable.

Marcus Aurelius

The Roman Emperor Marcus Aurelius (121–180 CE) was a keen student of philosophy and an admirer of, and influenced by, the *Discourses* of Epictetus, a copy of which he borrowed from one of his teachers. Thus he may be seen to stand within the tradition founded by Musonius. Yet Marcus could not be more different from either Musonius or Epictetus.

The emperor was obviously no professional teacher of philosophy nor a full-time sage in the marketplace. Yet in the texts that come down to us under the title *Meditations* (in English convention; the Greek title that has come down to us translates as "To Himself") we find someone who clearly spent much time in philosophical speculation. Marcus deals with a variety of themes in a non-technical manner in texts not conceived for wider circulation, so it is usually assumed, but perhaps written with some eye on future posterity.

Perhaps the one theme that dominates is the relationship between the individual and the cosmos. Here is just one example:

> In human life, our time is a point, our substance flowing, our perception faint, the constitution of our whole body decaying, our soul a spinning wheel, our fortune hard to predict and our fame doubtful; that is to say, all the things of the body are a river, things of the soul dream and delusion, life is a war and a journey in a foreign land, and afterwards oblivion.　　　　　　　　　　　　　　　(*Med.* 2.17)

There are many other passages similar to this in the *Meditations* and to some readers they may seem excessively repetitive. But this in part perhaps reflects their role as a philosophical notebook in which Marcus is working through ideas with himself, going over the same topics again and again in order to help himself digest the ideas with which he is grappling.

Hierocles and Cleomedes

The works of Seneca, Epictetus and Marcus Aurelius have been in wide circulation since the Renaissance (and Seneca was relatively well known in the West even earlier, during the Middle Ages). Recent scholarship has also shed light on texts by two lesser-known late Stoic authors, Hierocles and Cleomedes.

Little is known about Hierocles. He is mentioned by Aulus Gellius and some texts attributed to him survive in the anthology of Stobaeus. He probably lived in the second century CE. He is important, however, as the author of a work entitled *Elements of Ethics* (*Elementa Ethica*), discovered on a papyrus found in Egypt, and published for the first time in 1906. This text offers a very interesting and valuable account of the foundations of Stoic ethics. It is also important in so far as it takes the form of a school treatise, in contrast to the popular moral works of Seneca or Epictetus, and so offers an insight into what the myriad of other lost Stoic treatises might have looked like. It is "the closest thing we have to an uncontaminated text-book or series of lectures on mainstream Stoicism by a Stoic philosopher" (Long 1993: 94).

Even less is known about Cleomedes, the author of a Stoic cosmological text entitled *The Heavens* (*Caelestia*). This text did survive antiquity and was transmitted via manuscript, but unfortunately no other information about Cleomedes survives in any other ancient source. It is generally thought that he lived in either the first or second century CE, although there is no firm evidence, and he might have lived later. His treatise deals with astronomy and cosmology (its scientific character may help to explain its survival), and displays the influence of Posidonius. It stands, along with Seneca's *Natural Questions*, as a rare example of an extant Stoic text treating physical topics. Its existence also counters the traditional assumption that Stoics in the first few centuries CE were preoccupied solely with ethical questions.

Recent scholarship on both Hierocles and Cleomedes has done much to amend the traditional view of "late Stoicism". In that view the popular moralizing of Seneca, Musonius and Epictetus, along with the notebook ramblings of Marcus, merely illustrated a school in decline, no longer interested in the serious matters of logic and physics, no longer innovative, no longer fully aware of orthodox Stoic theory and happy to draw from other schools in an unsystematic manner. The treatises of Hierocles and Cleomedes offer us a glimpse of a continuing school tradition that paid serious attention to Stoic ethical and physical theory. Moreover, recent scholarship on Epictetus has drawn attention to his interest in logic and other aspects of the traditional Stoic curriculum (see e.g. Barnes 1997). Scholars are increasingly sensitive to the partial nature of our information about Musonius and Epictetus, who may well have also engaged in more theoretical classroom discussions ranging over the entire Stoic syllabus. We know from the testimonies of Plutarch and Galen, as well as from Epictetus himself, that the treatises of Chrysippus remained in circulation and were read throughout the first and second centuries CE. When reading the late Stoic "moralists", then, we should not read them as isolated works but rather approach them within the context of, and taking as read, the complex philosophical system of the early Stoa.

Other sources

Although these late Stoic texts are valuable sources for Stoic philosophy, for information about the ideas of the early Stoics it is necessary to rely on reports and quotations in other authors, authors who were often hostile to Stoicism. Anyone studying Stoic philosophy will inevitably find themselves reading works (or passages excerpted from works) by the following ancient authors. It is important to know something about these authors and their own philosophical tendencies in order to consider their reports of the Stoics in context.

Cicero

The earliest accounts of Stoic philosophy that survive are those of Cicero, dating from the first century BCE (and so even earlier than Seneca). Marcus Tullius Cicero (106–43 BCE) was a Roman statesman with an aristocratic background. As such he was schooled at an early age in Greek rhetoric and philosophy. He studied in Athens and Rhodes, attending the lectures of Posidonius. A prodigious author, he produced a large number of orations, letters and rhetorical works, as well as an important body of philosophical works.

Of his philosophical works the following contain valuable accounts of Stoic ideas: *Academics* (*Academica*), *On Divination* (*De Divinatione*), *On Duties* (*De Officiis*), *On Ends Good and Bad* (*De Finibus Bonorum et Malorum*), *On Fate* (*De Fato*), *On the Nature of the Gods* (*De Natura Deorum*), *Paradoxes of the Stoics* (*Paradoxa Stoicorum*) and the *Tusculan Disputations* (*Tusculanae Disputationes*). Impressively, many of these were written in just one year towards the end of Cicero's life (45–44 BCE). Collectively they form one of the earliest and most important sources for Stoic philosophy.

Scholars in the nineteenth century were often dismissive of Cicero as a philosophical author, pillaging his works for fragments of earlier Greek thinkers while paying little regard to Cicero himself. But Cicero was personally familiar with the leading philosophers of his day and there is little doubt that he had an able philosophical mind. His philosophical works, even when approached primarily as sources of information about Stoicism, deserve to be read as well crafted and unified essays rather than merely compendia of other people's opinions.

Cicero's own philosophical position was broadly Academic (that is, sceptical), but he also inclined towards a certain eclecticism. Although he certainly rejected Stoic epistemology, in places he endorses Stoic ethics, or at the very least admires the Stoic ethical ideal. Not a Stoic himself, Cicero is a relatively sympathetic and well-informed onlooker.

Plutarch

Plutarch of Chaeronea (c. 50–120 CE), famous for his *Parallel Lives* of eminent Greeks and Romans, also produced a substantial body of philosophical works, now gathered together under the collective title *Moralia*. Plutarch was a Platonist and, in comparison to Cicero, was fairly hostile towards the Stoics. Throughout the *Moralia* the Stoics often receive a mention, but in two works in particular Plutarch focuses all of his attention on Stoicism. These are *On Stoic Self-Contradictions* (*De Stoicorum Repugnantiis*) and *Against the Stoics on Common Conceptions* (*De Communibus Notitiis Adversus Stoicos*). In these two essays Plutarch devotes his efforts to showing the problems and inherent contradictions within Stoic philosophy and in order to achieve this aim he quotes extensively from earlier Stoics, especially Chrysippus. Consequently Plutarch has ironically become one of the most important reporters of direct quotations from Chrysippus, and so an important source for our knowledge of early Stoic philosophy. There is a third essay by Plutarch on the Stoics (*Compendium Argumenti Stoicos Absurdiora Poetis Dicere*), but this is much shorter and so of less significance.

Galen

Another important source for direct quotations from Chrysippus is Galen of Pergamum (c. 129–199 CE), the famous and prolific medical author. Galen wrote a number of works dealing with Stoic philosophy – a commentary on Chrysippus' *First Syllogistic* and a book on Epictetus among others – all of which are unfortunately lost. However, among his surviving works there are two texts that are especially important for the study of Stoicism.

The first is *On the Doctrines of Hippocrates and Plato* (*De Placita Hippocratis et Platonis*). This is a detailed study of physiology and psychology that attempts to combine ancient medical theories that locate the soul in the brain with Platonic tripartite psychology. In the process Galen attacks both Chrysippus' claim that the commanding faculty is located in the heart and his monistic psychology. For the second of these attacks Galen draws on the work of Posidonius and presents Posidonius as a heterodox Stoic who rejects Chrysippus' psychology. Galen quotes extensively from both of these Stoics and in the process offers us one of the most important discussions of the Stoic theory of the soul to survive from antiquity. He also preserves some of the longest passages from Chrysippus that have come down to us.

The second Galenic work to note is his *Introduction to Logic* (*Institutio Logica*), which contains some useful material about Stoic logic. However to a certain extent this merely supplements the far more important account in Sextus Empiricus.

Sextus Empiricus

Sextus Empiricus – probably active *c.* 200 CE – was a follower of the sceptical philosophical tradition that claimed descent from the Hellenistic philosopher Pyrrho (and so is known as Pyrrhonian Scepticism, to distinguish it from Academic Scepticism). He may also have been, like Galen, a medical doctor. His principal works are the *Outlines of Pyrrhonism* (*Pyrrhoniae Hypotyposes*) and *Against the Professors* (*Adversus Mathematicos*), the second of which may in fact consist of two different works. The contents of these two works mirror each other to a certain extent, with the subject matter of Books 2 and 3 of the *Outlines* repeated (at greater length) in Books 7–11 of *Against the Professors*.

Sextus is an important source for a number of aspects of Stoic philosophy but he is especially important when it comes to Stoic logic, for there are so few other sources. His account of Stoic logic is in Book 2 of the *Outlines of Pyrrhonism* and Book 8 of *Against the Professors*.

Alexander of Aphrodisias

Alexander of Aphrodisias held a chair in Peripatetic (Aristotelian) philosophy at Athens around the year 200 CE. This may well have been one of the four chairs in philosophy that are reported to have been created by Marcus Aurelius a couple of decades earlier (the recent discovery of an inscription in Alexander's native Aphrodisias supports this). Alexander wrote a number of commentaries on the works of Aristotle along with a wide range of shorter texts. Hostile to the Stoics, Alexander argues against them and in the process reports some of their doctrines in a number of his works. Two of his shorter works in particular stand out as important sources for Stoicism: *On Fate (De Fato)* and *On Mixture (De Mixtione)*.

Alexander's engagement with Stoicism suggests that it remained a serious intellectual force in Athens as late as 200 CE. Indeed, alongside Alexander's chair in Peripatetic philosophy there was also a chair in Stoic philosophy (the two others being chairs in Platonic and Epicurean philosophy). Presumably Alexander engaged in debates with the holder of this chair in Stoic philosophy, and it is likely that students were able to attend the lectures of more than one chair holder if they so wished. Much of this is inevitably speculation, but the detailed attention that Alexander paid to Stoic ideas suggests that Stoicism was far from being simply of antiquarian interest.

Diogenes Laertius

One of the most important sources for Stoicism is Book 7 of the *Lives and Opinions of the Philosophers (Vitae Philosophorum)* by

Diogenes Laertius. Unfortunately we know nothing about Diogenes as an individual. He is usually dated to some point in the third century CE. It has sometimes been supposed that he was an Epicurean, for the final book of his *Lives* is devoted entirely to Epicurus, who is quoted at great length. This last book may have been conceived by Diogenes as the culmination of the history of philosophy that he has presented.

Diogenes' account of the Stoics draws upon an earlier source whom he names: Diocles of Magnesia. Diocles has been dated to the first century BCE, although this date may well be as uncertain as the date for Diogenes.

Stobaeus

John of Stobi (Ioannes Stobaeus), a late pagan who probably flourished in the fifth century CE, gathered together a wide collection of philosophical and literary material to aid him in educating his son. This collection, the *Anthology* (as modern editors have called it), contains a number of important sources and fragments relating to Stoicism. By far the most important of these is the *Epitome of Stoic Ethics* by Arius Didymus (from the first century BCE). However, Stobaeus is also the source for Cleanthes' *Hymn to Zeus* and the *Discourses* of Musonius Rufus, not to mention a whole host of other fragments reporting the opinions of the Stoics.

Simplicius

Stoic ideas remained alive in philosophical discussions right up to the end of antiquity. In 529 CE the Emperor Justinian ordered the closure of the remaining pagan philosophical schools in Athens. By this date it is highly unlikely that any Stoic school had existed for some time. But a Neoplatonic school led by Damascius did still survive, and its members felt the pinch of Justinian's decree. According to the historian Agathias, Damascius and the last Neoplatonists fled to Persia, although they did not stay there long, and where they went afterwards remains a matter of controversy.

One member of this group of itinerant Neoplatonists was Simplicius, author of a number of important commentaries on works by Aristotle. In these commentaries Simplicius reports Stoic doctrine on a wide range of philosophical topics (as well as material from many other earlier philosophers whose works are now otherwise lost). Simplicius also wrote a commentary on the Stoic Epictetus' *Handbook*. This commentary is unique in so far as it is the only commentary on a Stoic text to survive from antiquity. However, the commentary itself is more concerned with developing Neoplatonic ethical themes than explicating Epictetus on his own terms. Nevertheless it does attest to the fact that Epictetus continued to be read right up into the sixth century CE.

Simplicius also reports a range of Stoic doctrines in his various commentaries on works by Aristotle. However, in his commentary on Aristotle's *Categories* he remarks that most Stoic writings are unavailable in his time (*in Cat.* 334,1–3). It seems likely, then, that his knowledge of Stoicism beyond Epictetus derived from second-hand reports, such as the Aristotelian commentaries of the third-century Neoplatonist Porphyry, which Simplicius says contained much about Stoicism (*in Cat.* 2,5–9).

Decline and loss of texts

As we have seen, the vast majority of early Stoic texts have been lost. For Zeno, Cleanthes, Chrysippus, Panaetius and Posidonius all that survive are fragments quoted by later authors and second-hand accounts of their ideas. More recently, we are fortunate to have some further texts by Chrysippus that have been discovered at Herculaneum, but otherwise the texts of Stoic authors before Seneca are all lost. Why? And how might this loss of so many Stoic texts be related to the decline in the Stoic school in late antiquity?

Traditionally the decline in the fortunes of Stoicism from around 200 CE onwards has been linked with the rise in the popularity of

Neoplatonism, whose founder, Plotinus, was born in 205 CE. But this is not an entirely satisfactory explanation. It is not obvious why someone philosophically attracted to the immanent materialism of Stoicism would be equally drawn to the otherworldly metaphysics of Neoplatonism just because the latter was rising in popularity. Rather than look for an external reason such as competition from another school it might be worth considering a cause internal to Stoicism. One such possible cause may be found in Epictetus.

Epictetus is named by a number of second-century authors as the pre-eminent Stoic of the day. Aulus Gellius hails him as the greatest of the Stoics (*NA* 1.2.6), Fronto called him a sage (in his *Epistulae* 2.52), while Celsus reports that he was more famous than Plato (Origen, *Contra Celsum* 6.2). His texts are reported to have circulated widely. His fame at this point is highlighted in an anecdote reported by Lucian in his dialogue against ignorant book collectors:

> I believe the man is still alive who paid three thousand drachmas for the earthenware lamp of Epictetus the Stoic. I suppose he thought he had only to read by the light of that lamp, and the wisdom of Epictetus would be communicated to him in his dreams, and he himself assume the likeness of that venerable sage. (*Adversus Indoctum* 13)

As with modern-day film stars, fans were apparently prepared to pay large sums of money for items handled by their idols. Any aspiring Stoic in the second century would no doubt have eagerly sought out Epictetus' *Discourses* as recorded by Arrian, or even one of Epictetus' pupils, if any of them turned themselves to teaching. And Epictetus' posthumous success may well have been the decisive factor in the demise of ancient Stoicism as a continuing tradition. In order to develop this suggestion it will be necessary to consider Epictetus' conception of philosophy and his attitude towards earlier school texts.

Epictetus' conception of philosophy places value on deeds rather than words. The real Stoic is not one who merely learns to recite the words of Chrysippus; rather he is one who can display actions in harmony with those words. The task of philosophy is to understand Nature, so that one can live in accordance with Nature and so achieve happiness or *eudaimonia*. The study of philosophical theories is always – for Epictetus – subordinate to this practical goal. Thus he presents philosophy as an "art of living", an art (*technē*) that, like other arts and crafts, will be orientated towards a practical outcome. And like other arts and crafts it will be necessary not only to learn the principles underpinning the art of living but also to practise or exercise in order to learn how to put those principles into action. He says:

> After you have digested these principles, show us some resulting change in the commanding faculty of your soul, just as the athletes show their shoulders as the results of their exercising and eating, and as those who have mastered the arts can show the results of their learning. The builder does not come forward and say "Listen to me deliver a discourse about the art of building"; but he takes a contract for a house, builds it, and thereby proves that he possesses the art.
>
> (*Diss.* 3.21.3–4)

The philosopher should do exactly the same, Epictetus suggests, exhibiting his or her abilities not in fine words but in fine deeds. It should come as no great surprise, then, that Epictetus displays a fairly ambivalent attitude towards school texts. There is indeed evidence that Epictetus used canonical Stoic texts such as treatises by Chrysippus in his own classroom, but this evidence is more often than not embedded within a passage warning his students not to take the study of these texts too seriously:

> Is this, then, the great and admirable thing, to understand or interpret Chrysippus? Who says that it is? But what, then, is the admirable thing? "To understand the will of Nature." Well, then, do you understand it on your own account? In that case, what need have you for anyone else? ... But, by Zeus, I do not understand the will of Nature. Who, then, interprets that? They say Chrysippus. I go and inquire what

this interpreter of Nature says. Then I fail to understand
what he means and seek somebody who can interpret him.
... For it is not on his own account that we have need of
Chrysippus [or his interpreters], but to enable us to follow
Nature ....   (*Diss.* 1.17.13–18)

One should not lose sight of the philosophical task at hand and get
lost in textual interpretation, Epictetus suggests. Nor should one
consider textual interpretation a skill worthy of praise:

"Take the [Chrysippean] treatise *On Impulse*, and see how
thoroughly I have read it." That is not what I am looking
for, slave, but how you exercise your impulse to act and not
to act, how you manage your desires and aversions, how
you approach things, how you apply yourself to them, and
prepare for them, and whether in harmony with Nature or
out of harmony.   (*Diss.* 1.4.14)

Mastery of subtle and complex philosophical arguments is not the
ultimate goal of philosophy: "If you could analyse syllogisms like
Chrysippus, what is to prevent you from being wretched, sorrow-
ful, envious and, in a word, being distracted and miserable? Not
a single thing" (*Diss.* 2.23.44). For Epictetus, then, the task of the
philosopher is quite different from that of the philologist. The successful student of philosophy will not waste time on the analysis of
texts; rather they will concentrate their attention on transforming
the ruling part of their soul in conformity with the philosophical
principles that they have learned. Of course, the student will study
philosophical texts, but only as a means to an end. Books are thus
signs or maps that direct us to where we want to go; the traveller
who spends all of their time analysing maps and never goes anywhere has failed as a traveller. The philosopher who spends all their
time analysing texts and never putting their contents into practice
is equally a failure. For Epictetus, it is not the voluminous author
Chrysippus who stands as his philosophical role model; rather it is
Socrates, who expresses his philosophy in deeds rather than words.

And, like Socrates, Epictetus himself chose not to write, reserving his philosophy for his way of life.

Stoic students who successfully grasped Epictetus' philosophy would focus all of their attention on the transformation of their way of life in an arduous attempt to approach the life of the sage. Like Epictetus, they would aspire to be like Diogenes the Cynic and, above all, like Socrates. But what they would not do is engage in philological studies of school texts or write commentaries on them. It is this ambivalent attitude towards textual studies and the production of commentaries, quite unlike the Platonists and Aristotelians of the same period, that may be one of the reasons why Stoicism declined so quickly and why so many early Stoic texts have been lost. For it only requires a generation or two of students to pay little or no attention to the preservation of school texts to make it literally impossible for the subsequent generations of potential Stoics to study Stoicism at all.

This ambivalent attitude towards texts clearly did not mark the entire Stoic tradition. Early Stoics such as Chrysippus wrote copiously and may even have produced commentaries on earlier Stoic texts, if his *On the Republic* was in fact a commentary on Zeno's *Republic*. Cleanthes wrote a commentary on Heraclitus (DL 7.174), who was an important source for Stoic physics, and, later on, Athenodorus the Stoic wrote a commentary on or polemical response to Aristotle's *Categories* (Porphyry, *in Cat.* 86,22–4). Perhaps more significantly, the Byzantine encyclopedia known as the *Suda* includes an entry on an Aristocles the Stoic who wrote a commentary on Chrysippus' *How We Name and Conceive Each Thing*. Thus not all Stoics appear to have had ideological objections to the commentary form as such. And later Stoics roughly contemporary with Epictetus, such as Hierocles and Cleomedes, did not appear to share Epictetus' focus on practical philosophy at the expense of more academic discussion of philosophical topics. But Epictetus' somewhat unfavourable attitude towards texts combined with his subsequent popularity may have been the decisive influence on Stoics in the late second and early third centuries. Any aspiring Stoic in this period would have read Epictetus, the most famous Stoic of the day, and would have learned not to pay excessive attention to the interpretation of school texts at the expense of practical philosophical exercises. They certainly would not have spent time writing lengthy commentaries on earlier Stoic texts, despite the fact that Alexander of Aphrodisias reports that at that time the commentary was becoming the standard form of philosophical writing (*in Top.* 27,13–16). Epictetus' success in the second century – or, to be more precise, the success of Arrian's literary account of Epictetus' lectures – may well have contributed to the tragic loss of so many early Stoic texts and the then inevitable decline of Stoicism. Ironically, we have to thank opponents such as Plutarch and Galen for recording material from the Chrysippean corpus that would otherwise be totally lost. Even more ironically, it looks as if we should at least in part blame Epictetus (but equally, Arrian) for the decline in the fortunes of Stoicism and the loss of so many Stoic texts.

TWO

The Stoic system

How did the Stoics conceive philosophy?

In the final section of Chapter 1 we touched upon Epictetus' conception of philosophy and how it may have unwittingly contributed to the subsequent loss of early Stoic texts. As we have seen, for Epictetus philosophy is not merely about being able to understand and interpret philosophical texts; it is also something more practical and existential. As such, philosophy for him is an activity quite different from the modern academic discipline.

Before turning to Stoic philosophy directly it is important to consider precisely how the Stoics conceived philosophy and how their conception of philosophy differs from our own. If we assume that the Stoics were philosophers simply in the same sense in which a modern academic is a philosopher then we run the risk of countless misunderstandings and distortions. In particular, we may well end up simply abstracting those parts of Stoic philosophy that fit neatly into modern categories of philosophy and ignoring everything else that does not. While such an approach may be intellectually fruitful, it will not enable us to understand Stoic philosophy on its own terms. So let us begin by considering some Stoic thoughts about the nature and function of philosophy. The following passage comes from Epictetus:

Philosophy does not promise to secure anything external for humans, otherwise it would be admitting something that lies beyond its proper subject matter. For just as wood is the material of the carpenter, bronze that of the statuary, so each individual's own life is the material of the art of living.

(*Diss.* 1.15.2)

Here Epictetus presents Stoic philosophy as an art (*technē*), an art concerned with transforming one's way of life. Elsewhere (*Diss.* 2.19.20–25) he suggests that the best indicator of a person's philosophy is not what they say but how they behave. He suggests that his students should try to observe themselves in their daily actions in order to discover to which school of philosophy they really belong. He predicts that most of his students – all of whom are, of course, studying Stoicism – will find themselves to be Epicureans (holding pleasure to be the key to happiness), and a few will discover that they are Peripatetics (holding virtue to be the key to happiness, but requiring favourable external circumstances). But Epictetus doubts that he will find many Stoics among the students in his classroom (holding virtue to be the key to happiness regardless of circumstances). Of course, all of his students will be able to recite Stoic arguments and doctrines, but as we have seen for Epictetus that is not enough. The real Stoic must be able to translate those doctrines into concrete behaviour. It is not enough to say that one can be virtuous, and thus happy, regardless of circumstances; one must actually *be* happy regardless of circumstances, whether one is in danger, disgraced, sick or dying.

This last thought is echoed in a rather chilling passage from Seneca:

How do I know with what equanimity you would bear the loss of children, if you see around you all that you have fathered? I have heard you offering consolation to others. If you had been offering it to yourself, if you had been telling yourself not to grieve, then I might have seen your true character.

(*Prov.* 4.5)

For Seneca as much as for Epictetus, actions speak louder than words. Indeed, Seneca is himself explicit about his conception of philosophy. In one of his letters he writes:

> Philosophy is no trick to catch the public; it is not devised for show. It is a matter, not of words, but of facts. It is not pursued in order that the day may yield some amusement before it is spent, or that our leisure may be relieved of a tedium that irks us. It moulds and constructs the soul; it orders our life, guides our conduct, shows us what we should do and what we should leave undone ... without it, no one can live fearlessly or in peace of mind. (*Ep.* 16.3)

Similar thoughts can be found in the works of Musonius Rufus (see *Diss.* 5). In response to a question about the relative importance of theory and practice, Musonius asks to whom one would prefer to entrust one's life: an inexperienced doctor who can talk very well about medicine, or an experienced but not very articulate doctor with a good track record? Again, would one rather listen to music played by someone versed in the theory of music who has never played an instrument before, or one who knows nothing about musical theory but who is an experienced player? The answers to both questions are obvious. The same applies in philosophy; we should value far more highly someone who manages to put his philosophy into practice than someone who merely talks about philosophy.

Sadly, the lack of any complete texts from earlier Stoics makes it difficult to know for sure whether Zeno or Chrysippus held this very practical conception of philosophy outlined by Musonius, Seneca and Epictetus. It is conceivable that it might have been a later innovation. But that seems unlikely. If Zeno studied with Crates the Cynic, then we should expect him to have an equally practically orientated approach to philosophy. The fact that Zeno did not remain a Cynic, however, choosing instead to study with Polemo, and eventually founding his own school, is fairly clear evidence that he had no desire to become an orthodox Cynic. But nevertheless, the practical orientation of Cynicism no doubt left its mark. And despite some ancient attempts to argue that this Cynic influence was limited to the youthful Zeno, modern scholars have shown that Cynic themes can be found throughout the early Stoa (see Goulet-Cazé 2003). With a strong practical orientation in both those Cynics immediately preceding the early Stoics and in the later Stoics, it seems reasonable to suppose that this orientation marked the approach to philosophy of the early Stoics as well.

In fact, there is some evidence in favour of this supposition. In an account that draws on a lost work by Chrysippus, Cicero outlines an early Stoic use of a medical analogy (*Tusc.* 3.1–21). Echoing discussions by Socrates that one can find in the early Platonic dialogues, it is suggested that just as there is health and sickness of the body so too there is health and sickness of the soul. But although there is an established art of medicine for the body, less attention has been paid to developing an art of medicine for the soul, even though sickness of the soul is far more serious than sickness of the body. The art concerned with the cure or therapy of the soul is philosophy, Cicero suggests, following Chrysippus. Philosophy, then, is an art devoted to curing the soul of diseases just as medicine is an art devoted to curing the body of diseases. What might these diseases of the soul be? For the Stoics these diseases are famously the emotions, and the emotions are themselves the product of faulty judgements (on which more in Chapter 5). The process of uncovering the faulty judgements that create unwelcome emotions is a process of diagnosis similar to the physical diagnoses undertaken by a doctor. In fact, the emotions are strictly speaking merely the symptoms of a deeper mental disturbance, namely false beliefs that are the product of faulty judgements. The task of philosophy, conceived as this art of medicine for the soul, is to cure us of those false beliefs by teaching us how to avoid making faulty judgements. The philosopher, for Chrysippus, is thus a physician of the soul (Galen, *PHP* 5.2.23).

Unlike physicians who treat the body, however, the Stoic physician of the soul will be less concerned with curing the mental diseases of others and more concerned with the condition of his own soul:

> Assuredly there is an art of healing the soul – I mean phi-
> losophy, whose aid must be sought not, as in bodily diseases,
> outside ourselves, and we must use our utmost endeavour,
> with all our resources and strength, to have the power to be
> ourselves our own physicians. (*Tusc.* 3.6)

This conception of philosophy as an art for treating the diseases of the soul that one can only practise on oneself forms the context for our opening passage from Epictetus (*Diss.* 1.15.2). When Epictetus said that each individual's own life is the material of the art of living, he was responding to a man who asked him how it might be possible to stop his brother being angry with him. Epictetus' response was to say that the man should be more concerned with his own emotional reaction to his brother's anger than with his brother's anger itself. If the man wants to take up philosophy himself to treat his own mental diseases then he should do so, but he should not think that he will then be able to cure his brother's anger. Only his brother can do that. Here the Stoics may be seen to develop a theme originating with Socrates, namely the thought that the most urgent task we face is that of taking care of our own souls (see Sellars 2003: 36–9). No one can do this for us; we must all master the art of "taking care of oneself" for ourselves. Thus the Stoic physician of the soul is not some form of evangelical therapist who is intent on trying to cure the souls of everyone he meets; rather he is focused on a more personal and private task, although – like Socrates and Diogenes the Cynic – he may try to encourage others to embark on that very same personal work for themselves.

As we shall see later on, the Stoics are materialists and the soul is conceived as a certain kind of matter in a certain state. Any discussion of curing the soul of bad emotions, false beliefs or faulty judgements may equally be described in terms of altering the physical disposition of the soul. Chrysippus also gives us an analogy designed to show that any such alteration in the disposition of the soul will have a necessary impact on the way that we act (Aulus Gellius, *NA* 7.2.11). He suggests that we imagine a cylinder lying on the ground. In order for the cylinder to move it will require an external push, but the way that it moves, by rolling, will depend on its internal nature or form, namely its circular cross-section. The movement of the cylinder will thus be the product of the interaction of both the external cause (the push) and the internal cause (the shape). For Chrysippus, the disposition of the soul is analogous to the shape of the cylinder, while external stimuli are analogous to the push. Whenever someone acts in response to an external event, their action will necessarily be shaped by the disposition of their soul as well as the external event itself. In other words, transforming the disposition of an individual's soul will have a direct impact on their actions and so their way of life. This is the sense in which philosophy conceived as an art of curing the soul is also an art of living; we transform our lives by transforming the habitual dispositions of our souls.

As we shall see in later chapters, the early Stoics developed a complex philosophical system including formal logic, theories of language and knowledge, ontology and cosmology, as well as ethical theory. However, it is important to remember that these various aspects of the Stoic philosophical system were developed within this highly practical context. The aim of philosophy, for the Stoics, was to transform one's whole way of life. This process of transformation was focused on becoming as much as possible like their image of the idealized individual: the Stoic sage.

The role of the Stoic sage

Central to Stoic philosophy is the ideal of the Stoic sage. If philosophy is an art of living devoted to transforming one's way of life, then the ultimate goal of that art is to turn one's life into the life of a sage. All the various parts of Stoic philosophy are, in their own way, directed towards this end.

The sage is described in a variety of sources as someone who is never impeded, who is infallible, who is more powerful than everyone else, richer, stronger, freer, happier and the only person truly deserving the title "king" (see e.g. Cicero, *Fin.* 3.75; also *Tusc.* 3.10–21). Arius Didymus adds the following in his summary of Stoic ethics:

They say that the sage also does everything he does well. This is obvious, in the way that we say that the flute-player or the lyre-player does everything well ... so in the same way the sensible person does everything well with respect to whatever he does .... For they have thought that the belief that the sage does everything well is consistent with his completing everything in accord with correct reasoning and in a fashion which is in accord with virtue, which is the art that deals with life as a whole.   (Arius Didymus 5b10)

The sage, then, is an individual who has mastered the art of living and so always acts well in all areas of his life, just as the flute-player who has mastered the art of flute-playing always plays well whenever he is flute-playing. Having mastered the art of living, the sage will be completely free from the diseases of the soul, and his wisdom will be defined simply in terms of having a perfectly healthy soul (*Tusc.* 3.10). Or, following Galen, we might say that the soul of the sage will be completely immune from such diseases, while some others will be healthy but not immune, others will be easily prone to illness, while those currently overcome by emotions will be sick (*PHP* 5.2.9). In general, though, Stoic accounts tend to present everyone who is not a sage as impious, foolish and mad (e.g. Plutarch, *St. Rep.* 1048e).

If the sage is as rare a creature as we would expect, then these unflattering terms will apply to almost everyone. Not surprisingly, this did not go down well with some of the Stoics' opponents. The peculiar attributes of the sage led to a number of conclusions that came to be known as the "Stoic paradoxes". Cicero provides us with a helpful short text summarizing some of these: the *Paradoxa Stoicorum*. Among the topics discussed by Cicero are the Stoic claims that "every non-sage is mad", that "only the sage is rich" and that "only the sage is free and so every non-sage is a slave". Dealing with the last of these he writes: "If slavery means, as it does mean, the obedience of a broken and abject spirit that has no volition of its own, who would deny that all fickle and covetous people and indeed all the vicious are really slaves?" (*Parad.* 35). Despite the popularity of Stoicism in the Roman world, one can understand why wealthy slave-owning Roman nobles would not have appreciated listening to arguments claiming that in fact they were poor and slaves themselves because they had not reached the (possibly unattainable) ideal of the Stoic sage.

The Stoics did acknowledge a third, intermediate class of individuals: those who are "making progress" (*prokopē*). These are philosophers in the etymological sense of the word: lovers of wisdom who aspire after wisdom but who are not themselves wise. However, such individuals remain strictly speaking among the foolish, as is graphically illustrated in a passage by Chrysippus:

> Just as in the sea the man a cubit from the surface is drowning no less than the one who has sunk 500 fathoms, so neither are they any the less in vice who are approaching virtue than they who are a long way from it … so those who are "making progress" continue to be stupid and depraved until they have attained virtue.
>
> (reported in Plutarch, *Com. Not.* 1063a)

So, even the philosophers remain slaves, impious, foolish and mad. Indeed, none of the early Stoic philosophers appear to have presented themselves as sages, even if some of their later followers may have been tempted to venerate them as such (see Brouwer 2002). If this is so even for the philosophers then who might possibly be counted as an example of a sage? Not surprisingly, there was some doubt as to whether any such individual actually existed, or indeed could ever exist. In the light of this doubt one question that arises is whether the ideal of the sage is a real practical possibility that can actually be achieved in reality or whether it is a purely abstract regulative ideal that one can only work towards but never actually reach. This second response has formed the basis for a common criticism of Stoicism down the ages, articulated by Erasmus and Kant among others, and already made in antiquity. This is obviously closely related to the question of whether any Stoic sages have ever existed. We only need to be able to point to one concrete example of a genuine Stoic sage in order to be able to say that it is a real possibility to become a sage, no matter how difficult it may be to achieve this. In order to counter the charge that the sage is an impossible ideal, supporters of Stoicism suggested the names of individuals whom they believed had attained the status of the sage. Among Roman Stoics, the preferred example was Cato the Younger.

Cato the Younger (95–46 BCE), a political opponent of Julius Caesar, whose life is recounted in Plutarch's *Cato the Younger* and Lucan's *Pharsalia*, is most famous for committing suicide in Utica, the north African town he governed during Rome's civil war, rather than face capture by Caesar. When pushed for an example of a Stoic sage, Seneca's response was always to point to Cato. Seneca's admiration for Cato was so great that he suggested that Cato might even surpass the ideal of the sage:

> You have no reason to make your usual remark that this wise man of ours cannot be found anywhere. We are not inventing him as a sort of imaginary glory of human nature, nor is he just a lofty image of some false conception of ours; but we have shown him existing as we portray him, and we shall show him again – rarely perhaps, and only an isolated example at long intervals of ages. For greatness that surpasses ordinary common limits does not occur frequently. But I wonder whether this same Marcus Cato, with whom our discussion started, may not even surpass our ideal.   (*Const.* 7.1)

While Cicero remained to a certain extent critical of this Stoic ideal, he nevertheless acknowledged that Cato had indeed managed to live his Stoicism rather than merely to argue about it (*Pro Murena* 62), and described him as a perfect example of a Stoic (*Parad.* 2). The Stoic poet Lucan is even more emphatic about Cato's pre-eminent status:

> Cato was a true father of his country, and far worthier than others who have since been granted this title, to have altars raised in his memory. One day when we are finally freed from slavery, if that ever happens, Cato will be deified; and Rome will then have a god by whose name it need not be ashamed to swear.   (*Pharsalia* 9.601–4)

Whereas Roman Stoics such as Seneca and Lucan admired Cato the Younger as a possible example of a sage, in the Greek-speaking world it was Socrates who was often presented as an example of a sage. We saw in Chapter 1 the story claiming that Zeno was first inspired to study philosophy after reading about Socrates in Xenophon's *Memorabilia*. Indeed, one might say that Stoic philosophy literally began with Zeno's admiration for the life of Socrates. Philodemus reports that some Stoics actually wanted to be called "Socratics" (*De Stoicis* 13,3-4). In the works of a later Stoic such as Epictetus, Socrates forms an authoritative paradigm for the ideal philosophical life: "Even if you are not yet a Socrates, you should live as if you wish to become a Socrates" (*Ench.* 51.3).

It is also clear that Socrates stood as an important role model for many of the early Stoics (see Long 1988), similar to the way in which Epicurus functioned as a role model for the Epicureans. But of course Socrates was no Stoic sage, nor could he ever have been, living before Stoicism had been conceived. He was simply a model of wisdom that some Stoics took to embody the principal attributes of their own philosophical ideal. Other non-Stoics who were adopted in this way as models of the sage included the legendary Heracles (or Hercules) and Diogenes the Cynic. Epictetus offers Diogenes as just such an example to a sceptical interlocutor:

> But can I show you one who was free, that you may no longer have to seek for an example. Diogenes was free. "How so?" Not because he was born of free parents, for he was not, but because he was free himself, because he had cast away all that gives slavery a hold on a person, so that there was no way that anybody could come up to him or seize hold of him to enslave him. (*Diss.* 4.1.152)

Despite these examples, the great problem for the Stoa was that none of the early Stoics presented themselves as sages and later Stoics seemed hesitant to canonize the school's founders. Both parties should of course be credited for their caution here. But it meant that the school did not have an internal figure that it could hold up as a living example of its own philosophical ideal. Neither Socrates nor Diogenes were Stoics, while Cato was a specifically Roman hero, the product of a particular political context, who would not have been an obvious role model for Stoicism as a whole. Ancient critics were quick to point out that there is a potential problem in a philosophical system that is primarily directed towards becoming something that has never and perhaps can never exist. There is something inevitably futile about devoting one's life to trying to become a sage if that is an impossible goal to reach. Despite their great qualities, there is something ridiculous about the claim that Socrates or Cato never made a mistake in their lives, which would follow from the claim that they were infallible sages. Indeed, it appears that some later Stoics took these concerns seriously and Panaetius, for instance, shifted attention away from the hypothetical actions of the perfect sage and focused more on the actions of imperfect individuals trying to improve their lives in the here and now (see Seneca, *Ep.* 116.5).

In response to these sorts of concerns one might say that although the Stoic sage may appear to be an impossible abstract ideal, it was in fact an ideal based on particular concrete examples. As we have seen, the most important of these would have been Socrates, perhaps followed closely by Diogenes. Although it is unlikely that either Socrates or Diogenes would have claimed to have lived up to some of the more abstract accounts of the sage's perfected attributes, they nevertheless did embody a range of qualities that the Stoics considered praiseworthy. If we approach the image of the sage within this context, bearing in mind the concrete examples on which it is based, then it will not seem quite so unrealistic an ideal. While it may be impossible to become perfect to the point of infallibility, it is conceivable, in the words of Epictetus, "to become like Socrates", no matter how difficult that task may be, and even if the "Socrates" in mind is no longer identical to the historical figure. The most important point to stress here, however, is the way in which this concern with the sage in Stoicism emphasizes its primarily practical orientation. The fundamental philosophical task for Stoicism is to transform one's way of life into the life of a sage.

The "three parts" of philosophy

So far we have focused on the practical dimension of Stoic philosophy. For ancient philosophers such as the Cynics, this was all that
mattered. The Stoics, by contrast, combine this practical approach
with a keen interest in philosophical theory. Indeed, the most important figure in the history of the Stoa, Chrysippus, was probably best
known in antiquity as a logician. Ancient accounts of Stoic doctrine
such as the one given by Diogenes Laertius outline a complex taxonomy of philosophical theories with numerous divisions and subdivisions. Here is just one example:

> Some [Stoics] divide the logical part of the system into the
> two sciences of rhetoric and dialectic ... rhetoric itself, they
> say, has three divisions: deliberative, forensic and panegyric
> ... dialectic (they hold) falls under two heads: subjects of
> discourse and language. And the subjects fall under the
> following headings: presentations ..., propositions [and
> so on].   (DL 7.41–3)

At the summit of this Stoic taxonomy is a basic division of philosophy into three main parts: "They say that philosophical discourse
has three parts, one of these being physical, another ethical and
another logical" (DL 7.39). It is important to stress at the outset
that these three terms – logic, physics and ethics – were being used
slightly differently from the way in which they are used today. Logic,
for instance, was conceived in a much wider sense than it is now,
encompassing not only formal logic, but also rhetoric and epistemology. Similarly, physics was understood to cover not only natural
philosophy but also ontology or metaphysics and theology.

Various Stoics offered different similes in attempts to explain the
relationship between the three parts of logic, physics and ethics:

> Philosophy, they say, is like an animal, logic corresponding
> to the bones and sinews, ethics to the fleshy parts, physics
> to the soul. Another simile they use is that of an egg: the

shell is logic, next comes the white, ethics, and the yolk in the centre is physics. Or again they liken philosophy to an orchard: logic being the surrounding fence, ethics the fruit, physics the soil or the trees.   (DL 7.40)

Some commentators have looked at these accounts and tried to see whether they imply any priority of one part of Stoic philosophy over the others. But what all of these images seem to suggest is a fundamental interdependence between the three parts of philosophy. This is evident in the case of the egg simile, but it is perhaps most obvious in the comparison with a living being. Indeed, another source reports that Posidonius rejected the comparison with an orchard precisely because it was too easy to conceive of the parts existing independently from one another, and he explicitly preferred the comparison with a living being because it stressed that the three parts of philosophy are inseparable (see Sextus, *Adv. Math.* 7.19).

Accepting this fundamental interdependence, might it still be possible to place the three parts in some form of order of priority? One context in which that might be done is when trying to determine their order of teaching. It is reported that various Stoics disagreed over the order in which the three parts should be taught (DL 7.41). Chrysippus thought that students should be taught logic first, then ethics, then physics (and then theology, the highest part of physics). Yet, as Plutarch comments, many of Chrysippus' discussions of ethics presupposed and would have been prefaced by discussions of physics (*St. Rep.* 1035a–f). Other sources report that Zeno, Chrysippus and others all placed logic first, followed by physics and finally ethics. Others suggested that no part should be given priority over any other, and that they should be taught in a mixed form in order to emphasize this (DL 7.40). Any teaching programme introducing Stoicism cannot do everything at once, and so some ordering seems inevitable. But from the albeit limited accounts that we have it seems likely that the orders of priority are merely concerned with arranging a curriculum and do not imply any more fundamental philosophical priority of one part over any other. As we shall see, each of the three parts of Stoic philosophy depends upon the others and cannot be understood fully without them.

Philosophy and philosophical discourse

We have seen how Stoic philosophy was divided into the three parts of logic, physics and ethics. This is not strictly speaking correct, however. Diogenes Laertius tells us that it was philosophical *discourse* that was divided in this way (DL 7.39), whereas Plutarch says that this division applies to philosophical *theorems* (*St. Rep.* 1035a). This is important as it may help us to reconcile the claims that, on the one hand philosophy is a practical art concerned with transforming one's life into that of a sage, while on the other hand it is a seemingly theoretical subject divided into logic, physics and ethics, each of which is further subdivided into a complex taxonomy of doctrines. We can now see that this complex taxonomy is of philosophical discourse or theory, but not necessarily of philosophy itself. Philosophy itself, as we have seen with Epictetus, is an attempt to transform one's way of life. Arius Didymus writes:

> It is not the person who eagerly listens to and makes notes of what is spoken by the philosophers who is ready for philosophizing, but the person who is ready to transfer the prescriptions of philosophy to his deeds and to live in accord with them. (11k)

We have a clear distinction, then, between philosophical discourse, what is spoken and written by the philosophers, and philosophy itself, a way of life in which philosophical doctrines are expressed in one's behaviour. But how are these two things related to one another? Do the Stoics give an account of how they thought their complex philosophical theory could be put to work in a way that would enable one to progress towards the ideal of the sage?

Epictetus gives us just an account. He outlines a two-stage model for philosophical education:

> The philosophers first exercise us in theory, where there is less difficulty, and then after that lead us to the more difficult matters; for in theory there is nothing that holds us back from following what we are taught, but in life there are many things that distract us. (*Diss.* 1.26.3)

First we study Stoic doctrines or theory, divided under the headings of logic, physics and ethics, and then we turn to the much harder task of trying to put those doctrines into practice, of transforming our lives in the light of what we have learned. The first stage involves, in Epictetus' classroom at least, the study of the famously difficult writings of Chrysippus. The second stage involves a series of exercises (*askēseis*) that are designed to accomplish an even harder task, namely translating the philosophical doctrines contained within the works of Chrysippus into actions. Here Epictetus is following his old teacher Musonius. As we have seen, Musonius emphasizes the value of practice over theory. However, he qualifies that claim by stressing the necessity of practice grounded in theory: "Theory, which teaches how one should act, is related to application, and comes first, since it is not possible to do anything really well unless its practical execution be in harmony with theory" (*Diss.* 5). So, the study of philosophical doctrines is an essential first stage in philosophical education, even for the highly practically orientated Musonius. But what about Epictetus' second stage? I have suggested that this second stage will be constituted by some form of exercise designed to translate the content of those doctrines into actions. In a text entitled *On Exercise* Musonius fleshes out this second stage. He begins by presenting the exercises that will be necessary as exercises for the soul – what Pierre Hadot has called "spiritual exercises" (in e.g. Hadot 1998) – analogous to the exercises for the body that an athlete might undertake. With regard to these "spiritual exercises", Musonius says:

> Exercise for the soul consists first of all in seeing that the proofs pertaining to apparent goods as not being real goods are always ready at hand and likewise those pertaining to

> apparent evils as not being real evils, and in learning to
> recognize the things that are truly good and in becoming
> accustomed to distinguish them from what are not truly
> good.   (*Diss.* 6)

In other words, these exercises are aimed at transforming our
habitual ways of acting in the light of the philosophical theories
that we have mastered in the classroom. It is one thing to be able
to say what is truly good and what is only apparently good; it is
quite another to act immediately and consistently in the light of
that understanding. We have, Musonius says a little further on,
built up a large number of bad habits that we must overcome if
we are to make genuine philosophical progress. That is why we
can acknowledge one course of action to be the best, and yet follow another. The task for this second stage, then, is to habituate
the soul so that one's consciously chosen philosophical beliefs can
shape one's unconscious habits, and so determine one's everyday
behaviour. This process is often presented in terms of habituation
and digestion. Marcus Aurelius presents this as a process of dyeing
the soul a new colour, just as one might dye a piece of cloth a new
colour (*Med.* 5.16). The task is what we might call the digestion of
philosophical theories, analogous to the digestion of food. Epictetus writes:

> Sheep do not bring their fodder to the shepherds and show
> how much they have eaten, but they digest their food within
> them, and on the outside produce wool and milk. And so
> you too should make no display to the layman of your philo-
> sophical principles but let them see the results that come
> from the principles when digested.   (*Ench.* 46)

But how do you digest philosophical theories? One way to assimilate information is to write it out a number of times, just as students write out revision notes a number of times in order to help
them remember their contents. It has been suggested that the
often repetitive passages of the notebooks that we now know as

the *Meditations* of Marcus Aurelius are an example of this sort of writing. Indeed, Epictetus advises that this is precisely how philosophers should exercise themselves, namely by writing out key doctrines every day (*Diss.* 1.1.25). Seneca proposes another strategy. He suggests that at the end of each day we should take time to call ourselves to account and go over the events of the day. We should cross-examine ourselves and ask whether we have remained faithful to the philosophical principles that we consciously hold, whether we have overcome any bad habits and whether we have resisted any unwelcome desires (*Ira* 3.36.1–3). In both cases, such exercises should take place *after* one has left the philosophy classroom, that is, after one has already studied the philosophical doctrines that one is now trying to digest.

At this point one might raise an objection. As we shall see in more detail in later chapters, the Stoics follow Socrates in holding a unified, monistic conception of the soul and an intellectualist account of the relationship between knowledge and action. Socrates is famous for asserting that virtue is constituted by knowledge, that if one knows that x is right then one will necessarily do x. This, in turn, forms the basis for Socrates' famous denial of weakness of will: no one ever does wrong willingly and always acts in accordance with what they believe to be right. Now, if the Stoics are intellectualists in this Socratic sense then surely mastery of philosophical doctrines in the first stage of Epictetus' plan would be sufficient on its own to deliver the corresponding philosophical actions. If we know the doctrines, and know them to be right, then how could we not act in accordance with them? The second stage of habituation, exercise and therapy of the soul (as it is often described) should, for a Socratic intellectualist, be totally superfluous.

There are a number of ways to respond to this thought. One would be to distinguish between the early Stoics, who perhaps did remain faithful to Socratic intellectualism, and the later Stoics who introduced the ideas of exercise and therapy after having abandoned the Socratic position. However, this does not seem to be the right way to solve the problem, because later Stoics such as Seneca and Epictetus who *do* make use of the themes of exercise and therapy still hold on to the orthodox Stoic theory of the emotions that presupposes a monistic and intellectualist conception of the soul. Another way to respond would be to think further about the way in which knowledge is being conceived here. It is knowledge, remember, that Socrates held to constitute virtue. At the beginning of this chapter we saw Epictetus present philosophy as an art, a *technē*, and this thought also appeared in the Chrysippean medical analogy. In a number of ancient discussions of arts and crafts it is emphasized that in order to master an art it is necessary both to master the principles underpinning the art and then to undergo a period of practical training. In the case of becoming a doctor, for instance, a medical student will have to complete a lengthy apprenticeship after they have finished their theoretical classroom studies and before they can qualify as a doctor. One can see that there are two stages here – theoretical principles and practical training – and that these are similar to the two stages that we have already encountered in Epictetus. For Epictetus, philosophy is an art and mastery of that art will require both stages of education just as the art of medicine will.

The objection that, as Socratic intellectualists, the Stoics should have no need for exercises or therapy because knowledge should be sufficient on its own assumes that the theoretical principles underpinning an art will on their own constitute knowledge. In other words, it assumes that philosophical knowledge should be identified with mastery of philosophical doctrines. But a Stoic such as Epictetus does not conceive philosophical knowledge in this way. Because he conceives philosophy as an art then philosophical knowledge, like mastery of an art or craft, will require *both* mastery of philosophical doctrines *and* a subsequent period of training or exercise designed to digest those doctrines. For Epictetus, mastery of philosophical doctrines alone will not constitute knowledge, and so if someone with such mastery fails to act in accordance with them he will not be acting against his knowledge. We might say that he acts against the information that he has gathered, but not his knowledge, for at that point he has not yet gained any philosophical knowledge. In order to gain genuine philosophical knowledge, he will, like any other apprentice craftsman, have to undergo the second stage of training in order to assimilate that information. Only then will he attain knowledge conceived as knowledge of an art. In this sense, the second stage of education remains essential. However, Epictetus can remain a Socratic intellectualist while holding this conception of philosophical knowledge for, like Socrates, he can then argue that once one does have philosophical knowledge then it will necessarily inform one's behaviour. The sage will necessarily act well, just as the master builder will necessarily build good houses (excepting deliberate intent or external influence).

Indeed, this intellectualist objection against Stoic therapy was made by the heterodox Stoic Aristo right at the beginning of the school's history (and reported in Seneca *Ep.* 94), a fact that we might take as evidence for the claim that such therapy and exercises were a feature of not only the later Stoics but also the earliest Stoics. Aristo argued that exercises (in the form of general moral precepts) would be of no benefit to someone who remained ignorant, for their ignorance would cloud their judgement, whereas exercises would be superfluous to anyone who was free from ignorance, for such individuals would already know what to do (*Ep.* 94.11). It is the second of these claims that forms the intellectualist objection. In his reply to this objection Seneca implicitly draws attention to the fact that only the perfect sage will be completely free from ignorance. The vast majority of us, however, will have unwanted habits and emotions that will hinder our digestion of philosophical principles. Seneca also cites the opinion of Aristo's contemporary Cleanthes, who held that this second stage of philosophical education "is indeed useful, but that it is a feeble thing unless it is derived from general principles" (*Ep.* 94.4). This clearly pre-empts Epictetus' two-stage account of philosophical education.

So, we have a conception of philosophy as an art or craft that, like other arts and crafts, will involve two stages of education: first a study of philosophical discourse, followed by a practical training or apprenticeship conceived as a process of habituation and digestion. How might this two-stage model of philosophical education relate to the tripartite division of philosophy into logic, physics and ethics? Well, if we remember that it is philosophical discourse that is divided into these three parts then we shall be part of the way to an answer already. The three types of philosophical discourse – logic, physics and ethics – form the contents of the first stage of philosophical education. Thus, students in Epictetus' classroom will study texts on each of these three topics by eminent Stoic authors. What about the second stage? Will this be a unified practice, or will it also divide into parts? In order to answer this question let us consider what Epictetus calls the three *topoi* or "areas of study":

> There are three areas of study, in which a person who is going to be noble and good must be trained:
> [1] That concerning desires and aversions, so that he may neither fail to get what he desires nor fall into what he would avoid.
> [2] That concerning the impulse to act and not to act, and, generally, appropriate behaviour; so that he may act in an orderly manner and after due consideration, and not carelessly.
> [3] The third is concerned with freedom from deception and hasty judgement, and, generally, whatever is connected with assents. (*Diss.* 3.2.1–2)

It has been suggested that these three areas form three types of exercise in the second stage of philosophical education that correspond to the three types of discourse in the first stage. It would be very neat if they did, which makes the suggestion very attractive, but it should be noted that some scholars remain unconvinced and the issue is contentious (see e.g. Dobbin 1998: 94). With that proviso in place, we shall see how far it is possible to make sense of this suggestion. At the outset it should be stressed that the claim is not that these three "areas of study" are identical to the three parts of philosophy, but rather that they can be correlated with the three types of philosophical discourse. So the challenge is to show how they might in fact do so.

The second *topos*, concerned with impulse and appropriate behaviour, clearly correspond to ethics. After students have studied the Stoic theory of appropriate actions (which we shall encounter in

Chapter 5), they will require training outlined by the second *topos* to help them put that theory into practice. This correlation is probably the most obvious of the three.

The third *topos*, concerned with judgement and assent, corresponds to logic. Both judgement and assent (as we shall see in Chapter 3) are central topics in Stoic epistemology, itself part of Stoic logic.

That leaves the first *topos*. It also leaves physics. By a process of elimination, the first *topos* must correspond to physics, if the suggestion that there is a correlation is to stand. The first *topos* appears primarily to be concerned with desire and aversion, and it is not immediately obvious how training in relation to desire and aversion might put into practice Stoic physical theory. However, there is arguably a connection. The first *topos* is devoted to training one's desires and aversions, that is, it attempts to put into practice a philosophical analysis concerning what one should desire and what one should avoid. Understanding what one should desire and what one should avoid will involve physical theory on two levels. At the microscopic level it will involve a physiological analysis of the human organism, of what will be beneficial and harmful to its constitution. Such a physical analysis will tell us that, for instance, we should desire healthy foods and avoid poisons. At the macroscopic level it will involve an understanding of the order of causes in the cosmos as a whole, knowing what would and would not be a realistic outcome of events to desire. This sort of physical analysis, involving the Stoic theory of fate, will tell us that, for instance, we should only desire events that are in fact possible outcomes given the order of causes currently at play. In other words, if one were to ask what the practical implications of the study of Stoic physics might be, the answer would most likely be that a greater understanding of the way in which Nature works at both the individual and cosmic levels should have consequences for what we consider realistic objects of desire and aversion. In this sense, then, the first *topos* is indeed training that correlates with Stoic physical theory.

If we accept this correlation, and as I have noted not all scholars will, then what we have are three types of training in the form of the three *topoi* or "areas of study" that constitute the second stage of

Epictetus' programme of education, reflecting the threefold division of the first stage into logical, physical and ethical discourse.

Much of the foregoing account has been based on material in Epictetus. It is difficult to determine how much of it, if any, is innovative or whether it reflects much older Stoic discussions about the internal structure of philosophy. It would be prudent, then, to be hesitant before attributing it to the Stoa as a whole. Having said that, this material does constitute the fullest surviving Stoic account of the nature and function of philosophy.

The interrelated nature of the Stoic system

Although it is important to stress the practical orientation of Stoic philosophy, and to note the role played by training or exercises in some of the later Stoic texts, it is also important not to lose sight of the interrelation of the three parts of Stoic philosophy. The emphasis on practical matters in the late Stoic authors has traditionally led commentators to suggest that there was a shift away from concerns with logic and physics towards an almost total concern with ethics. The discussion in the previous section has shown that the division between philosophical discourse and training or exercise in fact cuts across all three of the traditional parts of philosophy, so that it is possible to talk of practical physics and practical logic alongside practical ethics (represented by the three *topoi*), as well as theoretical ethics alongside theoretical logic and theoretical physics (the three types of philosophical discourse).

Thus, a shift in focus towards practical matters need not necessarily involve prioritizing one of the three parts of philosophy over the others. It is important for the Stoics that this is so, because each of the three parts of the Stoic system is necessary for their philosophy to stand at all. No one part can be adequately understood without at least some grasp of the central concepts developed in the other parts. For instance, the ethical goal of "living in accordance with Nature" will naturally depend upon at least some understanding of the characteristics of Nature, the domain of physics. Similarly, the ethical goal of freedom from emotions will depend upon an understanding of the epistemological concepts of judgement and assent that give rise to emotions, which belong to the domain of logic. Ancient critics also understood this; for instance Sextus Empiricus thought that he could undermine the Stoic concept of an art of living if he could show that their epistemological concept of an "adequate impression" was questionable (*Pyrr. Hyp.* 3.242). Cicero has his expositor of Stoicism proclaim that the Stoic system is "so well constructed, so firmly jointed and welded into one … [with] such close interconnection of the parts that if you alter a single letter, you shake the whole structure" (*Fin.* 3.74). No doubt this was precisely Sextus' thought; all he need do is remove one brick from the structure and the whole edifice might fall down. The systematic interrelation of the three parts of Stoic philosophy was a strength but also potentially a weakness.

While it may be possible to distinguish between the three parts of philosophy in our discourse, in practice, whether that be theoretical speculation or human action, it is impossible for them to become completely separated from one another. As we have seen, the process of division is vital for the purposes of education, but Seneca reminds us that "it is useful that philosophy should be divided, but not chopped into bits" (*Ep.* 89.2). This close interrelation between the three parts of philosophy reflects an organic unity alluded to in the famous similes that we encountered earlier; philosophy is like an egg or it is like a human being. Posidonius' rejection of the orchard simile was precisely because it did not capture this organic unity in the same way. Indeed, if we were to be more precise, we should say that philosophy proper is an organic unity, an organic and material disposition of the soul that can transform the way in which we live. It is only philosophical discourse that can be divided into the three parts, but even then each part of philosophical discourse depends upon concepts that belong to the other parts.

It is in the light of the interrelated nature of the Stoic philosophical system that the ever-practically orientated Epictetus insists on the necessity of the study of logic (see *Diss.* 1.17). When one of his students interrupts and says that studying logic is a waste of time because it will not help him improve his character, Epictetus replies by saying that how can any of us hope to do that unless we are able to define what it is that we hope to improve and are able to distinguish between truth and falsehood. Elsewhere (*Diss.* 2.25), Epictetus responds to someone who demands to be convinced of the necessity of logic by saying that the only way he can do that is by using an argument, so if the questioner wants to know whether logic is necessary or not he must first be able to judge whether that argument is valid or not. Thus logic is necessary even to answer the question whether logic is necessary. It is clear, then, that even the most practical Stoics explicitly acknowledged the necessity of a potentially non-practical part of the Stoic system such as formal logic (see Barnes 1997). It is to logic that we shall turn first in our exposition of the Stoic system.

THREE
Stoic logic

Logic in antiquity

Following the Stoic division of philosophical discourse into logic, physics and ethics, we shall begin by looking at Stoic logic. By the term "logic" today we usually mean the formal analysis of arguments. While this sort of abstract reasoning was an important part of logic in antiquity, ancient logic was much broader than its modern counterpart. "Logic" translates *logikē*, and *logikē* is that part of philosophy that examines *logos* – reason, language or argument – in all of its forms, including formal arguments, rhetorical arguments, speech, grammar, philosophy of language and truth (i.e. epistemology). The formal abstract reasoning that now constitutes logic was known in antiquity as one part of dialectic, and dialectic was just one part of *logikē*.

For the Stoics, logic comprised dialectic and rhetoric as two principal divisions. Other Stoics added definition and canonic (epistemology) as further parts, and some added canonic but not definition (see DL 7.41–3). In what follows I shall look first at Stoic dialectic, then what we might call their philosophy of language and finally their epistemology. But I shall leave to one side their discussions of rhetoric and their important work on grammar.

Stoic dialectic

Stoic logic did not fare well in subsequent history. It is fair to say that its significance was not really comprehended until fairly recently by the Polish logician Łukasiewicz in the early twentieth century (Bocheński 1951: 80). The most important ancient sources for our knowledge of Stoic logic are Diogenes Laertius, Sextus Empiricus (*Pyrr. Hyp.* 2, *Adv. Math.* 8) and Galen (esp. *Institutio Logica*).

The founder of Stoicism, Zeno, is reported to have studied with the Megarian philosopher Stilpo. This is significant here because the Megarians have a considerable reputation for their work on logic (see Kneale & Kneale 1962: 113–17). Famous Megarian logicians include Euclides (founder of the Megarian school), Eubulides (creator of a number of famous paradoxes including "the liar" and "the heap"), Diodorus Cronus (inventor of the famous "master argument") and Philo (Zeno's fellow pupil under Stilpo). Zeno's education in Megarian logic no doubt proved a vital influence in the early development of Stoic logic. However, the Stoic philosopher most closely associated with logic is Chrysippus and it seems probable that Chrysippus did much to shape Stoic logic as we now know it. Indeed, it has been suggested that Chrysippus even rivals Aristotle in stature as a logician.

Before turning to discuss Stoic logic directly, it may be helpful to begin with a brief account of Aristotle's logic, as this will enable us to see how Stoic and Aristotelian logic differ from one another. Consider the following argument:

> All human beings are animals;
> All animals are mortal;
> Therefore, all human beings are mortal.

This type of argument is known as a syllogism and Aristotle's famous account of the syllogism may be found in his *Prior Analytics*. The final line (the conclusion) follows necessarily from the first two lines (the premises). If one accepts that both premises are true then one must also accept that the conclusion is true. This is because the formal structure of the argument is what is known as "valid". If we replace the terms in the argument with letters then the formal structure will become clearer:

> All *A* are *B*;
> All *B* are *C*;
> Therefore, all *A* are *C*.

Any argument that has this form, regardless of what the letters are replacing, will be a valid argument. For example:

> All bananas are fruit;
> All fruit are purple;
> Therefore, all bananas are purple.

This argument is still valid in its logical form, even though we may doubt the truth of one of its premises. The conclusion follows necessarily from the premises, and if we were to accept both the premises as true, we would also have to accept the conclusion as true. This form of argument (all *A* are *B*; all *B* are *C*; therefore all *A* are *C*) is an example of an Aristotelian syllogism. Other examples include:

> All bananas are fruit;
> Some bananas are green;
> Therefore, some green [things] are fruit.
> (All *A* is *B*; some *A* is *C*; therefore some *C* is *B*.)

> No fruit are black;
> All coals are black;
> Therefore, no coals are fruit.
> (No *A* is *B*; all *C* is *B*; therefore no *C* is *A*.)

As we can see, Aristotle's logic makes use of four basic logical terms: "all", "some", "is/are" and "is/are not" (or "no"). There are a number of other features of Aristotle's syllogistic logic that we should also note. One is that it is concerned solely with universal terms. Thus the well-known example "Socrates is a man; all men are mortal; therefore

Socrates is mortal"' is not in fact an Aristotelian syllogism because "Socrates" is a particular rather than a universal. The second is that when these arguments are formalized the letters are used to replace terms. This will become important shortly.

Let us now turn to consider some other types of arguments. Take the following example:

> If it is raining this afternoon, then I shall not go out for a walk;
> It is raining this afternoon;
> Therefore, I shall not go out for a walk.

As with the examples above, it is possible to formalize this argument, thus:

> If p, then q;
> p;
> Therefore, q.

This is an example of a Stoic syllogism. Notice that, in contrast to the Aristotelian syllogisms, the letters replace not terms (e.g. "human beings") but propositions (e.g. "it is raining this afternoon"). These propositions are called "assertibles" (*axiōmata*).

An assertible is a complete sayable, and we shall consider sayables in the next section. They can be either true or false (DL 7.65). Indeed, the ability of being able to be either true or false is an important characteristic of assertibles. Their truth-value can also change depending on *when* they are asserted. So, the assertible "it is night" will be true when it is night, but not when it is day (*ibid.*). They can also be either simple or complex (literally, "not simple"); an example of a simple assertible would be "it is night", while "if it is night, it is dark" would be complex because it contains within itself more than one simple assertible. The Stoics catalogue different types of both simple and complex assertible (DL 7.69–74). Examples of the former would be affirmation and negation; examples of the latter would be conditionals and conjunctions. In our example above, the first premise is complex ("If it is raining this afternoon, then I shall not go out for a walk"), while the second is simple ("It is raining this afternoon"). Assertibles can also be distinguished according to their modality – whether they are possible, impossible, necessary or non-necessary – and here the Stoics were probably building upon earlier Megarian interests in this area, especially the work of Diodorus Cronus.

Stoic syllogisms are built out of assertibles rather than terms, as we have seen. In our first example, the letters p and q replace propositions rather than individual words as they did in Aristotelian syllogisms. The ancient sources (e.g. Sextus, *Adv. Math.* 8.227) suggest that the Stoics themselves preferred to use ordinal numbers when formalizing arguments:

> If the first, the second;
> The first;
> Therefore, the second.

Once formalized in this way, an argument structure such as the one above was known as a "mode" (and strictly speaking a "mode" (*tropos*) is not an argument itself, but rather the structural form of a certain type of argument that particular arguments can have). Just as Aristotle outlined a number of different forms for valid arguments, so the Stoics offered a number of types of argument. In particular, they proposed five basic "undemonstrated" or "indemonstrable"' (*anapodeiktos*) syllogisms to which all others could be reduced (see Sextus, *Pyrr. Hyp.* 2.157–8). The five basic arguments were held to be obviously valid and so not in need of any further proof. They are:

1. If p, then q; p; therefore, q.   (*modus ponendo ponens*)
2. If p, then q; not q; therefore, not p. (*modus tollendo tollens*)
3. Not p and q; p; therefore, not q.
4. Either p or q; p; therefore, not q.   (*modus ponendo tollens*)
5. Either p or q; not q; therefore p.   (*modus tollendo ponens*)

As one can see, each of the five undemonstrated syllogisms has a complex assertible as its first premise, and a simple assertible as its second premise. They make use of the logical connectors "if", "and" and "or". An argument involving an "if" is known as a conditional; arguments involving "and" and "or" are known as conjunctions and disjunctions respectively. Note also the use of "not" for negation. So whereas Aristotle's syllogisms depend on four key logical terms – "all", "some", "is" and "is not" – Stoic syllogisms have their own set of four key terms: "if", "and", "or" and "not".

In order to give a sense of how a much wider range of arguments may be extrapolated from these five basic types, let us briefly focus on the first type: "if p, then q; p; therefore, q". In this example the first premise, a complex assertible, contains two simple assertibles, both of which are affirmative. However, either or both of these could equally be negative. So as well as "if p, then q", this opening premise could alternatively be "if not-p, then q", or "if p, then not-q" or "if not-p, then not-q". This immediately gives us four slightly different versions of the first undemonstrated argument. Similar permutations are possible for the other four undemonstrated arguments as well.

Faced with an argument that is *not* of the form of one of the five undemonstrated arguments, the task will be to show how it can be reduced to one of those five types. This task will need to be carried out according to a set of logical principles that the Stoics called *themata* or "ground-rules", of which it is reported that there were four. If one is faced with an argument and one wants to test its validity, one must use the *themata* to reduce its structure to that of one (or a combination) of the five undemonstrated arguments whose validity is intuitively obvious.

Without going any further into the complexities of Stoic syllogistic arguments, we can see that they differ considerably from Aristotelian syllogistic arguments. Whereas Aristotle's syllogisms deal with terms, Stoic syllogisms deal with propositions. Moreover, these two ancient systems of logic deal with quite different types of arguments, and may be seen as complementary. However, in antiquity they were sometimes seen as rival systems.

Philosophy of language

Formal logic or "dialectic" is just one part of the study of *logos*. Another part might best be described as the philosophy of language. The Stoics' account of language is closely bound up with their ontology (on which see Chapter 4), reflecting the interrelated nature of their system. At this point all we need to bear in mind is that the Stoics are materialists who claim that only physical bodies exist. How might such materialists account for language?

The Stoic theory of language begins with the voice or utterance (*phōnē*). A vocalization is a physical movement of air caused by the mouth. It must be something physical because it can be a cause and (as we shall see in Chapter 4) only bodies can be causes. In the case of an animal cry this is merely a noise, but in the case of human beings it is something articulate (see DL 7.55–6). As something articulate, it is no longer merely voice but also speech (*lexis*).

Consider the example of someone saying "here is Socrates". The spoken words are something purely physical, a movement of air caused by the mouth. Another purely physical element is Socrates himself, the thing that is being referred to in the statement. There is also a third element, though, and this is not physical: the meaning or sense of what is being said, namely that Socrates is here. The meaning or sense expressed by the physical act of speech is called a "sayable" (*lekton*). For the Stoics, "sayables" are one of four types of entity that they classify as "incorporeals" (*asōmata*). These are not bodies and so do not exist, but they are still in some sense real, so they are said to "subsist". Sextus Empiricus reports the following:

> The Stoics said that three things are linked together, the thing signified and the thing signifying and the thing existing; and of these the thing signifying is the utterance ("Dion" for instance); and the thing signified is the actual thing indicated thereby and which we apprehend as subsisting in dependence on our intellect, whereas foreigners although hearing the utterance do not understand it; and the thing existing is the external object, such as Dion himself. And of

these, two are bodies – that is, the utterance and the existing thing – and one is incorporeal, namely the thing signified and sayable, and this too is true or false.

(*Adv. Math.* 8.11–12)

So, if I were to listen to someone speaking a language I did not know (e.g. Japanese), although they would be making a physical utterance I would not be able to comprehend the *meaning* of what it was that they were saying. The physical cause, the movement of the air produced by their utterance, would still be present, but it would not communicate anything to me. This illustrates the Stoic distinction between voice and speech, between the utterance and what gets said. A better example, however, would be someone performing a nonsense poem that *no one* could understand. In this case there would certainly be an utterance but nothing would be being said. The utterances would not be utterances of a sayable, something with meaning or sense.

So, a sayable is that which is expressed by an utterance that has meaning. Not all sayables have meaning in a helpful sense, however. The Stoics draw a distinction between complete and incomplete sayables. An example of an incomplete sayable would be "… is walking"; whereas "Socrates is walking" would be a complete sayable that actually tells us something without us having to ask for further information (see DL 7.63).

The ontological status of sayables led the Stoics into a number of paradoxical positions that their critics were keen to exploit. For instance, strictly speaking "being wise" is not good according to the Stoics, even though wisdom obviously is. Seneca reports the standard Stoic explanation of this, even though he is not inclined to adopt it himself:

> We of the Stoic school believe that the Good is corporeal, because the Good is active, and whatever is active is corporeal. … They declare that wisdom is Good; it therefore follows that one must also call wisdom corporeal. But they do not think that "being wise" can be rated on the same

basis. For it is incorporeal and accessory to something else,
in other words, wisdom; hence it is in no respect active.

(*Ep.* 117.2–3)

Seneca has little time himself for this sort of linguistic subtlety and is
happy to accept a more down to earth understanding of the phrase
"being wise". Yet these sorts of counterintuitive accounts of language
are a consequence of the Stoics' rigorously materialist ontology. For
them, meaning or sense including the meaning or sense of the phrase
"being wise", literally does not exist, for only bodies exist. So why did
they feel the need to posit these sayables at all?

At one level we might say that the Stoics in particular did not
posit sayables. Everyone acknowledges that the words that we speak
carry meaning and that an account of human communication cannot rely on utterances alone. This is clear from the earlier example
of me hearing the utterances of someone speaking in Japanese but
not understanding the *meaning* of those utterances. So a distinction
between utterance and meaning seems fairly intuitive and would by
no means be limited to the Stoics.

What is perhaps unique to the Stoic position is their rejection of
meaning as something that exists. As incorporeals, sayables only
subsist. We shall return to this distinction in Chapter 4, but at this
point it is perhaps worth noting just how odd this claim is. If sayables
are not bodies then they cannot act and be acted upon. So the meaning of an utterance – such as "watch out, the tree is falling" – strictly
speaking should not cause me to do anything at all, such as move
out of the way. It cannot cause me to move because only bodies can
be causes, and sayables are not bodies. In short, the meaning of all of
our language has no causal efficacy at all, according to the Stoics.

So if someone shouts "watch out, the tree is falling" and I move out
of the way, how might the Stoics give an account of the causal process
at work here? Well presumably they would do so by saying that the
physical utterance made by the person shouting caused sounds in
the form of a movement of air, which then impacted upon my ear,
which then caused an impression in my soul, and that my assent to
that impression then caused me to move. In other words, the causal

explanation will be solely with reference to bodies (or modifications to bodies in the case of an impression in my physical soul). But the *meaning* of what was said will not figure in the causal explanation.

How do sayables relate to thoughts? One would certainly not want to say that *thoughts* can have no causal impact. A thought will be a disposition of the material soul, and so something material. So thoughts are clearly distinct from incorporeal sayables and can be causes. But if a sayable is said then it must also be thought, if only by the person saying it. The meaning conveyed by someone's utterance will reflect the meaning of their thought, but the utterance and the thought will both be material entities, distinct from their meaning or content.

Beyond their account of meaning in the theory of sayables, the Stoics had wide interests in language, ranging from rhetoric to the details of grammar. The Stoics are also famed for an interest in etymology, and Chrysippus may well have coined the term (see DL 7.200). They were equally interested in questions of poetical interpretation and it is reported that Chrysippus tried to reconcile traditional Greek mythology with his own theology, which as we shall see is fundamentally his physics (see Cicero, *ND* 1.41). Thus the Stoics were interested in allegorical interpretations in which traditional mythical stories or figures were presented as processes or elements in Nature. These two interests came together in Stoic etymological accounts of the origins of the names of the traditional gods, and this can be seen in the work of Cornutus in the first century CE. However, the precise status of these allegorical and etymological interests has been the subject of disagreement among scholars.

Stoic epistemology

So far we have considered syllogisms, assertibles and sayables. We have been working backwards, so to speak, from complete logical arguments, through propositions within arguments, to the linguistic content of those propositions. But standing behind all of these is the process by which the individual gains knowledge that can form the content of propositions. It is to this that we shall now turn, namely epistemology, the theory of knowledge.

The point of departure for Stoic epistemology is the impression (*phantasia*). An impression is literally imprinted on the soul (DL 7.45), similar to the way in which a seal makes an impression in a piece of wax (although not too literally, later Stoics suggested, in order to account for the imprinting of new impressions over old ones; see DL 7.50). Whereas most impressions are assumed to come from sensation, and so the Stoics might broadly be characterized as empiricists in epistemology, they do also acknowledge impressions received from the mind that are the product of reasoning (DL 7.51). And, like later empiricists, they deny the presence of any innate knowledge, saying that at birth the human mind is like a blank sheet of paper (Aetius 4.11.1–2), although this is a topic that we shall come back to in the next section.

Once an impression has been received it is then turned into a proposition. So, the impression of a man sitting under a tree is presented to the mind as a proposition such as "there is a man sitting under the tree". The mind then accepts or rejects this proposition. This is an act of assent (*sunkatathesis*). Let us consider an example of this process, an example that is used to illustrate a fragment from the fifth book of Epictetus' *Discourses* that is preserved in an account by the Latin author Aulus Gellius (*NA* 19.1.1–21).

Gellius recounts the following story. He was once making a journey by sea in the company of a Stoic philosopher. During the sea voyage they encountered a storm, which became increasingly violent. As the storm worsened and the passengers became increasingly afraid, Gellius turned to the Stoic philosopher to see how this wise man was keeping his composure during this moment of danger. However, he was disappointed with what he saw, for the Stoic philosopher appeared to be just as terrified as everyone else on board; so much for Stoic philosophy as an antidote for unwelcome emotions such as fear. After the storm had passed, Gellius turned to the Stoic philosopher and asked him why he seemed so afraid given that as an adherent of Stoicism he presumably claimed to be indifferent to all external circumstances and to have overcome the emotions. In response to this question the Stoic philosopher proceeded to take out of his bag a copy of the (now lost) fifth book of Epictetus' *Discourses* and pointed out to Gellius a passage that he thought would explain his apparent fear.

According to Gellius' account, the passage from Epictetus said the following. It argued that the impressions we receive that present external objects to us are not within our control. We do not have the power to choose them; instead they force themselves on us. However, we do have the power to choose whether to assent to these impressions or not. But in a situation such as the storm at sea, the mind of even the Stoic sage will be disturbed by the sudden impressions it receives against its will. In an interesting discussion of Gellius' account, Augustine glosses this point by saying that it is as if the resulting emotion is just too quick for the mind (*De Civitate Dei* 9.4.2). However, although the Stoic philosopher might be briefly overcome by the force of the sudden impression, he will not give his assent to the impression. Instead he will stand firm, reject the impression that something terrible is happening, and affirm that in fact nothing bad has occurred. In contrast, the other passengers in the storm will just unthinkingly assent to the impression that something terrible is indeed happening. It was by referring Gellius to an account of this sort in Epictetus that the Stoic philosopher tried to explain his apparent fear during the storm. Although the philosopher may have momentarily been overcome by what looked like fear as the impression suddenly forced itself on his mind, he did not give his assent to that impression once he had the chance to consider it properly. Consequently he did not form a genuine emotion of fear but rather simply experienced a "first movement" (on which see Sorabji 2000: 66–75).

This example nicely illustrates the nature of the relationship between impressions and assents. However it also differs in an important way from the example with which we began. Let us return to the example of a man sitting under a tree. If we were to come across such a man then we would have an impression of this state of affairs and that impression would be presented to our minds in the form of the proposition "there is a man sitting under the tree". We would then either assent to this proposition or reject it. In the case of the storm at sea, though, something else has happened before we receive the proposition. If we were on the boat with Gellius then what we would actually receive by way of impression would be an image of a huge wave about to crash over our heads. But in Gellius' discussion it is clear that the propositions that are being assented to or rejected are not of the form "there is a wave above my head" but rather "there is a wave above my head *and this is something terrible*". It is something like this second proposition that the terrified passengers have assented to, and it is something like this that the Stoic philosopher has been briefly overcome by, even if he will later refuse to assent to it. But of course the Stoic philosopher will happily assent to the former proposition "there is a wave above my head".

So, we need to add to our account a further stage. First there is a perception of an external event or state of affairs, such as the man sitting under a tree or a wave above our heads. Secondly there is (in some instances) an almost involuntary and seemingly unconscious value judgement that is made about the content of the perception, such as "this is terrible". Thirdly there is the presentation to the conscious mind of an impression in the form of a proposition that is composed of *both* the perceptual data received from outside *and* the unconscious value judgement. Finally there is the act of assent or rejection of the impression.

In usual accounts of epistemology the principal concern is with determining what is and is not reliable as a source of knowledge. The concern is with the reliability of the senses, for instance. Thus examples are usually fairly mundane, such as whether there is really a man sitting under a tree or not. But real life is rarely so uninteresting. The example from Gellius is important because it shows how acts of assent to the senses are intimately bound up with the value judgements that we make about the information we receive from the senses. People regularly assent to propositions about events that include implicit value judgements: "his death was a terrible thing"; "I wish that had not happened"; "the interview did not go well". But for the Stoics every external event is, strictly speaking, a matter of indifference; they can never be inherently good or bad (we shall return to this in Chapter 5). So, whenever anyone assents to an impression of an external state of affairs that contains within it some form of value judgement, they are making an epistemological mistake. Marcus Aurelius makes this point, using the phrase "first impressions" to refer to a perception before an unconscious value judgement has been added to it:

> Do not say more to yourself than the first impressions report. You have been told that someone speaks evil of you. This is what you have been told; you have not been told that you are injured. I see that the little child is ill; this is what I see, but that he is in danger I do not see. In this way, then, abide always by first impressions and add nothing of your own from within …
> (*Med.* 8.49)

Whenever we are faced with an impression that contains a value judgement we should reject that impression as false. So we should reject impressions such as "there is a wave above my head and this is something terrible". But what about the simpler impression "there is a wave above my head"? We can hardly accept this as reliable simply because it does *not* contain a value judgement. The Stoics still need to give an account of how we can distinguish between true and false impressions among these sorts of more mundane examples.

As we have seen, impressions can be both true and false. We can give our assent to both true and false impressions. In the former case we shall have a true belief; in the latter case we shall have made a mistake. But how do we know which impressions are true, and so deserve our assent, and which are false? The Stoics characterize true impressions to which we should assent as "adequate" or "cognitive" (*kataléptiké*) impressions. This term is notoriously difficult to translate; it is literally a "grasping" impression. The epistemological task, then, will be to learn how to recognize adequate impressions when we encounter them.

An adequate impression is defined as an impression that comes from "what is", agrees with "what is", and is imprinted in such a way that it could not have come from what is not (see e.g. DL 7.50).

Here it is natural to assume that "what is" refers to a real existing object, although it may be more accurate to say that "what is" refers to a fact rather than an object (see Frede 1999: 302). An adequate impression is an impression that is so clear, vivid and distinct that it is its own guarantee of its accuracy. At first glance this sounds a little like Descartes' notion of a "clear and distinct idea", and some have suggested that these two concepts share something in common (see Brooke 2004: 94). However, unlike Descartes' clear and distinct ideas, the Stoic adequate impressions are instances of *empirical* cognition rather than *a priori* cognition. But how might one understand an *empirical* impression that can guarantee its own accuracy? It has been suggested that this should be understood in terms of the impression's causal history – in other words, with reference to the physical condition of all of the objects involved in its production. So, if one's sense organs, the object in question, and all the other variables involved are not obstructed or in an abnormal state, then the resulting impression will be an adequate impression (see Frede 1983: 71–2). This sounds as if it might be something that one could check. One could examine the causal history of an impression and look to see if anything may have interfered with its production. If nothing has, then one could accept the impression as being adequate. But, of course, the sceptic could simply reply by saying that all the impressions used to test the initial impression would *also* need to be tested in order to ensure that they were reliable, and so on *ad infinitum*. This no longer sounds as though we are dealing with impressions that are their *own* guarantee of their accuracy.

So, how might we conceive of an adequate impression that can truly guarantee its *own* veracity? What the Stoics are trying to suggest with this concept is something that will require no further proof or justification beyond itself, something that can form the foundation for all of our knowledge. Are there any unproblematic examples of such impressions? In fact, Epictetus offers us just an example. He suggests that in the middle of the day one should try to assent to the proposition "it is night time" (see *Diss.* 1.28.2–3). He argues that it is simply not possible to do this in all good faith. The impression that we receive telling us that it is day time, as the midday sun burns down on our heads, is simply too strong for us to deny. We might say that this impression simply *demands* our assent. We might, in the confines of the seminar room, consider the possibility that this impression is merely a trick from an evil demon or an elaborate computer game, but once we are back outside in the sun the overwhelming power of the impression means that not one of us will refuse to assent to the impression that "it is day time". Here we have an example of an adequate impression, for which we require no further proof or justification. If, on the other hand, we found that we *could* assent to the opposing proposition "it is night time" then this would be enough for us to doubt the veracity of the impression and for us to withhold our assent.

The truth of the impression "it is day time" is indisputable when it is day time, at least at midday, if not at sunrise and sunset. There will, of course, always be exceptional occasions, such as eclipses, but these are examples of impressions where the causal history has been interrupted and where further information about the context and so on can correct any confusion. Naturally the truth of many other impressions will not be so immediately obvious. Indeed, the sceptic might argue that the vast majority of our impressions will be nowhere near so obviously true. But the Stoic can reply by saying that over time it will become possible to develop a certain ability to recognize adequate impressions. One might not be infallible at first, but one might eventually be able to become highly accurate with certain sorts of impressions, just as a trained piano tuner can consistently recognize particular sounds by ear to the point of rarely, if ever, making a mistake. We do not have an infallible perceptual faculty, nor do adequate impressions come with a special characteristic that immediately marks them out, but nevertheless it is possible to distinguish adequate impressions from those that are false. Yet in some cases, such as it being day time, ability will not be an issue and anyone will confidently be able to assent to an impression knowing that it is adequate.

Each act of assent to an adequate impression might best be described as an instance of cognition (*katalēpsis*). However it is not strictly speaking an instance of knowledge. For the Stoics knowledge (*epistēmē*) is something far more substantial; it is an organized and structured system of assents to adequate impressions, something close to what we would today call systematic scientific knowledge. Not surprisingly, this fully comprehensive and consistent sort of systematic knowledge is reserved only for the sage. Zeno is reported to have illustrated the distinction between cognition and knowledge by using a gesture: he held out his hand with the fingers stretched out and said "this is like an impression"; then he closed his fingers in and said "this is like an assent"; then he pulled his fingers in tighter to make a fist and said "this is like cognition (*katalēpsis*)"; finally he clenched his other hand over the fist and said "this is like knowledge, which is restricted to the sage" (Cicero, *Acad.* 2.145). Knowledge for the Stoics is thus not so easy to come by, but cognition is something that anyone can achieve. I can, for instance, assent to a whole host of adequate impressions relating to the movement and position of the sun and the moon, and the planets in the night sky. Each of these will be a cognition. But bringing all of these cognitions together into a systematic unity and *understanding* how they relate to one another so that I have a proper grasp of the way in which the solar system functions is altogether another matter and significantly harder to achieve.

Although this sort of systematic knowledge may be reserved for the sage, as we have seen anyone can achieve cognition by assenting to an adequate impression. For the Stoics the adequate impression formed the criterion of truth (DL 7.54). In antiquity the claim that there was any such criterion of truth received much criticism, especially from members of Plato's Academy, who at that time adhered to a form of scepticism. The ensuing debate between the Stoics and Academic Sceptics on this topic was one of the high points in inter-school debate in ancient philosophy. We are fortunate to have an account of this philosophical dispute in Cicero's dialogue the *Academics*. The principal argument of the Academic philosophers, people such as Arcesilaus and Carneades, was that one would always run the risk of mistaking a false impression for an adequate impression: "But he [Arcesilaus] pressed the point at issue further in order to show that no impression proceeding from a true object is such that an impression proceeding from a false one might not also be of the same form" (*Acad.* 2.77).

Let us suppose that we are faced with two very similar impressions, one that is accurate and one that is not. How do we choose between the two? To which should we assent? The problem for the Stoics, according to the Academic Sceptics, is that if adequate impressions are themselves the criterion of truth then there will be nothing further beyond them to which one might appeal when trying to distinguish them from false impressions. If adequate impressions are to be the criterion of truth for the Stoics then they must be self-evidently true. We should not need to appeal to anything further in order to be able to distinguish them from false impressions. If adequate impressions *cannot* perform this function, if we *do* find ourselves needing to appeal to something further in order to recognize them, then this foundation for Stoic epistemology will be undermined, and their entire philosophical system will come crashing down.

Sextus Empiricus reports that in order to overcome this problem later Stoics stressed that adequate impressions will accurately reflect objects but only provided that there is no obstacle (see *Adv. Math.* 7.253). As we have seen, the thought is that if one's sense organs, the object in question, and all the other variables involved are not obstructed or in an abnormal state, then the resulting impression will be an adequate impression. But this implies that the Stoics *did* acknowledge that in those circumstances when one of these elements is in an abnormal state then it may well be possible to mistake a false impression for an adequate impression. But if their epistemology is to stand they will have to argue that this will not be a typical occurrence. For the most part, impressions will be the product of normal conditions, and so will be adequate impressions. It should only be in relatively unusual cases that we might want to refer to the causal history of an impression in order to explain a potential confusion. Often the way in which such a confusion is explained away is by placing a particular impression within a wider context involving other impressions.

For instance, individuals rarely mistake two-dimensional representations of three-dimensional objects for real three-dimensional objects, unless those representations are of the highest quality. If we do think that we have a three-dimensional object in front of us, when in fact we are looking at a two-dimensional representation, we are likely to be misled only for a moment. Further scrutiny will soon reveal the true nature of what is in front of us. We need only move a little to the left or to the right and glance at the representation from a slightly different angle in order to realize that what is in front of us is *not* a three-dimensional object. The confusion – that is, the mistaken assent to a false impression – is quickly corrected. So, although it may be possible to make a mistake, it is equally possible to correct the mistake.

Further, the sceptical objection that it is *sometimes* possible to make a mistake with impressions does not force us to accept the conclusion that we can *never* be sure about our impressions. While it is certainly possible sometimes to be mistaken, this is not enough to support the claim that when a rational being experiences a true impression under normal conditions that he will *never* be able to recognize it as such. We can all recognize the truth of the impression that it is day time when it is day time, as we have seen. If the Stoic can point to at least some cases such as this where there is no room for doubt, owing to the overwhelming power and vividness of the impression, then the Stoic notion of there being adequate impressions can survive the sceptical attack. The Stoic need not claim that he is *never* mistaken (see Cicero, *Acad.* 2.19).

There will, of course, be plenty of other circumstances in which it will not be so easy to be sure about the status of the impression that one has received. In those cases the Stoic, like the Pyrrhonian Sceptic, will choose to withhold his assent and to suspend his judgement. We have already discussed Epictetus' example of an impression that *demands* our assent, namely "it is day time" when it is day time. In this case it is obvious that we are faced with an adequate impression. Epictetus also gives us an example of a case in which it is equally obvious that we are *not* faced with an adequate impression. Consider the impression that "the number of stars in the night sky is even" (*Diss.* 1.28.2–3). Is there any way in which we could justify assenting to this impression instead of the impression "the number of stars in the night sky is odd"? Let us assume that counting is simply not a viable option. If we are confronted with either one of these impressions then it is immediately obvious that it is not an adequate impression; it clearly does not demand our assent.

No matter how many situations that we might find ourselves in where there is some doubt about whether an impression is adequate or not, if we can point to at least some examples where we can be absolutely sure that either we *do* have an adequate impression ("it is day time") or that we *do not* have one ("the number of stars is even"), then the Stoics' concept of an adequate impression as the criterion of truth and foundation for their epistemology will withstand the sceptical attack. Indeed, the Stoic could well go on the counter-attack and challenge the Sceptic to claim sincerely that he is *never* sure whether it is day time or not. He could also challenge the assumption behind the sceptical objection that claims that it is in fact possible to be faced with two identical impressions, one of which is true and one of which is false. The Stoics could reply, following their theory of the identity of indiscernibles, that no two impressions will ever be *absolutely* identical, and so there will always be some unique distinguishing features that in theory the sage could use to differentiate them and judge their veracity correctly. But of course the Stoics' philosophical system depends upon a wide range of adequate impressions, many of which, the sceptic might argue, are far less obvious and far more controversial than simple cases such as "it is day time".

Stoicism and empiricism

Everything that we have seen thus far would lead one to conclude that the Stoics are empiricists, claiming that all of our knowledge derives from experience. In Chapter 4 we shall see that the Stoics also reject the existence of universals, adding further weight to this conclusion. Indeed, many commentators have suggested that the Stoics are broadly speaking empiricists and some have drawn parallels between Stoicism and ideas in Locke and Hume (see e.g. Hankinson

2003: 63). Beyond the general character of their epistemology that we have just considered, probably the most important piece of evidence in support of the claim that the Stoics are empiricists is a passage from the doxographer Aetius: "When a man is born, the Stoics say, he has the commanding part of his soul like a sheet of paper ready for writing upon. On this he inscribes each one of his conceptions. The first method of inscription is through the senses" (4.11.1–2). This clearly pre-empts Locke's famous characterization of the mind as a blank sheet of paper in his *Essay Concerning Human Understanding* (2.1.2). Locke's intention was to argue against those who claimed that there exist in the mind innate ideas at the time of birth:

> It is an established opinion amongst some men that there are in the Understanding certain innate principles, some primary notions, *koinai ennoiai*, characters, as it were stamped upon the mind of man, which the Soul receives in its very first being and brings into the world with it.
>
> (*Essay* 1.2.1, in Locke 1975: 48)

But here we face an apparent problem. The *koinai ennoiai* that Locke refers to here also have their origin in Stoicism. They are the Stoics' "common conceptions", these being generalizations held by everyone. So, although the Stoics appear to pre-empt Locke in presenting the mind as a blank sheet of paper, they also appear to be the source of the position that Locke is explicitly attacking. Indeed, Leibniz was well aware of this, as we can see in the Preface to his *New Essays on Human Understanding*, conceived as a reply to Locke:

> There is the question about whether the soul in itself is completely empty like tablets upon which nothing has been written (*tabula rasa*), as Aristotle and the author of the *Essay* maintain, and whether everything inscribed on it comes solely from the senses and from experience, or whether the soul contains from the beginning the source of several notions and doctrines .... The Stoics call these principles *prolepses*, that is, fundamental assumptions, or what is taken

> as agreed in advance. Mathematicians call them common notions (*koinai ennoiai*).   (Leibniz 1989: 292)

How does Leibniz arrive at this image of the Stoics as innatists, given the evidence that we have already seen from Aetius? As we can see, he makes reference to the Stoic idea of a "preconception" (*prolēpsis*). According to Diogenes Laertius, a preconception was for Chrysippus a general notion (*ennoia*) that comes about by nature (DL 7.54). However, it has been argued that rather than conceiving these as *innate* ideas we should instead think of them as naturally occurring first conceptions of things, unconscious conceptions that we have automatically, in contrast to consciously developed rational conceptions by which they should ideally be replaced (see Sandbach 1930: 46–7). On this account, both unconscious preconceptions and conscious rational conceptions will be *a posteriori*, that is, the product of our experiences. As such, these preconceptions will not be necessarily universal to all, but given what humans share in common physiologically with one another, many of them will occur in more or less everyone. To a certain extent this account undercuts the claim made by Leibniz that the Stoics believed in innate ideas.

How do these preconceptions relate to the "common conceptions" mentioned by both Locke and Leibniz? It has been suggested that they should simply be identified with one another (see e.g. Sandbach 1930), although others are wary of this claim (see e.g. Todd 1973: 57). But what about the following passage from Epictetus:

> Whoever came into the world without an innate conception (*emphuton ennoian*) of what is good and evil, honourable and base, becoming and unbecoming, and what happiness and misery are, and what is appropriate to us and forms our lot in life, and what we ought to do and ought not to do?
> (*Diss.* 2.11.3)

Here we appear to have a reference to conceptions that are innate or inborn (*emphutos*); something slightly different from a preconception. In the immediately preceding text Epictetus acknowledges that we do not have innate ideas of triangles or other things that we learn via experience, but here he seemingly does go on to imply that we have innate ideas concerning moral notions. Epictetus goes on further to suggest that with these notions we are already instructed by Nature (*Diss.* 2.11.6), and so do not need to be taught them in the way that, for instance, we do need to be taught geometry. This claim is echoed in Diogenes Laertius where he reports that our notions of goodness and justice are said to come about naturally (DL 7.53). But having a conception of goodness develop naturally, being instructed by Nature as Epictetus puts it, is somewhat different from being born with an innate conception of goodness. But however one might conceive this, and deciding how best to translate *emphutos* will be an important factor, we also have other evidence to suggest that the Stoics thought that individuals would naturally tend towards a virtuous life and that our all too common deviations from virtue are the product either of external influences leading us astray or of faulty reasoning. As Diogenes Laertius puts it, "the starting points of Nature are unperverted" (DL 7.89; see also Arius Didymus 5b8).

This is taking us some distance away from the question of empiricism, although it does nicely illustrate the way in which questions about one part of the Stoic system soon lead into the other parts, highlighting its interrelatedness. Our principal question is this: are the Stoics "blank sheet" empiricists as Aetius reports, or do they claim that we possess at birth certain innate ideas and, in particular, innate moral concepts? The claim that if we are left to our own devices then we shall naturally tend towards virtue may be understood as a claim presupposing the existence of either (a) innate moral concepts or (b) an innate moral tendency. Alternatively it might presuppose (c) the claim that, although born without any innate moral concepts or tendency, the natural course of events after birth will inevitably lead to the formation of an inclination towards virtue.

Cicero offers testimony that supports the rejection of option (a) in *On Ends*:

> Notions of things are produced in the mind when something has become known either by experience or combination of

> ideas or analogy or logical inference. The fourth and last
> method in this list is the one that has given us the concep-
> tion of the Good. (*Fin.* 3.33)

Although Cicero does not explicitly state this, it seems reasonable to assume that the last three methods that he lists are dependent upon the first, namely that notions produced by combinations of ideas or analogy or inference all presuppose the data of experience (this is implied by the examples given in a parallel discussion in DL 7.53). In other words, our notion of "the Good" will not be *a priori* (independent of experience); it will be the product of inferences based upon experiences, building upon an unconscious preconception of what we take to be good that is also the product of experience.

Seneca briefly addresses this issue in a letter dealing with the question of how we first acquire knowledge of goodness. He says that Nature does not teach this to us directly; Nature does supply us with the *seeds* of knowledge of goodness, but not with that knowledge itself (*Ep.* 120.4). He goes on to suggest that it is via observation that we develop knowledge of goodness proper. If Nature does not furnish us with knowledge of goodness directly then this suggests that we do not have innate moral concepts (option (a)), despite Epictetus' claim. We might understand Seneca's reference to a *seed* as referring to an innate tendency or disposition, one that might lead us to develop knowledge of goodness after birth, via observation (option (b)). Alternatively we might understand this as a reference to a naturally arising unconscious preconception, a postnatal *product* of experience that forms the foundation of a fully developed conception of goodness (a version of option (c)). It is difficult to be sure which of these last two readings is best, given how brief the discussion is.

It has been suggested that despite the shared "blank sheet" imagery, the Stoic position is in an important sense innatist, and as such is quite different from that of Locke. Although the Stoics may not be conceptual innatists, it has been suggested that they are "dispositional innatists", proposing the existence of innate appetites and aversions (Scott 1988: 146), option (b). We shall return to this idea of an innate disposition in the opening section of Chapter 5.

Summary

In this chapter we have been working our way backwards through the Stoic account of the acquisition of knowledge, the central theme in Stoic logic. By way of summary let us recap by going forwards. For the Stoics the mind at birth is like a blank sheet of paper. It is via sensory experiences or impressions that we gain information, and it is via assent to adequate impressions that we achieve cognitions, instances of knowledge. The impressions that we assent to are presented to the mind in the form of propositions; thus our cognitions are also in the form of propositions. A proposition is a physical entity – the movement of air when spoken, an inscription when written – but it also carries meaning or sense, which is incorporeal. The meaning or sense of a proposition is a sayable. Sayables can be both complete and incomplete. Complete sayables, such as "it is raining this afternoon", are assertibles, and assertibles are the propositions that can be brought into combination to form syllogistic arguments. Such arguments form the foundation for systematic scientific knowledge of the world. Here we can see the way in which the Stoics account for the origin and development of our knowledge. In Chapter 4 we shall consider precisely what the Stoics claimed to know about the nature of the physical world.

FOUR

Stoic physics

Ontology

For the Stoics, physics is that part of philosophical discourse that deals with all questions concerning the physical world, from foundational ontology to the empirical sciences such as astronomy and meteorology. The fundamental assertion underpinning all of Stoic physics is the claim that only bodies exist, a claim that dates back to Zeno himself. This may be seen as a direct challenge to the Platonic claim that the material world that we experience is merely a shadow of another realm where real existence lies. Indeed, it echoes a position attributed to one of the parties in the discussion of the nature of existence in Plato's dialogue the *Sophist* (on this see Brunschwig 1988).

In the *Sophist* Plato mounts a famous attack on materialism as an ontological position (245e–249d). He refers to a battle between giants and gods over whether "being" pertains only to physical objects or whether it pertains to non-physical entities. The materialist giants insist that being is "the same as body". Anything that they cannot touch or squeeze in their hands, as they can with bodies, does not exist at all. Thus they must deny the existence of non-bodily entities such as soul, intelligence, justice and virtue. For Plato, these conclusions are not only unpalatable but also probably disingenuous, for no one seriously denies the reality of these things. This extreme position is tempered, Plato suggests, by more moderate materialists who claim that the soul does exist but that in order to exist it must be a special kind of body.

For Plato, it will be possible to catch out the materialists, of whatever sort they may be, if he can force them to admit to the existence of something that is not a body (247c). Such an admission would destroy the materialist claim that being a body is the only true mark of existence. Notice that Plato explicitly assumes that for something to be something at all it must have "being" or existence (237d). Now, with regard to intelligence, justice and virtue, Plato's more moderate materialists find themselves embarrassed, and have to accept that perhaps these things can exist without being bodies. Plato then expands upon his conception of existence by characterizing it as a capacity to act or be acted upon, and suggests to the moderate materialists that perhaps this should be the true mark of existence rather than being a body. Yet Plato's materialists appear to have rejected this characterization (248c).

Now let us turn to the Stoics. Zeno follows the giants in the *Sophist* by insisting that being or existence should be identified with body, despite the concession by Plato's moderate materialists. He reaffirms that only bodies exist. Rather than fall into the Platonic trap of being forced to admit that the soul or justice or virtue do not exist, however, he is prepared to claim that all of these things exist and are indeed bodies. He also accepts Plato's characterization of existence as the capacity to act or be acted upon, but reserves this solely for bodies, against Plato's intention. Finally, he calls into question Plato's assumption that for something to be something at all it must exist. For Zeno, there can be real things that are not bodies, and so do not exist according to his materialist ontology, but yet are nevertheless in some sense real, as we shall see shortly.

So, for the Stoics if anything exists or has the capacity to act or be acted upon then it is a body (see e.g. Cicero, *Acad.* 1.39). This will be as true for the soul, justice, virtue or wisdom as it will be for more tangible physical objects such as sticks and stones. In this way, Zeno faces Plato's challenge to materialism head on, refuses to compromise as Plato's moderate materialists had, and reaffirms the uncompromising materialism of the giants.

Despite this fairly uncompromising materialism, there are a few entities that cannot be conceived as bodies and yet that the Stoics would not want to say are nothing at all. One such example would be the sense or meaning of an utterance, the "sayables" that we encountered in the previous chapter. Another would be void, which is clearly not a body but yet is presumably something in some sense if it is to be an object of thought at all. In fact, the Stoics suggest four types of entity that fit into this category of being "something" (*ti*) yet not being bodies: void, time, place and "sayables" (*lekta*). As they claim that only bodies exist, these other entities are in some sense real but cannot be said to exist. Instead, they are said to "subsist". Stoic ontology posits a supreme genus of "something" under which there are two subdivisions of existing bodies or corporeals and subsisting incorporeals (Alexander, *in Top.* 301,19–25):

something (*ti*)
REALITY
{
corporeals (*somata*)
EXISTENCE

incorporeals (*asōmata*)
SUBSISTENCE
}

For the Stoics, then, existence or "being" is not the highest ontological genus. It is, contrary to Plato's assumption in the *Sophist*, possible for something to be something at all without having to assume that it exists. These non-existing somethings, the incorporeals, do not exist but nevertheless they are real. We have, then, a highest genus covering all real entities, some of which are existing bodies and some of which are non-existing (but subsisting) incorporeals.

The idea of an existing body is fairly straightforward; we have touched upon its definition and we shall consider Stoic bodies further in the next section. But what about these incorporeals? As we have just seen, there are four types of incorporeal: void, time, place and "sayables" (*lekta*). The Stoics want to be able to say that these incorporeals are real, for in order to be an object of thought they must at least be "something" (Sextus, *Adv. Math.* 1.17), but in so far as they are not bodies, the Stoics cannot say that they exist. Instead, they say that these incorporeals subsist; they are real, but they are *non-existent* realities. Moreover, in certain circumstances these subsisting incorporeals are said not to subsist but to "belong". For instance, whereas the past and the future "subsist", the present moment "belongs"; the present moment is in some sense more real than moments in the past or future but it is not as real as a physical object. Critics of Stoicism would argue here that this uncomfortable ontological category of incorporeal, containing four seemingly unrelated entities, simply highlights the inadequacy of their materialism, which is unable to give a proper explanation of these four types of entity.

So, only bodies exist, and these four incorporeals subsist. It is worth noting what this ontological scheme leaves out. Significantly it leaves out universals in the form of Platonic Ideas. For the Stoics, such Ideas neither exist nor subsist. As existence and subsistence appear to be the only two categories of "something", such entities are dismissed as "not-something" (Simplicius, *in Cat.* 105,9–11), and classed alongside hallucinations and phantoms of the imagination. However, it would perhaps be a mistake to think of "not-something" as another clearly defined category within the Stoic ontological scheme. Instead, being labelled "not-something" precisely means that the item in question has no place at all in Stoic ontology, failing to find a place under the Stoic supreme genus of "something".

The Stoics thus explicitly reject universals conceived as Platonic Ideas. Every entity that falls under their highest genus of "something" must be something particular; only individual particulars exist (Syrianus, *in Metaph.* 104,21). Consequently they have often been presented as the first nominalists, rejecting the existence of universal concepts altogether. But presumably they, like anyone else, would want to be able to give at least *some* sort of account of universal concepts such as the colour "red", an account of what it is that this particular red object and that one share in common. Recent work on this thorny issue has suggested that an important shift occurred between Zeno and Chrysippus here (see Caston 1999); we shall focus our attention in what follows on Chrysippus' account, which laid the foundation for subsequent Stoic orthodoxy on the subject.

For Chrysippus there are no universal entities, whether they be conceived as substantial Platonic Forms or in some other manner. We are often led to think that there are such entities by the way in which we use language, especially common nouns such as "man". Thus, when we say "man is a rational animal" we often assume that there must be a generic "man" to whom we are referring. Chrysippus attempts to get round this problem by reformulating such statements in a way that will not lead us to make this assumption. So, instead of saying "man is a rational animal", we should instead say "if something is a man, then that thing is a rational animal" (see Sextus, *Adv. Math.* 11.8). Putting it this way enables us to indicate a common property shared by all particular men without assuming the existence of a generic entity "man".

Within this context, Chrysippus developed a well-known argument: the "no one argument" (Simplicius, *in Cat.* 105,7–16; also DL 7.187). The argument goes like this:

> If someone is in Athens, he is not in Megara;
> "man" is in Athens;
> therefore, "man" is not in Megara.

The aim of this argument is to deny that the generic name "man" refers to anything at all. The assumption standing behind the argument is the claim that "man" is someone (or "something" in the Stoic ontological scheme). The argument is primarily directed towards the Platonists. A Platonist will accept the intuitive first premise, and has no reason to argue with the second premise. However, he will not want to accept the conclusion. In order to avoid doing so he must reject the implicit assumption that "man" is someone (or "something"). If he does so, then he will have fallen into the Stoic trap and admitted that Platonic Forms such as "man" are "not-something" (see Caston 1999: 202–3).

Presumably Chrysippus will need to give his own account of the term "man", even if he is not willing to admit that there exist substantial universals such as Platonic Ideas or even generic concepts. He will do so by presenting such things as qualities that are attributable to a number of existing particulars. The qualities in any *particular* physical entity will themselves be physical, and we shall see how the Stoics account for this in the next section. Indeed, a *particular* entity will be both "commonly qualified" (*koinōs poion*) and "peculiarly qualified" (*idiōs poion*). For instance, Socrates is "commonly qualified" as a human being, and this is something that he shares with all human beings. Being "commonly qualified" as a human being is what makes Socrates a human being rather than, say, a dog or a horse. But Socrates is also "peculiarly qualified" as Socrates, and no one else is "peculiarly qualified" in exactly the same way. The former accounts for what Socrates shares in common with other human beings; the latter accounts for what makes Socrates unique among human beings. When we talk about the concept of "human being" or "man" all we are really talking about is a mental construction that we have created in order to describe a certain physical quality of being "commonly qualified" that exists in a number of different particular individuals (see e.g. DL 7.61).

Principles

Having considered the division in Stoic ontology between the corporeal and the incorporeal, we shall now turn to consider the corporeal in more detail. As we have seen, only bodies are said to exist. Central to Zeno's definition of a body is that it is something that can act and be acted upon.

The Stoics propose two material principles (*archai*) as the foundation for their physics, two principles that are presented in the surviving fragments using a variety of terms. They are that which acts (*to poioun*) and that which is acted upon (*to paschon*), or we might say the active and the passive; they are God and matter (see e.g. DL 7.134). The origins of this theory are no doubt complex but recent scholarship has noted a parallel with the physics of the early Academy (see Cicero, *Acad.* 1.24–9 with Sedley 2002), and Zeno may have found inspiration there during his time studying with Polemo. Another precursor often cited is Heraclitus (see Cicero, *ND* 3.35).

The earliest formulations of this theory appear to have identified the active principle with fire. Later versions of the theory, associated with Chrysippus, replace fire with the concept of "breath" or *pneuma*, possibly reflecting the increasing importance that this latter concept was gaining in the sciences of the day, especially biology. These two characterizations are not unrelated, in so far as breath or *pneuma*, conceived as the principle of life within a living being, was thought to be intimately related to warmth or heat.

Central to understanding Stoic physics is determining the nature of the relationship between these two principles. We have already seen that the Stoic definition of a body is something that can act or be acted upon. Anything that can act or be acted upon cannot be incorporeal (Cicero, *Acad.* 1.39). This implies that both of these principles will be bodies, one acting, the other being acted upon. However, a number of ancient sources (e.g. Calcidius, *in Tim.* 293) and modern commentators (Lapidge 1973; Todd 1978) suggest that the Stoics proposed a strict monism, that is, a conception of a single unified material reality. If this is so, then the distinction between the two principles is perhaps something merely abstract or conceptual, and consequently something less important than it might at first seem.

Why would the Stoics want to make such an abstract distinction, especially if they are also keen to assert a strict monism? One answer might be this. They want to give an account of the material world that does not have to refer to anything outside Nature in order to explain its movement or development. In other words, they do not want to conceive the material world as purely passive and inert, for if they did they would then need to give an account of its activity with reference to some other, supernatural, entity. By drawing this conceptual distinction they are able to say that the material cosmos both acts and is acted upon; it is both active and passive, acting upon itself.

This may go some way to explain the motivation for the distinction, but we are still left with a question. Are the two principles two *bodies* in a total mixture, or are they two *aspects* of a single unified body? Unfortunately the ancient sources are not entirely consistent on this point, in part because some of them are hostile to the Stoic position. Moreover, one key passage in Diogenes Laertius (7.134) contains a disputed textual variant; it could be read as saying that the two principles are bodies, or that they are incorporeals. I suggested earlier that both principles must be bodies because only bodies can act and be acted upon. But perhaps we should read this as saying that bodies can *both* act *and* be acted upon, whereas the principles each have only one of these attributes, and so cannot be bodies themselves (Brunschwig 2003, however, suggests that it should be read as act *or* be acted upon). But it would seem odd to say that the principles are incorporeal, and we have already seen an apparently exhaustive list of items that the Stoics thought were incorporeal – time, void, place, sayables – in which the principles do not appear.

If, however, we accept the claim that the principles form a conceptual distinction between two aspects of a unified material body then they will be concepts, and as such will be examples of sayables or *lekta*. As *lekta*, they will be incorporeal. This is clearly *not* to say that the material cosmos is composed of two incorporeals, which would be absurd, but rather that the division of the unified material cosmos into these two principles is merely a mental abstract division that has the ontological status of a thought or statement only. On this account the principles are not two independent entities that could, in theory, be separated from one another; rather they are verbal descriptions of different characteristics of a single entity.

Let us consider briefly the alternative hypothesis. Let us suppose that these two principles *are* two distinct material entities in some form of mixture with each other. A number of sources describe the cosmos as matter in mixture with the active principle *pneuma* (e.g. Aetius 1.7.33). How should we understand this? The Stoics' own theory of mixture is relevant here. They suggest that two material entities might be mixed together in three different ways (see Alexander, *Mixt.* 216,14–217,2). The first of these is "juxtaposition", in which grains of the two entities are mixed together but remain distinct from one another, as in the case of salt and sugar mixed together in a bowl. The second is "fusion", in which a new entity is created out of the two entities, which cease to exist independently, as when using a number of ingredients when cooking. The third the Stoics call "total blending", in which the two entities are mixed together to the point that every part of the mixture contains both of the original entities, yet each of the original entities retains its own distinctive properties and can in theory be extracted from the mixture. For instance, it is reported that if one mixes wine and water in a glass it is possible to extract the wine out of the mixture by using a sponge soaked in oil – and this has been supported by experimentation (Stobaeus 1,155,8–11 with Sorabji 2004: 298–9). Although the wine and water are completely mixed, in a way that the grains of salt and sugar are not, it is still possible to separate the two liquids. One slightly paradoxical consequence of this theory of total blending that the Stoics appear to have accepted was the thought that if one added a single drop of wine to the sea then that single drop of wine would have to mix with *every* part of the sea, in effect stretching itself out over a vast area (see DL 7.151). The Stoics described this third kind of mixture as a process in which the two original entities are destroyed and a new third entity, the mixture, is created. However, this new entity contains within it the qualities of the two original entities, and so it is possible to extract the original entities from the mixture (in a way that is not possible in the case of fusion, the second kind of mixture).

How does this relate to our concern with the relationship between the two principles? If the cosmos were conceived as a total blending of the two principles then in the light of this theory the principles would no longer exist as separate entities. We would be back to a monistic unified material cosmos. It seems, then, that even if we did try to insist on the physical independence of the two principles we would still end up with a monistic conception of the cosmos in the light of the Stoic theory of total blending. Indeed, it seems likely that the theory of total blending was proposed precisely to show how it would be possible for the two material principles to be in a total blend with one another. In particular, it was probably proposed in order to offer an explanation for the Stoics' counter-intuitive claim that two bodies, matter and God, can both be in the same place at once (see Sorabji 1988: ch. 6).

In sum, we might say that the Stoic cosmos is a material entity that does not have an active principle mixed throughout but rather simply is active itself. Breath or *pneuma* is not a special kind of distinct matter intermingled with passive matter; rather the material world itself has pneumatic qualities. Although we might be able to distinguish between the two principles in thought, in reality they are merely aspects of a single unified material cosmos. Taken in these terms, we have a distinction that sounds close to Aristotle's analysis of material objects into matter and form (in e.g. *Metaphysics* 7.7–9). But there are important differences as well, not least that the Stoic *pneuma* is itself in some sense material in a way that Aristotelian form is certainly not. Moreover, although the cosmos may be a unified material entity, it is nevertheless conceived as a total blend of two distinct components that, like the wine and the water, may be separated from one another at some point in the future. Indeed, as we shall see shortly, the Stoics did in fact think that such a separation took place at periodic moments of conflagration.

This is a complex and potentially confusing theory. It attracted a number of hostile attacks in antiquity. Like many of their predecessors, the Stoics held on to the traditional analysis of the physical world into four component elements: earth, water, air and fire. But their theory of the principles seemed to posit *pneuma* as a fifth element in mixture with the other four (see Alexander, *Mixt.* 225,3–10). The early identification of the active principle with fire caused later confusion; is this fire conceived as one of the four traditional elements, or is it some other "creative fire" in mixture with matter composed of the four elements? We shall return to this question later. Other sources divide the four elements between the two principles, *pneuma* being identified with fire and air, with water and earth constituting matter. No doubt Stoic physical theory developed at the hands of the different heads of the early school, and no doubt our doxographical reports do not always distinguish carefully between claims that belong to its different stages of development.

God and Nature

It is possible to give two quite different readings of Stoic physics. One reading would focus on the role of *pneuma* as a force that, in various degrees of tension, forms the material objects of Nature. The Stoics outline three principal conditions of *pneuma*, each reflecting a different level of "tension" (*tonos*). The first is "cohesion" (*hexis*), and this is the force that gives unity to a physical object; it is the force that holds together a stone, for instance. The second is "nature" (*phusis*), and this is the force by virtue of which something may be said to be alive. It is *pneuma* as *phusis* that constitutes the principle of life in biological organisms such as plants. The third is "soul" (*psuchē*), and this form of *pneuma* constitutes the principle of life in animals that have the powers of perception (impressions), movement (impulses) and reproduction (see Philo, *Legum Allegoriarum* 2.22–3). The difference between these three types of natural entity is simply one of differing levels of tension in their *pneuma*. This has been characterized as a difference in organizational complexity. They stand on a continuum, the difference between them being one of degree rather than kind. One could thus imagine an evolutionary account of the development of life and higher forms of life purely in terms of increasing complexity within Nature. It is thus possible to make Stoic physics sound quite modern and thoroughly naturalistic (see e.g. Sambursky 1959). And such a reading seems perfectly reasonable given that, as we have seen, the Stoics are uncompromising materialists.

Alternatively one might read the Stoics as quite religious philosophers, as pantheists who conceive God as the providential ruling force in Nature, echoing the role played by the Demiurge in Plato's *Timaeus*. Such a reading has plenty of support in the ancient texts, such as the discussion of Stoic theology in Cicero's *On the Nature of the Gods* and in Cleanthes' *Hymn to Zeus*. Here is an extract from Cleanthes' *Hymn* in order to give a flavour of this aspect of Stoicism:

> Zeus, giver of all, you of the dark clouds, of the blazing thunderbolt,
> save men from their baneful inexperience

and disperse it, father, far from their souls; grant that they
may achieve
the wisdom with which you confidently guide all with justice
so that we may requite you with honour for the honour you
give us
praising your works continually, as is fitting for mortals ...
(translated in IG II-21)

These sorts of sentiments are seemingly a world away from the naturalistic account of Stoic physics. For us, there is a strong tendency to
want to distinguish sharply between the philosophical or scientific
on the one hand and the religious on the other. This modern Western
tendency has often been noted as a hindrance when, for instance,
Western readers try to approach Eastern philosophies in which such
a division does not straightforwardly apply. But we are not in this sort
of situation with the Stoics, who stand squarely within the Western
intellectual tradition. The Stoic conception of God is clearly a *philosophical* God, a conception based upon arguments (of the sort that are
reported by Cicero in *On the Nature of the Gods*) and not the product
of myth, superstition or faith. Nevertheless, there remains a certain
tension between the two possible readings that I have mentioned.

The difference between these two readings is one concerning precisely how we are to conceive the Stoic God. The naturalistic reading
would not want to attribute any conscious purpose to the material
pneuma that holds together rocks and stones. The religious reading, by contrast, will want to assert God's conscious providential
ordering of the cosmos. So, is the Stoic God a conscious being that
orders the cosmos, or is the word "God" merely a traditional label
that has been retained for a primarily unconscious physical process
that orders and shapes Nature?

Before approaching this question directly there are a few points
that we ought to bear in mind. The first is that, no matter how we
conceive the relationship between the two principles, the Stoic God
is very much *in* Nature. It is very easy for us to think of God as
an external creator of Nature, an external force that shapes Nature.

But for the Stoics God simply *is* Nature. Whereas the late ancient Church Fathers and early modern Christian readers of Stoicism were often keen to stress the *difference* between God and Nature in the light of Christian teaching (and so stress the distinction between the two principles), numerous ancient sources note that the Stoics were happy to *identify* God with Nature, even if that claim might sometimes be qualified to say that God is the active force *within* Nature. For the Stoics, the cosmos is a living being (DL 7.142). So our question is as much about whether the cosmos as a living being is conscious or not. We should also bear in mind that some ancient critics took the Stoic identification of God with Nature to be a manoeuvre designed to enable them to continue to use the label "God" even though their naturalistic philosophy had no need of it. As Plotinus put it, "they bring in God for the sake of appearances, [a God] who has his being from matter in a certain state" (*Enneads* 6.1.27). Similar criticisms were later raised against Spinoza's identification of God with Nature, for whenever one uses the word "God" one could simply replace it with "Nature" and so "God" no longer has any explanatory force. Spinoza was attacked by his early readers as being an atheist who held on to the label "God" merely for the sake of appearances, just as Plotinus had criticized the Stoics for doing the same.

With these points in mind, let us return to our question: is the Stoic God, identified with Nature conceived as a living being, conscious or unconscious? Cicero reports that Zeno offered the following argument in support of the claim that the cosmos as a whole was indeed conscious:

> These expansive arguments of ours were condensed by Zeno like this: "that which employs reason is better than that which does not. Now nothing is superior to the cosmos; therefore the cosmos employs reason". By a similar argument it can be established that the cosmos is wise, and blessed, and eternal, for all embodiments of these attributes are superior to those without them, and nothing is superior to the cosmos. (*ND* 2.21)

Thus Zeno held that the cosmos as a whole must be conscious, for we are conscious and the cosmos, being superior to us, will not lack this attribute. Indeed, Cicero goes on to quote another, similar argument by Zeno: "Nothing which is devoid of sensation can contain anything which possesses sensation. Now some parts of the cosmos possess sensation; therefore the cosmos is not devoid of sensation" (*ND* 2.22). Of course, there is an important difference between saying that the cosmos possesses or contains sensation and saying that the cosmos is itself a sensible living being. The cosmos may possess sensation simply by virtue of the fact that some of its parts – you and I – possess sensation. But that does not seem to be the point that Zeno is trying to make. Instead the claim is that if you and I have sensation then the cosmos itself must have sensation as well. We might take this as an argument against the existence of emergent properties; an unconscious cosmos cannot give rise to conscious beings, so if there are any conscious beings in the cosmos then consciousness must also be an attribute of the cosmos itself.

Diogenes Laertius provides further evidence for the claim that the Stoics held the cosmos as a whole to be conscious:

> The doctrine that the cosmos is a living being, rational, animate and intelligent, is laid down by Chrysippus in the first book of his treatise *On Providence*, by Apollodorus in his *Physics*, and by Posidonius. It is a living thing in the sense of an animate substance endowed with sensation; for animal is better than non-animal, and nothing is better than the cosmos, therefore the cosmos is a living being.
>
> (DL 7.142–3)

However, Diogenes also reports that some Stoics rejected this claim. In particular Boethus of Sidon is said to have denied that the cosmos is an animate being (DL 7.143). When discussing this issue in the seventeenth century, Ralph Cudworth came to the conclusion that whereas the early Stoics such as Zeno were clearly theists, later Stoics such as Boethus were in fact atheists because although they still conceived the cosmos as a living being their notion of

God was merely of a vegetative process in Nature, devoid of all consciousness.

In answer to our question, then, it seems clear that, with the exception of Boethus and perhaps a few others, the orthodox Stoic position was that God is indeed conscious. (We might hesitate before using the modern term "conscious" here; I use it as shorthand for DL's "rational, animate, and intelligent".) In the terms of the division that I suggested between naturalistic and religious readings of Stoic physics this might seem to favour the religious reading. Yet we have also seen that this conscious God should not be conceived as a personal deity external to Nature. Rather, this conscious God *is* Nature conceived as a living being. Thus, much of Cleanthes' language evoking a personified Zeus is to a certain extent misleading. The same could be said for references to a personified God in Seneca, Epictetus and Marcus Aurelius. The dichotomy between reductive naturalism and theism falls apart when faced with Stoic physics. The Stoics are thoroughgoing naturalists who want to give an account of the movement and order in the cosmos that does not depend on any entity *outside* the cosmos. Versions of materialism that conceive matter as something passive or inert need to give an account of the movement of matter and can be forced into admitting the existence of either transcendent causes of motion or a first cause that sets things in motion. The great virtue of the Stoic version of materialism is that it does not need to refer to anything outside Nature in order to account for Nature's movement and order. While remaining naturalists, they conceive Nature as a living being that organizes and regulates itself. Their cosmology has thus been described as a "cosmobiology" (Hahm 1977: 136). This ancient theory is echoed in some modern discussions of Nature, or "Gaia", as a self-regulating biological system. Where the Stoics go further is to claim that Nature, conceived as a living organism, is also conscious. It is in so far as the cosmos is held to be conscious that one might call it "God". But one might equally side with Plotinus and those later critics of Spinoza by saying that to a certain extent this is simply holding on to the label "God" for the sake of appearances.

Cosmology

For the Stoics, then, the cosmos is a living being, and their cosmology is also a cosmobiology. This living cosmos is conceived as a spherical being, surrounded by infinite void (DL 7.140). The Stoic author Cleomedes offers a series of arguments in favour of the claim that the earth is spherical and that it rests at the centre of a spherical cosmos (*Cael.* 1.5). He also provides us with what is the most important discussion of the extra-cosmic void surrounding the cosmos (see *Cael.* 1.1). Void, as we have seen, is one of the four incorporeals. But why do the Stoics feel the need to posit this incorporeal extra-cosmic void? They could simply have conceived the cosmos as a finite entity, limited in extent, just as Aristotle had done in his *Physics*. But the claim that the cosmos has an edge was famously attacked by the Pythagorean philosopher Archytas, who wanted to know what would happen if someone standing right at the edge of this finite cosmos stuck out their arm (Simplicius, *in Phys.* 467,26–35). The Stoics also took up this sort of objection to an outer edge of the cosmos, as Simplicius reports:

> The Stoics, however, wanted there to be void outside the heaven, and they established this through the following supposition. Suppose, they say, someone stands at the extremity of the sphere of the fixed [stars] and extends his hand upwards. If he does extend it, they infer that there is something outside the heaven into which he extends it; but if he cannot extend it, there will be something outside in such a way as to prevent his hand's extension.
>
> (*in Cael.* 284,28–285,1)

So in order to overcome this paradox inherent in the idea that the cosmos has an edge, the Stoics proposed a finite cosmos surrounded by an extra-cosmic void. Their cosmos, like Aristotle's, is limited in extent, but by positing a void beyond the cosmos they avoid Archytas' objection. This extra-cosmic void will be infinite, for if it were finite then one would simply face the same objection when one reached *its* edge. For Aristotle, the notion of an infinite body actually exist-ing all at once, in contrast to an infinite *process* that never ends, is absurd. But the Stoic infinite void is not a body; it is incorporeal (see Cleomedes, *Cael.* 1.1.104–11).

The Stoics had a further reason for positing this extra-cosmic void. They claimed that at certain moments the entire cosmos was dissolved entirely into fire. Just as the same quantity of water takes up more space as water vapour than it does as liquid water, so the Stoics held that at this moment of total conflagration the matter of the cosmos as pure fire would require more space than it does in its current state (see Cleomedes, *Cael.* 1.1.43–54). Consequently they needed to be able to account for this periodic expansion in the size of the cosmos, and extra-cosmic void offered them a way to do so.

In order to account for the extra-cosmic void, the Stoics drew a distinction between the "all" and the "whole". The "whole" (*holon*) refers to the cosmos and the "all" (*pan*) refers to both the cosmos and the infinite void surrounding it. The "whole" is thus finite, and the "all" is infinite (see Sextus, *Adv. Math.* 9.332).

So, the cosmos itself is a finitely extended living being, a spheri-cal continuum of matter held together by the breath or *pneuma* that pervades it. This *pneuma* is identified with God and reason. This is thus much more than, say, a magnetic or gravitational force. It is a conscious and rational organizing principle. It is the soul of the cosmos, analogous to the soul of any other living being. Like other living beings, the cosmos has a limited life span. We have just seen that the Stoics held that at certain moments the entire cosmos would be dissolved into fire. This is the moment of cosmic conflagration (*ekpurōsis*).

The Stoic account of the birth and destruction of the cosmos is complex. We shall face many of the problems that we have already encountered when discussing the two principles. Here, too, the theory may well have developed during the course of the early Stoa, and the doxographical sources may well conflate details from dif-ferent versions. Diogenes Laertius reports that when the cosmos is born its substance is transformed from its initial state of fire into air then water and then earth (DL 7.142). Or, rather, we might assume that *part* of the initial fire is transformed into air, and *part* of that is transformed into water, and so on, so that we end up with a mixture of all four elements. It is from this mixture of the four elements that the wide variety of mineral, vegetable and animal forms come into being. This might suggest that at the moment of birth the cosmos is constituted solely by the element of fire.

However, other accounts of the conflagration suggest that at the moment of birth and destruction the cosmos is constituted solely by divine reason, that is, by *pneuma*. The active principle of *pneuma* is clearly quite different from the element of fire, which is just one part of the passive principle. But if we return to Diogenes Laertius we shall see that he suggests that, in order to have all four elements, fire will also have to be generated:

> The cosmos comes into being when substance turns from fire through air to moisture, and then the thick part of it is formed into earth and the thin part is rarefied and this when made even more thin produces fire. Then by a mixing from these are made plants and animals ...   (DL 7.142)

We can schematize this process as follows:

$$
\text{fire} \rightarrow \text{air} \rightarrow \text{moisture} \underset{\text{(i.e. water)}}{\longrightarrow}
\begin{cases}
\rightarrow \text{thick part} \rightarrow \text{earth} \\
\rightarrow \text{thin part} \rightarrow \text{fire}
\end{cases}
$$

For the cosmos to develop all of its myriad forms, all four of the elements are required. Yet if the fire out of which all of the other elements are generated is elemental fire, then why do we need this final stage in which the thin part of moisture is rarefied into fire? An answer to this would be to say that the initial fire is not elemental fire, but rather some other form of fire, to be identified with God, and later described as *pneuma*.

Indeed, Aetius (1.7.33) reports that the Stoics described God as a "creative fire" (*pur technikon*), and he suggests that this is the same thing as the *pneuma* pervading the cosmos. It is necessary to draw a distinction, then, between the creative fire out of which the cosmos is born and elemental fire, which stands alongside the other elements of air, water and earth. Stobaeus, reporting Arius Didymus, confirms this distinction: "There are two kinds of fire: one is uncreative and converts fuel into itself; the other is creative, causing growth and preservation" (Stobaeus 1,213,17–19). The cosmos is born out of this creative fire, and it is resolved back into this creative fire at the end of its life cycle, the moment of conflagration. At that moment, the cosmos is pure fire, that is, pure *pneuma*. The cosmic animal will be pure soul, without body (see Plutarch, *St. Rep.* 1053b). This implies that at the moment of conflagration the cosmos will be pure active principle, the passive principle having been in some sense converted into active principle, and awaiting conversion back again. It is not clear how the Stoics thought that they could justify this claim.

After the conflagration the cosmos is reborn. It then passes through another life cycle, culminating in another conflagration. This process continues in an endless series of cycles. The life of the cosmos in each cycle is identical to its predecessor. The cosmos, governed by reason, has the best possible organization, and as there is only *one* best possible organization, this is repeated in each cycle. Thus, there is eternal recurrence of the same events. Rather than conceiving this as an endless *series* of cycles, one might instead conceive it as a *single* cycle, repeated endlessly.

Some later Stoics, notably Boethus of Sidon and Panaetius, rejected the doctrine of conflagration and instead held that the cosmos was indestructible and existed eternally (see e.g. DL 7.142).

Fate and providence

We have already seen a certain tension in the way that one might present Stoic physics and theology. On the one hand we might present the Stoics as thoroughly naturalistic materialists, on the other hand we might present them as deeply religious pantheists. This tension extends into Stoic discussions of fate and providence. On the one hand, the Stoics *qua* naturalists outline a theory of rigid causal determinism, but on the other hand, *qua* religious pantheists, they hold a doctrine of divine providence. To what extent is it possible to reconcile these two ideas? In order to answer this question we shall begin by considering the Stoic definition of fate.

For the Stoics, "fate" (*heimarmenē*) is simply a continuous string of causes, an inescapable order and connection between events (DL 7.149; Aetius 1.28.4). At first glance this suggests an almost mechanical conception of the cosmos running like a clockwork mechanism in which every event follows seamlessly from its predecessor. Unlike the Epicurean cosmos, this seemingly mechanical Stoic cosmos admits of no random or chance events, and thus no miracles and no acts of free will. Anything that appears to happen by chance or luck is simply determined by a cause that has escaped our attention (Aetius 1.29.7). However, alongside this theory of fate the Stoics also hold a doctrine of divine providence. God, who pervades the entire cosmos, forms the cosmos into a harmonious whole and orders events in a providential manner. The cosmos is "administered by mind and providence" (DL 7.138).

The perceived tension between these two claims, which became a major concern for early modern Christian admirers of Stoicism, created the following problem. If Stoic fate admits of no exceptions, then is God's providence restricted or limited by the necessary order of causes? Is Stoic providence subsumed under the order of causes that constitute fate? Or does providence itself determine the causes that constitute fate? If the last is the case, how can fate be a *necessary* order of causes if providence is the product of God's will? Some of these concerns reflect the problems inherent in trying to reconcile the Stoic theory of fate with a Christian conception of God. The problem, though, is that much of our source material for the ancient Stoics on this topic derives from early Christian or Neoplatonic authors, some of whom were already thinking of God in very non-Stoic terms. To complicate matters further, the evidence that we do have explicitly attributing opinions to the early Stoics suggest that there may have been some internal disagreement on this topic.

Despite these difficulties, let us begin with a passage from the Christian Neoplatonist Calcidius. According to Calcidius, Chrysippus (although apparently not Cleanthes) argued that fate and providence are in fact one and the same thing:

> For providence will be God's will; and furthermore his will is the series of causes. In virtue of being his will it is providence. In virtue of also being the series of causes it gets the additional name fate. Consequently everything in accordance with fate is also the product of providence, and likewise everything in accordance with providence is the product of fate. That is Chrysippus' view. *(in Tim.* 144)

The necessary order of causes and the will of God are thus one and the same thing. Other sources identify the order of causes not with God's will but with God himself: "The common nature and the common reason of Nature are fate and providence and Zeus" (Plutarch, *St. Rep.* 1050a–b). Is this identification entirely satisfactory? For some later Christian authors it is not, because it makes God's will into a necessary order of causes, implying that God could not have acted other than he did. In other words, the identification of fate and providence denies the freedom of God's will. For other Christian authors, however, this need not pose so much of a concern. For if God is supremely good and supremely rational, then there will surely be only one course of action open to him, namely the best and most rational course of action. God could not act in any way other than he does, but then he would not want to. It is presumably in this sense that the Stoics thought that fate and providence could be reconciled. There is a necessary and unalterable order of causes that we call fate; but this necessary order is providentially arranged by God to be the best possible order.

The claim that this is "the best of all possible worlds" was famously parodied by Voltaire in *Candide* and is refuted on a daily basis by a variety of seemingly vicious and violent events, the product of human beings and Nature alike. There are a number of ways in which a Stoic might try to respond to scepticism about this claim. One would be to argue that God *qua* active principle of the cosmos orders the cosmos according to its own best interests and not according to the interests of any particular human individual, or even human beings as a species. Although events might not always turn out in the way we would prefer, nevertheless the way in which they do turn out is in fact the best possible way, and we would realize this if we were able to adopt a cosmic perspective. Another way to respond would be to argue that the apparently unpleasant events that sometimes befall us are not as bad as we so often assume. This second type of response was adopted by Seneca in his essay *On Providence*.

Seneca's arguments concerning providence are designed to undercut the claim that unpleasant situations are bad and to show their potential advantages. He repeats the standard Stoic claim (on which more in Chapter 5) that all external events are morally indifferent, and so no event can possibly be inherently bad. He also suggests that many apparently painful things often have far greater beneficial consequences, such as surgery for instance (*Prov.* 3.2). But his principal claim is that adverse situations offer one an opportunity to test, practise and develop one's virtue. He quotes the Cynic Demetrius, who said that no one is more unhappy than the man who has never faced adversity, for such a man has never had the opportunity to test his virtue (*Prov.* 3.3). "Disaster is virtue's opportunity", Seneca suggests (*Prov.* 4.6). Moreover, continual good fortune is dangerous, for it makes one inexperienced and unable to cope with adverse events that are surely on their way (*Prov.* 4.9–10). Thus we should in fact be more wary of good fortune than bad fortune. Those apparently vicious events that form part of providential fate should in fact be welcomed with open arms.

Such arguments pre-empt a whole host of later, often unconvincing, Christian arguments that attempt to overcome the "problem of evil" and are unlikely to convince the hardened sceptic. The claim that the order of causes in the cosmos is the best possible order for human beings clearly has its limits, especially when faced with the competing interests of particular individuals. The claim that the order of causes is the best possible order from the perspective of the cosmos as a whole overcomes these sorts of objections but raises others. Why, for instance, is the present cosmos with green grass preferable to an alternative cosmos in which grass is pink? If this is the best possible world, then surely every minute detail will be implicated in its perfection.

The solution to this objection lies in the Stoic theory of cosmic sympathy. This suggests that there is continual interaction between all parts of the cosmos no matter how far apart they may be. The influence of the moon on the tides was held to be one such example of this sympathy (Cicero, *Div.* 2.34). This sympathy between all of the parts of the cosmos is a product of the fact that it is all permeated by breath or *pneuma*. But if every minute part of the cosmos has a sympathetic impact on every other part, then it will not be possible to alter even the tiniest detail without creating wider consequences.

This conception of a cosmos sympathetically arranged and providentially ordered into a necessary series of causes that admits of no exceptions does not seem to leave much room for human agency. How do the Stoics position human actions within their deterministic cosmos? Is there any room left for free will? These sorts of concerns were raised in antiquity. The classic response to thoroughgoing determinism was known as the "lazy argument" and it, along with the Stoic response to it, are reported by Cicero (*Fat.* 28–30). The "lazy argument" states that if it is fated for someone to recover from an illness, then they will do so whether they call out the doctor or not. Consequently all human actions will become irrelevant to the already determined outcomes of events, and so we might as well not bother acting at all.

The Stoic response to this argument, made by Chrysippus, draws a distinction between two types of fated things: simple fated things and conjoined fated things. For Chrysippus, a simple fated thing is necessary and a product of the essence of a thing. For instance, the fact that a mortal being will die is a simple fated thing because death is a necessary consequence of what it means for a being to be mortal. A conjoined fated thing is more complex, involving two types of causes that we might call internal and external. For instance, "Socrates will die" is a simple fated thing by virtue of the fact that Socrates is a mortal being (his nature, or internal cause), but "Socrates will die this afternoon", is not a simple fated thing because various external causes may also contribute to the outcome alongside the internal cause of his nature as a mortal being. If Socrates is ill, then whether we choose to call the doctor out or not may have a considerable impact on whether he dies this afternoon or whether he survives to see another day. We might say that Socrates' survival is "conjoined" with us calling the doctor. Similarly, a woman giving birth to a baby cannot be fated to do so regardless of whether she has slept with a man; rather the two events will be "conjoined" and "co-fated" (Cicero, *Fat.* 30).

Chrysippus uses this distinction between simple fated and conjoined fated things to argue that human actions can in fact make a contribution to the outcome of events in a deterministic cosmos. It *will* make a difference whether we call the doctor out or not, but the final outcome will nevertheless be completely determined, shaped by a range of both internal and external causes.

Psychology

This concern with the role of human actions within the larger cosmological processes of fate brings us down to the human scale. So far we have focused mainly on the cosmos as a whole and we have seen how the Stoics conceived the cosmos as a living being composed of two principles that constitute its soul and its body. For the Stoics this cosmic relation is mirrored at the human level. The human soul is *pneuma*, a fragment of the *pneuma* that constitutes God's soul. Similarly, the human body is a fragment of the matter that constitutes the cosmic body. The nature of the relationship between the human soul and body is thus the same as that between the cosmic soul and body.

Let us consider this relationship in a little more detail. As we have seen, all existing things involve the two principles of matter and *pneuma* and the qualities within any existing thing are owing to the tension (*tonos*) of the *pneuma* in it. Different degrees of tension will generate different qualities. We considered earlier the way in which the Stoics outline three principal qualities that are the product of differing degrees of tension: cohesion (*hexis*), nature or growth (*phusis*) and soul (*psuchē*). Cohesion is the force that holds together inanimate physical objects such as stones. Nature or growth is that which gives vegetative life to plants. Soul is the power of conscious life (with sensation and impulse) found in animals. The Stoic author Hierocles gives an account of the development of these qualities in the foetus (*El. Eth.* 1,5–28). To these three we may add a fourth, even higher, degree of tension – rational soul (*logikē psuchē*) – that generates the quality of rationality in adult human beings (conscious life with rational judgement as well as impressions and impulses). A rational human being, then, will contain *pneuma* at all four levels of tension. She will have *pneuma* as *hexis* giving cohesion to her bones, for instance; *pneuma* as *phusis* by virtue of being alive in the most basic biological sense; *pneuma* as *psuchē* giving her the animal faculties of impression and impulse; and *pneuma* as *logikē psuchē* giving her the rational power of judgement that can intervene between receiving impressions and acting on impulses.

The human soul, then, is just one part of the *pneuma* that pervades our bodies, alongside *pneuma* in the less complex forms of *hexis* and *phusis*. We contain all three forms of *pneuma*. The *pneuma* that constitutes the soul is said to permeate the whole body, like the tentacles of an octopus (Aetius 4.21.2). It comprises eight parts (DL 7.157). These are the five senses – touch, taste, hearing, sight and smell – plus the faculties of speech and reproduction, and the "commanding faculty" (*hēgemonikon*; DL has *logistikon*, the power of reasoning). The "commanding faculty" itself comprises three parts: the faculties of impression, impulse and assent. Of these, the faculties of impression and impulse are shared with non-rational animals. It is the faculty of assent that corresponds with what we might call the self or "I", that part of the mind that engages in conscious decision-making processes.

Chrysippus is reported to have located the "commanding faculty" in the heart rather than the brain (see Galen, *PHP* 1.6.12; also DL 7.159). To put this in context, at around the same time two Hellenistic scientists, Praxagoras and Erasistratus, developed a theory of the nervous system based on *pneuma* extending through the whole body. Praxagoras took the heart to be the centre of the nervous system; Erasistratus took the brain to be the centre (see *PHP* 1.6–7; Annas 1992: 20–26). Chrysippus favoured Praxagoras' theory and so located the commanding faculty of the soul in the heart. With over two thousand years of hindsight it is easy to say that Chrysippus made the wrong choice, but in doing so he was in good company, for he was following in the footsteps of Aristotle (see *PHP* 1.6). It is also worth noting that not all Stoics followed Chrysippus in following Praxagoras, and some did locate the commanding faculty in the brain (see Philodemus, *De Pietate* (*PHerc* 1428) 9,9–13, in Obbink 1996: 19–21).

The Stoic account of the soul remains true to their naturalism and materialism, as can be seen in Chrysippus' use of then current scientific theories. However, it is important to stress that the Stoics never try to give an account of the soul purely in terms of the body, despite the soul being constituted by *pneuma*, which is itself physical. Individuals are ensouled because the cosmos as a whole is ensouled, and the Stoics do not conceive of the properties of the soul, such as consciousness, to be emergent properties developing from inert matter. This close kinship between particular human beings and the cosmos as a whole is a distinctive feature of Stoic physics. It is also central to Stoic ethics, to which we shall now turn.

FIVE

Stoic ethics

Self-preservation and the origin of values

Material about Stoic ethics is reported in a wide range of ancient sources, not to mention in the surviving works of the late Stoics Seneca and Epictetus. But perhaps the most important accounts of Stoic ethics that survive are those in Diogenes Laertius (esp. 7.84–131), Arius Didymus and Cicero's *On Ends* (esp. 3.16–76).

The foundation for Stoic ethics is a doctrine that has its own basis in physics, that is, in the nature of living beings. This is the doctrine of *oikeiōsis* (but for some doubts about this as the beginning of Stoic ethics see Schofield 2003: 237–8). This term is especially difficult to translate with a single English equivalent. It has generally been rendered as "orientation" and "appropriation". This doctrine opens Diogenes Laertius' account of Stoic ethics (DL 7.85), and it appears at the beginning of the account of Stoic ethics in Cicero's *On Ends* as well (*Fin.* 3.16). Here is part of Diogenes' version, in which he quotes from Chrysippus:

> An animal's first impulse, say the Stoics, is to self-preservation, because Nature from the outset endears it (*oikeiousēs*) to itself, as Chrysippus affirms in the first book of his work *On Ends*; his own words are, "The dearest thing (*prōton oikeion*)

> to every animal is its own constitution and its consciousness
> thereof".   (DL 7.85)

According to the theory of *oikeiōsis* the basic desire or drive in all animals (including human beings) is for self-preservation. The one thing that is most important to us is our own existence and its continuation. Consequently our most primitive choices and actions are shaped by what we think will enhance or damage our own physical constitution. We choose what we think will be good for us and we avoid what we think will be bad for us. This seemingly selfish (or at least self-centred) attitude is the basis for all of Stoic ethics. Although this may seem to be paradoxical it is arguably one of the strengths of the Stoic position, for it is an ethical theory that takes seriously the primitive behaviour of animals and human beings, and does not try to pretend that selfish motivations are not at the heart of most people's actions.

On the basis of this instinct for self-preservation, individuals ascribe value. Thus what will enhance our constitution we term "good" and what will damage it we term "bad". Unlike Platonism, which posits the existence of an absolute, transcendent concept of "the Good" to which all value ascriptions may be referred, Stoicism grounds value ascriptions in this naturalistic and physiological theory of *oikeiōsis*.

For a non-rational animal, the objects that will contribute to the preservation of its existence (and so be "good" for it) are fairly obvious: food, water, shelter and so on. For a rational adult human being these basic physical needs are supplemented with others that are also vital for survival. If I am to survive as a rational being and not merely as an animal then I must pursue those things that will help to preserve my rationality as well as those things that will preserve my body. In other words I must take care of my soul as well as taking care of my body.

Let us consider an example. If I am doing my best to be a rational being who is free and independent of others, then I will sometimes have to make choices that may *appear* not to further my own self-preservation. For instance, if a tyrant threatens to kill me if I do not agree to do certain things that I find objectionable or think to be wrong, then – if I am to preserve myself as a rational being – I should stand up to the tyrant even if this may mean the loss of my life (see e.g. Epictetus, *Diss.* 1.2). But why? How could getting myself killed possibly contribute to my self-preservation? Well, it may not contribute to my self-preservation in so far as I am merely a living animal, but giving in to the tyrant will equally destroy me as an independent rational being. I may remain biologically alive if I give in to the tyrant, but I will have lost something far more important, having reduced myself to a slave. Thus the Stoic doctrine of self-preservation will, in cases of rational beings – that is, philosophers working towards the ideal of the sage – sometimes lead to choices that may actually threaten an individual's physical existence. But then as Socrates famously put it, it is not merely living, but living well that matters (Plato, *Crito* 48b). This thought stood behind Socrates' decision to face his execution rather than take advantage of the opportunity to escape. It should be stressed, however, that such choices are not *against* our natural impulse for survival; they remain the product of a desire for self-preservation, simply operating with a different conception of the self, one above basic animal needs and everyday human preferences. Cicero reports that as one develops one's understanding, one places greater priority on being consistent in what one does than on mere material benefits (*Fin.* 3.21). In the case of Socrates, living by a consistent set of principles was far more important than merely living at whatever the price. As Epictetus put it, "such a man is not to be saved by any shameful means; he is saved by dying, and not by running away" (*Diss.* 4.1.165).

Paradoxically, then, it is the Stoic theory of self-preservation that forms the basis for their later infamous defence of suicide (see Rist 1969: ch. 13). Suicide may well be the end for an individual *qua* animal, but it may be the most appropriate act of the individual *qua* rational being. In some circumstances, suicide may be the only rational action. Roman Stoics in particular became famed for their adherence to this doctrine, the most famous of all being Cato. Seneca's acceptance of his imposed suicide, forced upon him by Nero, has been cited as another example, echoing the choice made by Socrates. But a number of the early Stoics are also reported to have taken their own lives, including Zeno (DL 7.28) and Cleanthes (DL 7.176).

Real goods and "indifferents"

As a rational being, although one will want to preserve one's own physical existence, one will want to pay more attention to the preservation of oneself *as* a rational being, even if this might lead one to suicide. How did the Stoics try to explain this paradoxical claim?

According to Arius Didymus (5a), Zeno divided things that exist into three groups: things that are good, things that are bad and things that are indifferent. The only things classified as "good" are virtue and things that participate in virtue. Likewise, the only things that are "bad" are vice and those things that participate in vice. (Instead of "virtue" and "vice", we might translate *aretē* and *kakia* as "excellence" and "imperfection".) Everything else is "indifferent" (*adiaphoron*), including one's own life, reputation, health, poverty or wealth and all other external objects. If we accept this threefold division then we shall focus all of our attention on cultivating and preserving virtue (the only good), and considerably less on preserving our biological life (a mere indifferent).

How does this relate to the preceding account of self-preservation? Well, when someone says that something is good for them, we should perhaps rephrase this by saying that it has value for them, but is not strictly speaking "good". Food, water and shelter all have value for me but they are not "good", for only virtue is good. Virtue for the Stoics is an excellent disposition of the soul; we can identify it with perfect rationality. Yet as we have seen it is possible to give an account of the value of virtue also in terms of the theory of self-preservation. Virtue has value – is good – because it contributes to our survival as rational beings. It is that which ensures the excellent condition of the soul, similar to the way in which food and water ensure a good condition for the body. But if virtue and externals such as food and water can all have their value accounted for in terms of the theory of self-preservation, then why is virtue accorded the grandiose status of being "good", while the externals food and water remain mere "indifferents"?

There are three reasons why this is the case. The first is that for the Stoics we are by nature rational beings, so the only thing that is genuinely good for us is that which preserves us as rational beings, and this will be virtue. The second is that externals such as physical health and great wealth cannot be inherently good because they can also be used for bad ends. So they must be morally indifferent, neither good nor bad in themselves. The third, and perhaps the most important, is that the possession of externals cannot guarantee us happiness, but the possession of virtue can, claim the Stoics. We shall return to these issues in due course, especially the relationship between virtue and happiness. But first we need to consider further the status of the indifferents.

The threefold division of good, bad and indifferent as outlined above is credited to Zeno. But in the light of criticisms from other schools the Stoic position was developed further (by Zeno himself, according to Arius Didymus 7g). The category of "indifferents" (*adiaphora*) was itself subdivided into "preferred indifferents" (*proēgmenon*), "non-preferred indifferents" (*apoproēgmenon*) and what we might call genuinely "indifferent indifferents" or "neutral indifferents". Cicero provides a summary:

> All other things, he [Zeno] said, were neither good nor bad, but nevertheless some of them were in accordance with Nature and others contrary to Nature; also among these he counted another interposed or intermediate class of things. He taught that things in accordance with Nature were to be chosen and estimated as having a certain value, and their opposites the opposite, while things that were neither he left in the intermediate class. These he declared to possess no motive force whatever, but among things to be chosen some were to be deemed of more value and others of less: the more valuable he termed "preferred", the less valuable, "rejected" [i.e. "non-preferred"]. (*Acad.* 1.36–7)

Thus the original rather harsh position has been softened. Rather than claiming that *all* externals should be a matter of pure indifference, the Stoics now suggest that there is nothing wrong with preferring some indifferents over others. It is perfectly natural, they suggest, to prefer to be healthy rather than ill, or rich rather than poor. Health and wealth would be examples of "preferred indifferents", with sickness and poverty being "non-preferred indifferents". As for completely neutral indifferents with no motivating force whatsoever, an example would be whether one had an odd or even number of hairs on one's head.

In Stoic terminology, the preferred indifferents that contribute to our physical well-being have value (*axia*) but they are not good in the way that virtue is good. Health has a certain value (owing to its contribution to our physical self-preservation), but it is not good (see Cicero, *Fin.* 3.44). Things that have value, such as health, wealth, reputation and so on, are all things that can accumulate; one can be more or less healthy, more or less rich. But virtue, by contrast, does not admit of degrees and cannot be added to in this way (see *ibid.* 3.45–8). If something is right or wrong, good or bad, then there are no degrees of goodness. Thus a good life is equally good whether it is long or short, so death cannot affect it (another reason for the acceptability of suicide). Moreover, all bad actions are equally bad, say the Stoics, no matter how serious or trivial they may appear to be. This also means that the goodness of a good life cannot be *increased* by the addition of health or wealth. So although these things may have some value, they remain merely preferred indifferents and do not contribute to the goodness of a good life.

The Stoic position may become clearer if we situate it in relation to two other ancient ethical theories: the Cynic and the Aristotelian. The Cynics would agree with the Stoics that virtue is the only good, but they would reject any attempt to prioritize among the indifferents. Indeed, Zeno's original position may well have been inspired by his time studying with the Cynic Crates. But it was Zeno's introduction of the subdivision of indifferents that marks the beginning of a clearly distinguishable Stoic position. The Aristotelians, on the other hand, would agree with the Stoics that externals such as health and wealth should be accorded value. Indeed, Aristotle argued that such things are necessary along with virtue for a happy life (e.g. friends, in *Nicomachean Ethics* 9.9). But the Stoics would not want to go that far. Although externals such as health and wealth have value they are not *necessary* for a happy life, claim the Stoics. Virtue alone is sufficient for happiness, and in claiming this the Stoics remained in agreement with the Cynics. Their position is thus halfway between the Cynic and Aristotelian positions; virtue is the only good, but some externals should be preferred over others.

Zeno's development of the Stoic position was not unanimously accepted. The Stoic Aristo rejected this subdivision of indifferents (see DL 7.160), maintaining the original position, which was more in line with the position of the Cynics. Perhaps his concern was that Stoicism would all too quickly become indistinguishable from the Aristotelian position. Indeed, Academic philosophers such as Carneades, Antiochus and Cicero claimed that the distance between the revised Stoic position and the Aristotelian position was merely a matter of words rather than substantial philosophical content (see e.g. Cicero, *Fin.* 3.10, 3.41).

Among the later Stoics, Epictetus offers an interesting conceptual distinction that is also relevant here. For Epictetus, things may be divided into two categories: those that are "up to us" (*eph' hēmin*) and those that are "not up to us" (*ouk eph' hēmin*). "Up to us" are our opinions, desires and actions; everything else – our bodies, possessions, reputations – are "not up to us". For Epictetus, we should focus all of our attention towards those things that are "up to us", paying no attention to things that are out of our control:

> Some things are up to us, while others are not up to us. Up to us are conception, choice, desire, aversion and, in a word, everything that is our own doing; not up to us are our body, our property, reputation, office and, in a word, everything that is not our own doing. Furthermore, the things up to us are by nature free, unhindered and unimpeded; while the things not up to us are weak, servile, subject to hindrance and not our own. (*Ench.* 1.1–2)

One can see that all of the indifferents, whether preferred or non-preferred, fall into the "not up to us" category. Epictetus is keen to stress that while some of these externals may be nominally better than others, choosing between them is not really a task worthy of our close attention. Instead, we should focus all of our attention on developing the only thing that is genuinely good, namely our virtue or excellence, which resides in the only thing over which we have any real control, namely our faculty of "choice" (*prohairesis*). By happy coincidence, the only thing that is genuinely good resides in the only thing over which we have any real control.

For Epictetus, it is not that the distinction between preferred and non-preferred indifferents should be rejected. He has no problem with people preferring health instead of sickness, for instance. But when compared with the benefits that can be conferred by virtue, it is clear, he thinks, where our attention should be focused – on the acquisition and preservation of virtue, the only real good. He is also well aware of the risks involved in pursuing preferred indifferents. Not only will one be likely to end up attributing too much value to these things if one starts to pay them close attention, but also one is likely to be frustrated when one is unable to secure these externals. It is a short step from such frustration to a violent emotion and all of the psychological damage that such emotions can bring. Although Epictetus may acknowledge that it is preferable to be rich than poor, the risks involved in actively pursuing wealth are just too great. Instead we should focus all of our attention on cultivating virtue, an excellent and healthy state of the soul.

The emotions

As we have just seen, Epictetus suggests that we should pay attention only to what is "up to us" (*eph' hēmin*), and the only thing that is truly up to us is our faculty of "choice" (*prohairesis*), part of the commanding faculty (*hēgemonikon*) of our soul. The only things that we have complete control over are our judgements, made by this faculty of choice. But this is no bad thing, for this is the means by which we are able to secure the only thing that has any real value, namely virtue, and this virtue is the only thing that can bring us genuine happiness.

But one might object that this account leaves out a substantial part of our internal lives over which we seem to have no control whatsoever, namely our emotions (*pathē*), a vital influence on our happiness. But it does not. For the Stoics, the emotions are themselves judgements. As such, they also fall into the realm of things that are "up to us". To be more precise, it is reported that Chrysippus held emotions to be judgements (Cicero, *Acad.* 1.39; Galen, *PHP* 5.1.4), whereas Zeno had held emotions to be *the product* of judgements (DL 7.111; Galen *ibid.*). It seems reasonable to assume that Chrysippus was attempting to improve upon Zeno's position, perhaps responding to criticisms from other schools, but Zeno's position is the more plausible of the two. Consider the following example. A relative dies in a tragic accident, and as time passes one's emotions surrounding this event gradually diminish until eventually, perhaps only decades later, one is no longer emotionally upset about the event. However, one might still hold firmly to the judgement that what happened was indeed a terrible thing (that, perhaps, could easily have been avoided). It would not be possible still to hold on to that judgement after the emotion had gone if the judgement and the emotional response were identical. So it seems more plausible to suggest that emotions are the product of judgements rather than judgements themselves.

Leaving this internal Stoic debate to one side, how did the Stoics conceive emotions, whether they be judgements or the product of judgements? They did so by outlining a process leading to their formation. Let us recall the discussion of epistemology in Chapter 3. There we considered Gellius' account of his journey by sea in the company of a philosopher who explained away his apparent fear during a storm. The philosopher did so by referring Gellius to a passage from Epictetus that gave the following account of the formation of emotions. First, we receive impressions that present external objects to us, and we have no control over these. Then, we make a judgement about the impressions that we have received, and this judgement is an act of assent over which we do have control. As we saw, sometimes we add an unconscious value judgement to our impressions; rather than being faced with the value-neutral impression "there is a wave above my head" we are instead confronted with "there is a wave above my head *and this is a terrible thing*". Now, if we assent to an impression that includes one of these unconscious value judgements then we shall create an emotional response. Gellius' seafaring philosopher claimed not to have made such an assent, being only briefly shaken by a "first movement". However, the other passengers may well have assented to a value-laden impression and so suffered an unpleasant emotional reaction.

Before turning to emotions proper, let us consider "first movements". These are the immediate physical responses that people sometimes have to impressions *before* they have had a chance to form a judgement about what is happening and so have a proper emotion. It is important not to confuse these first movements with genuine emotions. We have already seen the seafaring philosopher's account of his own first movements in the storm. Another example would be when someone jumps when there is a sudden noise. Just because someone reacts in this way does not mean that, for instance, they are suffering from the emotion of fear. The fullest discussion of first movements can be found in the second book of Seneca's *On Anger*. He writes:

> Emotion does not consist in being moved by the impressions that are presented to the mind, but in surrendering to these and following up such a chance movement. For if any one supposes that pallor, falling tears, sexual excitement or a deep sigh, a sudden brightening of the eyes, and the like, are evidence of an emotion and a manifestation of the mind, he is mistaken and fails to understand that these are just disturbances of the body. (*Ira* 2.3.1–2)

These sudden physical reactions do not constitute emotions. An emotion involves a conscious act of assent to an impression. The seafaring philosopher, although pale and trembling in the face of the storm, did not suffer from an emotion because once these immediate physical movements subsided he did not assent to the proposition that anything bad had happened.

As the product of an assent, the Stoics claimed that the emotions are completely within our control. Not only are they things that we *can* control, they are also things that we *should* control. They are (as we have seen in Chapter 2) diseases of the soul analogous to diseases of the body, and it is the task of philosophy to cure us of these mental diseases. They are the product of mistaken judgements, namely assents to impressions that include unwarranted ascriptions of value. They are thus the consequence of poor reasoning on our part and so they should play no part in the life of a properly functioning rational being, and they certainly will not figure in the life of the fully rational sage. Epictetus goes so far as to suggest that these seemingly trivial errors in reasoning can ultimately cause great death and destruction, for it was a faulty assent that led Paris to run away with Helen, and a similar faulty assent that led Menelaus to chase after him and attack Troy (see *Diss.* 1.28.12–13). The events recounted in Homer's *Iliad* are merely the product of a series of faulty assents. The same applies to the events recorded in the great tragedies (*ibid.* 1.28.32). If there is anything tragic in these famous stories, Epictetus suggests, it is merely that the protagonists are so foolish that they assent to their value-laden impressions without first pausing to analyse them.

The Stoics offer a detailed classification of those emotions that they consider damaging and think should be avoided. Cicero, probably following Chrysippus, offers a fourfold division of emotions into beliefs about good and bad things, either present now or expected in the future (*Tusc.* 4.14):

$$
\text{emotion}
\begin{cases}
\text{good}
\begin{cases}
\text{present} = \text{delight} = \text{belief in a present good} \\
\text{absent} = \text{lust} = \text{belief in a future good}
\end{cases} \\
\text{bad}
\begin{cases}
\text{present} = \text{distress} = \text{belief in a present evil} \\
\text{absent} = \text{fear} = \text{belief in a future evil}
\end{cases}
\end{cases}
$$

All of the various normal emotions that we experience fall into one of these four categories. From this we can see that the Stoics held that even emotional responses to seemingly favourable situations should be avoided. It is just as mistaken and potentially damaging to assent to the impression that an external state of affairs is good as it is to the impression that it is bad. First it is simply an error in reasoning; impressions report states of affairs and any ascription of value, whether positive or negative, is an unwarranted addition. Secondly it claims that an external, that is, an indifferent, is good when in fact only virtue is good. Thirdly it is dangerous because it creates a situation in which a change in the external state of affairs could lead to even worse emotions. If we think that a particular event – our numbers coming up in the lottery, say – is good, then we shall be overcome by the emotion of delight, but when we realize that we cannot find our winning ticket, the distress that we shall suffer will be so much worse. So both positive and negative emotions should be avoided. Thus the Stoics propose an ethical ideal of *apatheia*, freedom from all emotions.

However, they do also suggest that there exist *eupatheiai*, good emotions, which can be part of a fully rational life:

> They say that there are three good emotions (*eupatheiai*): joy (*charan*), caution (*eulabeian*) and wishing (*boulēsin*). Joy, the counterpart of pleasure, is rational elation; caution, the counterpart of fear, is rational avoidance, for though the sage will never feel fear he will still use caution. And they make wishing the counterpart of desire, inasmuch as it is rational appetency. (DL 7.116)

These three types of good emotion contain others: for instance, wishing includes benevolence and friendliness; caution includes modesty and reverence; joy includes mirth and cheerfulness.

Some ancient critics dismissed the introduction of these good emotions as merely playing with words: joy is simply delight renamed; caution is merely fear recast; wishing is just lust under another name (see Lactantius, *Div. Inst.* 6.15.10–11). Do these so-called good emotions really differ from the other emotions?

At first glance simply adding the adjective "rational" when describing these three good emotions seems question-begging. But it would be a mistake to dismiss this too quickly. An emotion may indeed be rational if, for instance, it is the product of an assent that is correct. For an emotion to be produced the impression assented to must contain some form of value judgement. As we have seen, these are usually unwarranted additions by the unconscious mind: "there is a wave above my head *and this is a terrible thing*". But such an evaluation will be warranted, and so rational, when there is a genuine good present. As we know, the only genuine good is virtue. But virtue can be the basis for an emotion, a good emotion. Thus, the good emotion of joy will be the emotion experienced by the sage when he is fully aware of his own virtue. As Seneca puts it, joy is an elation of the soul that trusts the goodness of its possessions (*Ep.* 59.2). This will be a good emotion for three reasons, mirroring the three reasons why normal emotions are bad. First it will be rational rather than the product of an erroneous judgement. Secondly it will reflect the genuine goodness of virtue. Thirdly it will reflect an internal state of affairs and so not be vulnerable to changes of fortune. The good emotion of joy will thus be self-sufficient, whereas the normal emotion of delight, for instance, will be dependent upon external states of affairs. The sage can revel in his joy, knowing that it is not vulnerable to the vicissitudes of fortune. Similarly, caution would be rational in the face of a genuinely bad future scenario, namely the loss of one's virtue. Wishing would be a rational desire for a genuine good, again virtue. There is no good emotion that stands as a counterpart to the normal emotion of distress. Why? Well, the sage would only experience distress if faced with a present evil, and the only genuinely bad thing is vice. But as a sage he is free completely from vice.

We can see that the traditional caricature of the stony-faced Stoic devoid of all emotion does not tell the whole story. The Stoic certainly will reject certain emotions as the product of confused judgements, but he will not be completely joyless. He will experience good emotions as rational responses to genuine goods. But he will not suffer irrational emotions as the result of assenting to confused and unwarranted value-laden impressions.

The foregoing account of the emotions is broadly speaking the orthodox Stoic position. According to Galen, Posidonius deviated from this intellectualist account of the emotions, adopting a tripartite theory of the soul along the lines of that outlined by Plato in the *Republic*, in which reason and emotion occupy separate faculties. How reliable Galen's testimony is here is a matter of scholarly debate. What is clear, however, is that later Stoics – Seneca and Epictetus for instance – remained faithful to the orthodox position.

Appropriate actions

The Stoic account of the emotions gives us a good sense of one sort of behaviour that the Stoics deemed inappropriate, namely assenting to impressions that contain unwarranted ascriptions of value. But what would they claim to be appropriate behaviour? In the light of the theory of appropriation (*oikeiōsis*), the most fundamental action appropriate (*oikeion*) for all animals and human beings is to try to preserve their own existence (see Cicero, *Fin.* 3.20). We might call this a theory of natural egoism. As we have seen, for a rational being this will mean trying to preserve oneself as a rational being. The way one does this is by cultivating virtue, which is also the only thing that properly deserves to be called "good". However, the Stoics also offer a whole range of other types of what they call "appropriate action" (*kathēkon*; "proper function" in LS).

An appropriate action is one that it would be natural for an animal to undertake, such as one that would contribute to its survival and be in accordance with its own nature (see e.g. DL 7.108). Some appropriate actions will be immediately and obviously so, such as the pursuit of food and water; others will require thought and deliberation in order to determine their appropriateness. At first glance it looks as if these should be connected with the class of preferred indifferents. Thus we might say that it is appropriate to pursue preferred indifferents, but inappropriate to pursue non-preferred indifferents. Indeed, Arius Didymus reports that the topics of the preferred and the appropriate are consistent with one another (Arius Didymus 8). The Stoics go on to posit a further category of action: the "perfect" or "completely correct" (*katorthōma*). Just as appropriate actions might be seen to correspond to the pursuit of preferred indifferents, so completely correct actions might be seen to correspond to purely virtuous actions. Completely correct actions are themselves appropriate actions, but not all appropriate actions are completely correct. Those that are not are known as "middle" or "intermediate" appropriate actions (*meson kathēkon*). There are, then, it seems, two types of appropriate action: those that correspond to the pursuit of preferred indifferents and those that relate to virtue. Like the preferred indifferents, appropriate actions are value neutral, and, like virtue, completely correct actions are good.

In fact, we should perhaps limit the parallel between preferred indifferents and appropriate actions to the fact that neither are inherently good or bad, rather than try to claim that appropriate actions are *only* concerned with preferred indifferents. The important point to emphasize is that appropriate actions can be performed by anyone, even non-rational animals, whereas completely correct actions are limited to those who possess virtue.

Given that completely correct actions are instances of appropriate actions, how do they differ from other appropriate actions? What characteristics do completely correct actions possess that mark them off from other appropriate actions? In order to answer this question let us consider two examples. First, let us imagine someone who, without much conscious thought or consideration, acts throughout their life in a perfectly reasonable way, acting in accordance with their own nature. Such a person's actions would be appropriate. Secondly, let us imagine another person who acts in *exactly* the same way, but does so after having consciously deliberated and come to a firm conclusion that these are the most appropriate actions to undertake. This second person's actions would be not only appropriate but also completely correct, for they would derive from the right sort of internal mental disposition, namely virtue. Although the outcomes may be the same, the second person's behaviour is preferable for it springs from their virtue, and so will be more consistent.

Here we might recall the distinction that Plato made in the *Gorgias* between procedures that are the product of trial and error – a mere knack – and procedures that are the product of genuine expertise

– an art or craft (*Gorgias* 463b). Although the Platonic distinction is slightly different from the one under discussion here, there is a parallel. The first individual acts appropriately without much conscious deliberation; they have a knack, we might say, but they would not be able to give an account of *why* they are acting as they do. The second individual, however, would be able to give an account of their appropriate actions, for they spring from their virtue, which, as we have seen in Chapter 2, the Stoics conceived as an art or craft. Although the resulting actions may be the same, naturally it would be better for them to result from a genuine expertise rather than trial-and-error experimentation or just unthinking good luck. The person who acts appropriately owing to their possession of such expertise will be confident that they will be able to continue to do so in the future in a way that the lucky amateur will not. It is this that will make their actions not merely appropriate but also completely correct.

This focus on the internal disposition of the agent rather than the actual outcome of an action when assessing its value has led some to draw parallels between Stoic ethics and Kantian ethics (we shall return to Kant in Chapter 6).

Virtue and happiness

The Stoics, then, suggest that a whole range of actions may be appropriate, being in accordance with our nature, but not necessarily good. As we have seen, only virtue is held to be good. The Stoics also suggest that it is the only thing with which we should concern ourselves. Why? Do the Stoics think that there is something inherently good about being virtuous? In one sense they clearly do, claiming that it is choice-worthy for its own sake (see e.g. DL 7.89). Yet the Stoics do not follow Plato in positing the existence of a transcendent conception of "the Good". As we have seen, for the Stoics value judgements originate in the theory of self-preservation. Being virtuous is good because in some sense it is good *for me* to be virtuous.

This thought is developed in the claim that virtue can be identified with happiness. If we are virtuous we shall be happy. If we want to be happy we must be virtuous. The Stoics, like the vast majority of ancient philosophers, are "eudaimonists". The word that is usually translated as "happiness" in discussions of ancient philosophy is *eudaimonia*. Scholars regularly note that the meaning of *eudaimonia* is somewhat broader than the meaning of the English word "happiness". It refers to a substantive well-being in one's life, rather than a merely subjective feeling of contentment. Thus it is sometimes translated as "well-being" or "flourishing" rather than "happiness". The important point here is that the Stoics, like so many other ancient philosophers, think that *eudaimonia* is a good thing and that it is something universally desirable. It is the *summum bonum*, namely that "for the sake of which everything is done but which is not itself done for the sake of anything else" (see Long 1989: 77). There is no argument for this claim in any of the ancient schools; it is the great implicit assumption in ancient ethics. Yet this is no reason to be suspicious; on the contrary, we are more likely to be suspicious of the psychological well-being of someone who *does not* unequivocally accept that they want to be happy and to live well.

In the light of this we might say that Stoic ethics begins with a conditional. The conditional is "If you want to be happy, then …". As we have seen, the Stoics identify happiness with virtue, independent of all externals. So their position might be summed up as "If you want to be happy and to live well, then you should try to become virtuous, for only virtue can bring you happiness". If you *do not* want to live well then Stoicism offers no argument to convince you that you *should* and has nothing further to offer you.

Having touched on the translation of *eudaimonia* as happiness, we should also consider briefly the meaning of "virtue". The Greek word translated as "virtue" here is *aretē*. The word *aretē* has a much wider meaning than the English word "virtue" and does not necessarily have the latter's heavy moral overtones. It is, for instance, sometimes translated as "excellence". Indeed, Zeno and Chrysippus defined virtue as "a disposition and faculty of the governing principle of the soul brought into being by reason" (Plutarch, *Mor.* 441c). Thus we might say that for the Stoics virtue is this governing principle of the soul in an excellent or perfected condition. It is, says Aristo, a "health" (*ibid.*), that is, a healthy state of the soul. As we have seen in Chapter 2, philosophy for the Stoics is an art, analogous to medicine, that is concerned with the health of the soul. Thus we might say that if one wants to live well, then one should try to cultivate a healthy state of the soul. This is quite different from a certain traditional image of Stoicism in which it is suggested that the individual should sacrifice themselves to the pursuit of selfless virtue.

The account of the relationship between happiness and virtue offered here borders on what Long has called a "utilitarian" reading of Stoic ethics (see Long 1970–71: 95–6). It suggests that virtue should be pursued only in so far as it will bring one happiness. Long is correct to point out that the Stoics do also claim that virtue is something choice-worthy for its own sake, something inherently valuable that is not chosen for some other motive, such as happiness. But that suggests that virtue, and not happiness, has become the *summum bonum*, that which is not chosen for the sake of anything else. How can virtue be something choice-worthy for its own sake when happiness is the only thing not chosen for the sake of anything else?

When Diogenes Laertius reports that virtue is choice-worthy for its own sake, he adds that it is not chosen out of hope or fear or for the sake of some external motive (DL 7.89). Yet it would be odd to characterize happiness in any of these terms. To do so would imply that happiness is like external benefits such as wealth or fame. Perhaps one way around this problem, then, is to stress the intimate interrelation between virtue and happiness for the Stoics. Thus one might say that virtue is intrinsically valuable for the Stoics precisely because it *constitutes* happiness, the *summum bonum*, rather than being merely a means to happiness in some instrumentalist fashion. Indeed, this is precisely what Diogenes goes on to say in his report: "it is in virtue that happiness consists" (*ibid.*). Having an excellent disposition of the soul will guarantee happiness; conversely, it will not be possible to be happy without such a disposition. Virtue and happiness go hand in hand, despite remaining conceptually distinct.

Living according to Nature

If we want to be happy, to live well, then we should cultivate virtue or excellence. What this means in practice is focusing our attention on the internal state of our souls rather than external objects that are out of our control. Although great riches and a successful career might be nice, they will not bring us a fulfilled life if internally we are a chaotic jumble of confused opinions, violent emotions and contradictory beliefs. This ethical ideal proposed by the Stoics is famously presented as living in accordance with Nature.

According to the ancient sources, Zeno proposed living in harmony or consistently (*homologoumenōs*). Is this harmony with oneself? This is certainly what Arius Didymus suggests, and it fits well with the preceding summary. If we live consistently then we shall be internally consistent and rational, free from conflicting beliefs and emotions.

Zeno is also credited with the definition of the goal as living in harmony with Nature (DL 7.87), although other sources credit this fuller version to his successor Cleanthes (Arius Didymus 6a). If we assume that the fuller version is simply an attempt to make the original thought clearer, rather than an innovation in doctrine, then not too much hangs on this question of attribution.

Is living in harmony with Nature, living in harmony with one's own nature, or the nature of the cosmos as a whole? It is both (see DL 7.87–8). In fact, it is possible to discern three aspects to this doctrine. The first is the idea of living harmoniously with oneself, that is, of living consistently and free from internal emotional conflict. The second is the idea of living in accordance with one's own nature, of living according to one's nature as a rational being and, in particular, of following this rather than passively reacting to external forces. The third is the idea of bringing oneself into harmony with Nature as a whole. As Nature as a whole is organized by the active principle that is God, and as our own nature is but a part of this, there will be no conflict between living according to our own nature and living according to Nature as a whole.

In order to explore these ideas further let us begin by considering an entity living according to its own nature. An entity will act according to its own nature unless it is stopped by some external force, often another entity acting according to *its* own nature. In this sense, to act according to one's own nature is simply not to be hindered by external causes, and so to be free (in what we might call the political sense of freedom rather than the metaphysical sense). But of course every finite being will come up against external causes that will limit its freedom. Ideally one will want to reduce the number of these freedom-limiting encounters and to reduce the impact they have when they occur. One way of achieving this is to reduce one's reliance on external goods. If one's happiness depends solely on one's virtue, as Stoicism argues that it should, then one will become immune to a whole range of external causes that would otherwise create adverse affects, such as the thief who takes your wallet, for instance.

Of course, as a finite being it will never be possible to become completely free and invulnerable to external events. Only Nature as a whole, personified as God, is completely free because only Nature as a whole has nothing external to it. There are no causes external to Nature that can hinder its actions (see Cicero, *ND* 2.35). Moreover, while there can be many things that are against *my own* nature, there is nothing that is contrary to Nature as a whole, for everything is part of Nature as a whole.

One aspect of "living according to Nature" is cultivating a new perspective on the world that tries to see things from the point of view of Nature as a whole rather than merely from one's own limited perspective. This is what Marcus Aurelius tries to accomplish in a number of the sections of the *Meditations*:

> You have the power to strip away many superfluous troubles located wholly in your judgement, and to possess a large room for yourself embracing in thought the whole cosmos, to consider everlasting time, to think of the rapid change in the parts of each thing, of how short it is from birth until dissolution, and how the void before birth and that after dissolution are equally infinite. (*Med.* 9.32)

As we have already seen, our value judgements about external objects derive from our desire for self-preservation, which is itself based upon our personal perspective, on what is good or bad for *our own* nature. Marcus is suggesting that we try to transcend this limited perspective and in a sense adopt the point of view of Nature as a whole – the perspective of God, so to speak. If we can do this then we shall no longer judge external objects and events as good or bad "for me", and this will contribute to our fully grasping the status of all such things as "indifferents". Of course we shall never fully master this perspective, just as we shall never be completely free, owing to the fact that we are finite beings. Our basic biological needs will continue to force us to select those things that are good for us and avoid those things that are bad for us, even if we reclassify these as preferred and non-preferred indifferents. The presence of external entities will inevitably limit our freedom from time to time. Is this why the Stoic sage is so rare? Is the life of the sage literally impossible for us to achieve in so far as it requires a perspective and freedom that only Nature as a whole can have? This might help explain why no Stoics ever claimed to be sages themselves.

So, living according to Nature is an idea that has a number of dimensions to it. On the one hand it implies living according to our own rational nature, of focusing our attention on our virtue conceived as an excellent disposition of the soul. In practice this means analysing our judgements, making sure that we only assent to adequate impressions, so that we avoid the violent emotions that are the product of false assents. The more we manage to live according to our own rational nature, the fewer mental disturbances we shall suffer and the more independent, free and happy we shall be. On the other hand living according to Nature implies widening our circle of concern to encompass Nature as a whole, realizing that we are not isolated units but rather parts of a systematically integrated whole. The first of these suggests an inward-looking perspective; the second an outward-looking perspective. This might suggest a tension within the Stoic ideal. But there is none, for the outward-looking cosmic perspective will depend upon correct judgements about our place in Nature, and these correct judgements will only be possible if we first attend to ourselves via the inward-looking perspective. It is the same set of mistakes in our reasoning that gives rise to both unwanted internal emotions and a confused understanding of our place in Nature.

By way of example, let us return again to Gellius' seafaring philosopher. In the middle of a storm the philosopher may find himself faced with the impression "there is a wave above my head *and this is a terrible thing*". However, he will know not to assent to this impression because it involves a value judgement that is not warranted. So he will reject this impression and instead assent to the impression "there is a wave above my head". By refusing to assent to the value judgement he will avoid an unwanted and unwarranted emotion. So far this is an inward-looking exercise, concerned solely with the philosopher's own judgements. Yet if the philosopher had assented to the impression that something terrible was happening then he would have seen the wave as something external to him and so as something threatening. In other words, he would have laid the foundations for a barrier between himself and the rest of Nature. As we have seen, to some extent this is inevitable for a finite being if it is going to be concerned with its own preservation. Yet as we have also seen, in this case such a barrier would be the product of a mistaken judgement. In other words, the limited perspective in which we are isolated from the rest of Nature is a consequence of faulty judgements that we make. If we want to cultivate Marcus Aurelius' outward-looking cosmic perspective then we must first turn our attention inwards.

This is just one possible attempt to flesh out the Stoic goal of living in accordance with Nature. To complicate matters further, the Stoics are also reported to have defined the goal as selecting things that are in harmony with Nature (see e.g. Cicero, *Fin.* 3.20, 3.31). Thus it is in harmony with Nature (my own nature) to choose those things that will contribute to my own self-preservation, things such as health and wealth that have value but remain merely preferred indifferents. However, only *choosing* these things can be part of the goal; actually *obtaining* them is of course beyond our control and so not "up to us" at all. There is a sense in which this seems a fruitless exercise – desiring certain things while at the same time doing one's best not to be disappointed when one fails to obtain them. Surely it would be simpler not to lust after these externals in the first place. Indeed, this is the view to which Epictetus often comes close, expressing indifference even over whether he lives or dies. This focus on selecting things was a later innovation in Stoic ethics (probably by Antipater), and Epictetus' attitude may well be closer to the orthodox position.

The political dimension

A number of the themes that we have encountered in Stoic ethics form the background for Stoic thinking about politics. The most important of these are the theory of *oikeiōsis*, the priority of one's internal virtue over one's external circumstances and the idea that one should live in harmony with Nature. These ideas contribute to a political theory of cosmopolitanism, a theory that is perhaps most clearly expressed in the surviving works of the late Stoics. The idea of cosmopolitanism was not original to the Stoics, however. It had already been expressed by Diogenes the Cynic, and he may well have coined the word *cosmopolitēs*: "citizen of the cosmos" (see DL 6.63). It was while under the tutorship of Crates the Cynic (Diogenes' pupil) that Zeno is said to have written his infamous and now lost work the *Republic* (for the fragments see Baldry 1959). This work, the earliest and most famous work in Stoic political philosophy, has attracted controversy from antiquity onwards. Some Stoics in the centuries after Zeno were horrified by the "Cynic" doctrines that it contained and so tried to distance themselves from it. Some suggested that it was an early and immature work by Zeno, written when he was still under the influence of Crates, and so not part of his mature philosophical system. Although it certainly does contain some Cynic themes, it would be rash to dismiss it as not part of Zeno's own considered philosophy, regardless of when in his career it was written. Recent scholars have shown that these same Cynic themes can be found throughout the early Stoa and so are not limited to this one "early work" (see Goulet-Cazé 2003). Perhaps the most important of the surviving fragments relating to the *Republic* is the following from Plutarch:

The much admired *Republic* of Zeno, the founder of the
Stoic sect, is aimed at this one main point, that our house-
hold arrangements should not be based on cities or parishes,
each one marked out by its own legal system, but we should
regard all humans as our fellow citizens and local residents,
and there should be one way of life and order, like that of a
herd grazing together and nurtured by a common pasture.
Zeno wrote this, picturing as it were a dream or image of a
philosopher's well-regulated society. (*Mor.* 329a–b)

This passage suggests that Zeno followed his Cynic predecessors
by presenting a form of political cosmopolitanism in his *Republic*.
However, another text implies that he may have conceived of an ideal
State along the lines of the ideal State in Plato's *Republic*, but with
only the wise as citizens. This reading has gained currency in recent
scholarship (e.g. Schofield 1991), whereas others have preferred to
view the *Republic* as outlining a form of anarchist utopianism that
imagines a future world populated only by sages in which traditional
political States become irrelevant and disappear. This latter view
would certainly make sense if the *Republic* had been written under
the influence of Crates the Cynic. But alas the fragmentary reports
do not really give us enough information for us to be absolutely sure
one way or the other.

Although we may have to suspend judgement about the overall
design of Zeno's *Republic*, our passage from Plutarch introduces a
number of key themes for later Stoic political thinking. Our focus, it
says, should be not on individual States or cities but rather on a much
wider community, embracing all of humankind. Rather than there
being different groups of people following different sets of political
laws we should all follow one shared way of life (and note that the
phrase "common pasture" might also be rendered as "common law").
In order to flesh out these ideas we shall need to return to some of
the ethical themes that we have already encountered.

We opened our account of Stoic ethics with the theory of *oikeiōsis*
and the claim that the basic desire for all animals and human beings
is the desire for self-preservation. The Stoics use this theory as the

foundation for both their ethical and political theories. In the political context they develop what we might call a theory of "social *oikeiōsis*". As we have seen, our fundamental desire is for self-preservation, but as we develop as rational beings we do not narrowly associate our self-preservation with our own physical survival. One obvious example is a parent's desire to protect their children, which the Stoics conceive as a natural widening of our circle of concern. A further widening would be concern for one's extended family and friends, and then concern for one's whole community or society. For the Stoics, the natural love of parents for their children forms the starting-point from which we can trace the development of all human society (see Cicero, *Fin.* 3.62). Like Aristotle, the Stoics think that human beings are naturally social and political animals (*ibid.* 3.63).

This process of widening one's circle of concern should not stop once it encompasses all of human society, however. Eventually one's *oikeiōsis* should extend to include the entire cosmos, generating a concern for the preservation of all human beings and the natural world (although for some reason Chrysippus denied any human concern towards non-rational animals). When we reach this widest possible circle of concern we shall become cosmopolitans – citizens of the cosmos.

For the Stoics, then, the boundaries of traditional cities and States are arbitrary places at which to stop identifying other human beings as fellow citizens. Further, the constitutions and laws that define traditional States are equally arbitrary if they do not reflect the dictates of reason. Rather than live according to the laws laid down by (non-wise) legislators, the Stoic sage should live according to the natural law embodied in his or her virtue. In a Stoic utopia, in which everyone would be a sage, everyone would live according to this "natural law" and so live according to one shared way of life.

But we do not live in a Stoic utopia; we live in a political landscape defined in terms of traditional cities and States, and so did the ancient Stoics. Seneca was fully aware of this, writing in *On Leisure*:

> Let us take hold of the fact that there are two communities
> – the one, which is great and truly common, embracing gods

and humans, in which we look neither to this corner nor to
that, but measure the boundaries of our citizenship by the
sun; the other, the one to which we have been assigned by
the accident of our birth.   (*Ot.* 4.1)

As a Stoic, Seneca thinks that our primary political affiliation should
be to the cosmos as a whole rather than the country in which we
happened to have been born. But he cannot deny that we are also
citizens of traditional States, with the obligations and duties that
such membership entails. A Stoic sage living here and now will thus
have dual citizenship, being a member of both a traditional political
community and a cosmic city of "gods and humans" (we should not
place too much weight on the term "gods" here, given Stoic mono-
theistic theology). But only the cosmic city will be a true city: the
Stoics define a "city" (*polis*) as a community of virtuous people held
together by a common law; consequently they deny the existence
of any real cities, for such a community does not exist anywhere on
earth (see Clement of Alexandria, *Stromata* 4.26). Thus it is reported
that Diogenes of Babylon denied that Rome was a real city (see
Cicero, *Acad.* 2.137), saying that "among the foolish there exists no
city nor any law" (Obbink & Vander Waerdt 1991: 368).

   To become a member of the cosmic city one must possess virtue,
which itself forms the common law shared by its members. Although
the term "law" has overtones of obligation, members will willingly
live according to virtue, knowing that it is the path to their own
well-being and happiness. As we have seen, this cosmic city can exist
alongside traditional cities; one can be a citizen of a conventional
State and the cosmic city at the same time. Stoic sages scattered
across the globe will be fellow citizens of the cosmic city, united by
their shared way of life and common law, even if they never meet
(although equally they may choose to gather together in a particular
place).

   In the light of this focus on the cosmic city it is not surprising that
the question arose as to whether the Stoic sage would have much
interest in conventional politics. Should a Stoic engage in politics
(as Plato had tried) or should he or she avoid public life (as Epicurus

recommended)? This question was especially important for aristocratic Roman admirers of Stoicism, who were expected to play their part in politics. The standard Stoic response was to say that the sage should engage in politics, so long as this engagement does not compromise their virtue, but it is tempting to say that the Stoics only needed to state this explicitly precisely because many of their other ethical and political doctrines implicitly suggest otherwise. The Stoic outlook is broadly apolitical when it comes to conventional politics. The sage may well engage in politics but unlike Aristotle, for instance, the Stoics do not think that traditional States are vital for human well-being. Despite this, the Stoics do hold that human beings are naturally social, all with the potential to be members of one shared cosmopolitan community.

Summary

The Stoic ethical ideal, built upon Stoic physics and epistemology, is striking. The only thing that has any inherent goodness, and so the only thing with which we should concern ourselves, is virtue, conceived as an excellent internal disposition of the soul; a healthy mind, we might say. All external objects and states of affairs are strictly speaking neither good nor bad and so should be a matter of indifference to us. Many of the emotions that we suffer are based upon mistaken judgements on our part, judgements that attribute spurious value to indifferent externals. These emotions are diseases of the soul and they reduce our well-being or happiness. But if we learn to reason correctly and avoid mistaken judgements then we shall not suffer these emotions. Our happiness will then be dependent not on the presence or absence of external things, none of which are in our control, but rather on our own correct reasoning. We shall thus become impervious to the whims of fate and fortune. The ultimate message of Stoic ethics is that our own happiness is fully within our own power here and now, if only we are prepared to see the world aright, and that once achieved this happiness can never be taken away from us.

This is a powerful message but it is based upon some disconcerting proposals. It is not surprising that Stoicism has continued both to fascinate and to upset philosophers ever since. It is to the subsequent legacy of Stoicism that we shall now turn.

SIX
The Stoic legacy

Stoicism persisted as a living philosophical movement in antiquity for some 500 years. Its impact did not end there, however. Ever since the decline of Stoicism some time during the third century CE, Stoic ideas and texts have continued to exert their influence. In what follows I shall offer a brief sketch of the later impact of Stoicism, focusing on the transmission and influence of Stoic texts, along with their impact on later philosophers. I shall not attempt to consider all of the ways in which Stoic ideas have implicitly contributed to later philosophical developments. Rather, I shall focus on explicit engagements with Stoicism or Stoic authors. I shall not comment on the impact of Stoicism on later European literature and culture more generally, although this is an interesting topic in its own right and there has been much written on the subject.

Late antiquity and the Middle Ages

The last Stoic of note, Marcus Aurelius, died in 180 CE. Although there are a few reports of Stoics after that date – the third-century Neoplatonist Porphyry mentions a Stoic in his *Life of Plotinus* (§17) and the sixth-century Neoplatonist Damascius mentions someone of the "school of Epictetus" in his *Philosophical History* (46d) – it seems that Stoicism was no longer a vital force. Alexander of Aphrodisias' polemics against Stoicism, written in Athens around 200 CE, suggest that Stoicism remained part of the intellectual scene at that time (Marcus Aurelius had created a chair in Stoicism not long earlier, alongside the chair in Peripatetic philosophy occupied by Alexander), but probably not much later.

The next philosophical movement to rise to prominence was Neoplatonism, effectively founded by Plotinus (205–270), and developed by his pupil Porphyry (232–305). Stoicism clearly influenced Plotinus in the development of his own philosophy, both positively and negatively (see Graeser 1972). Porphyry writes that Plotinus' *Enneads* are full of hidden Stoic doctrines (*Life of Plotinus* §14), and from what we know about Porphyry's lost works, it seems that he also engaged considerably with the Stoics (see e.g. Simplicius, *in Cat.* 2,5–9).

The later Neoplatonists who followed Plotinus and Porphyry continued to discuss Stoic ideas, often to argue against them. This can be seen, for instance, in the sixth-century Neoplatonist Simplicius' commentary on Aristotle's *Categories*. More important, and in many ways more surprising, is the increased attention received by Epictetus. The Neoplatonist Olympiodorus makes a number of references to Epictetus in his commentary on Plato's *Gorgias*, and Simplicius devoted an entire commentary to Epictetus' *Handbook*, the only commentary on a Stoic text to survive from antiquity. As I have already noted, Damascius, writing in the sixth century, makes reference to someone from the "school of Epictetus" in his *Philosophical History*, and so these late Neoplatonic interests in Epictetus may have reflected a wider renewed interest in his works.

According to tradition, in 529 CE the Emperor Justinian closed the last pagan philosophical schools in Athens, probably around the same time that Simplicius commented on Epictetus. This date has come to mark the end of the history of ancient philosophy. Around the same year St Benedict founded the famous monastery in Monte Cassino, laying the foundations for medieval Western monasticism. Consequently this date has also been taken to mark the beginning of the Middle Ages. By this date, all of the early Stoic texts that are now lost were probably no longer available. Simplicius certainly had access to a far wider range of ancient philosophical texts than we do today, but much of his knowledge of the early Stoa was probably second-hand, deriving from now lost works by Porphyry and Alexander, for instance. By the sixth century there were very few Stoic texts in the Greek-speaking world.

One notable reader of Stoic texts in the early Byzantine world was Arethas (c.850–935), Archbishop of Caesarea. Arethas was an important collector of manuscripts at a time that proved to be important for the survival and transmission of ancient texts. Arethas is important to the history of Stoicism because it has been suggested that he owned copies of both Epictetus' *Discourses* and Marcus Aurelius' *Meditations*. All of the surviving manuscripts of Epictetus' *Discourses* derive from just one manuscript now in the Bodleian Library in Oxford. This manuscript contains marginal notes that have been identified as by Arethas. Although the Bodleian copy is unlikely to be *the* copy owned by Arethas, it may well be a direct copy of the text that he once owned and annotated. If Arethas had not found and preserved his copy of Epictetus' *Discourses*, then the Bodleian manuscript would not have been made and we might have lost this central Stoic text forever. Arethas tells us himself in one of his letters that he also owned an old and worn copy of Marcus Aurelius' *Meditations*, and that he planned to have a new copy of the text made. He is also the first recorded author to refer to the *Meditations* by their now standard Greek title – *ta eis heauton*, "to himself" – in a marginal comment added to a manuscript of the works of Lucian. But in his letter he does not use this title, and this has led some to speculate that Arethas may himself have coined the title. We can indeed only speculate, but it is clear that Arethas played a key role in the transmission of these two central Stoic texts during a crucial period in the transmission of classical literature. Without the intervention of Arethas it is possible that both of these texts might have been lost.

The next centuries saw the translation of a number of Greek philosophical texts into Arabic, notably the works of Aristotle. There has been some debate concerning the extent to which Stoic ideas might also have been transmitted to the Islamic world (see Jadaane 1968;

Gutas 1993). Unfortunately there is little evidence of texts being translated into Arabic that would have given their readers extensive knowledge of Stoic doctrines. One source might have been Galen, especially his *On the Doctrines of Hippocrates and Plato*. Another might have been Porphyry's now lost *History of Philosophy*. A more concrete influence can be found in a short work by al-Kindi, the first Arabic philosopher of significance, entitled *On the Art of Dispelling Sorrows*. In this text al-Kindi quotes Epictetus' *Handbook* (see Boter 1999: 117). If, as is generally supposed, al-Kindi did not know Greek himself, then this might be taken as evidence that the *Handbook* was translated into Arabic. The popularity of al-Kindi's text led a number of later Arabic philosophers also to quote Epictetus, and this formed one strand in what has come to be known as the "spiritual medicine" tradition in Arabic philosophical ethics (Fakhry 1994: 68).

So it is possible to sketch a tradition of reading Epictetus in the Eastern Mediterranean and Middle East, running through Simplicius, Olympiodorus, Arethas and al-Kindi. At the same time, Epictetus was also being used in the monasteries (see Boter 1999), his *Handbook* being adapted for use as a training manual for monks, with pagan references (e.g. Socrates) replaced by Christian ones (e.g. St Paul).

In the Latin-speaking West, the legacy of Stoicism was shaped primarily by the works of Seneca and Cicero. The Latin Church Fathers – such as Tertullian (*c.*160–240), Lactantius (*c.*250–325) and Augustine (354–430) – all engaged with Stoicism. Tertullian famously called Seneca "*our* Seneca" (*De Anima* §20), and this was often quoted by later Christian admirers of Seneca in order to justify their interest in the pagan moralist. Lactantius also admired Seneca to a certain degree (*Div. Inst.* 1.5.26 with Ross 1974: 127), although in general he was hostile towards Stoic doctrines, especially Stoic pantheism (e.g. *Div. Inst.* 7.3.1), not to mention pagan philosophy in general. Seneca's popularity was boosted by the existence of a series of letters between him and St Paul. This correspondence was mentioned by Jerome (*c.*348–420) and Augustine, and still survives today, although its authenticity has long been rejected.

The impact of Stoicism in the West as the Middle Ages progressed is much harder to trace. Some scholars have suggested quite a broad diffusion of Stoic ideas during this period, often unacknowledged as being specifically Stoic (see Ebbesen 2004). It is perhaps more fruitful, however, to focus on those cases where Stoicism was explicitly taken up in philosophical discussions.

The most striking medieval engagement with Stoicism is the one that can be found in the ethical works of Peter Abelard (1079–1142). In his *Dialogue between a Philosopher, a Jew, and a Christian* (also known under the title *Collationes*), Abelard puts into the mouth of his character the Philosopher a number of Stoic ideas, drawing on Stoic material in Cicero. In particular the Philosopher prefers the law of Nature over scriptural authority, and takes up the unity of virtue, the claim that virtue is the highest good and that there are no degrees of virtue (see Marenbon & Orlandi 2001: lii). He also cites the Stoic hero Cato the Younger as an example of an ethical role model (*Dialogue* §131). The Philosopher also describes Seneca as the greatest teacher of morals (*ibid.* §81), echoing comments in Abelard's letters to Heloise and in his *Historia Calamitatum*.

After Abelard, the medieval intellectual scene was dramatically transformed by the introduction of translations of Arabic scientific and philosophical works, notably translations of Aristotle and his new Arabic commentator Averroes. From then on Aristotelianism dominated philosophy in the West. This new tradition shaped the work of Thomas Aquinas, who in turn set the philosophical agenda for the later Middle Ages.

The Renaissance and early modern philosophy

At a certain point, one that would now be described as the beginning of the Renaissance, a new interest in the pagan classics developed, along with a desire to rediscover the culture of ancient Rome. Soon the works of Aristotle and his interpreters were no longer the only ancient philosophical texts available to readers. Now the philosophical texts of the Latin world gained a renewed importance, especially the works of Cicero. A key figure in this process that led to the emergence of Renaissance Humanism was Francesco Petrarca

(1304–74), commonly known as Petrarch. As we have seen, Cicero is an important source for Stoicism, and Petrarch's fascination with Cicero naturally led to a close familiarity with his accounts of Stoic philosophy. Not only that, Petrarch also found much of value in Stoicism, and the impact of Stoic ideas can be seen in a number of his works. Two in particular are worth noting. The first, *My Secret Book* (*Secretum*, written c.1347–53), takes the form of an imaginary dialogue between Petrarch the pupil and Augustine the master, in which Augustine recommends to Petrarch Stoic ideas taken from Cicero and Seneca. The second, *On Remedies for Both Kinds of Fortune* (*De Remediis Utriusque Fortunae*, written c.1354–66), was inspired by a work attributed to Seneca (the *De Remediis Fortuitorum*) and draws heavily on the account of the Stoic theory of emotions in Cicero's *Tusculan Disputations*. It offers a Stoic-inspired therapy for the emotions conceived as a medicine for the soul (see Panizza 1991).

Also around this time Petrarch's Greek teacher, the monk Barlaam of Seminara (c.1290–1348), wrote a short compendium of Stoic ethics, the *Ethica Secundum Stoicos*, focusing on Stoic accounts of happiness and the emotions.

Some time around 1450, Niccolo Perotti translated Epictetus' *Handbook* into Latin, along with the preface to Simplicius' commentary (see Oliver 1954). A little later, in 1479, Angelo Poliziano (known as Politian) also translated the *Handbook*, and this was published in 1497. Politian's translation soon became a classic and was included in numerous later printed editions of Epictetus. His translation was accompanied by a prefatory letter to Lorenzo di Piero de' Medici and a letter to Bartolemo Scala in defence of Epictetus, and in both of these he makes it clear that he read Epictetus with the aid of Simplicius. Indeed, in the latter, Politian attempted to make Epictetus more palatable to Scala by suggesting that Epictetus owed much to Plato, claiming that "our Stoic fights boldly, using Platonic arguments as his shield" (Kraye 1997: 198).

A more substantial engagement with Stoicism was made by Pietro Pomponazzi (1462–1525), perhaps better known as an Aristotelian. His distaste for the then dominant Averroist interpretation of Aristotle led Pomponazzi to Aristotle's ancient commentator Alexander of

Aphrodisias in search of a purer reading of Aristotle's texts. Although Pomponazzi did not follow Alexander in detail, he did share with him a more naturalistic approach to Aristotle. More importantly though, Pomponazzi would have learned much from Alexander about Stoicism, and it has been suggested that Pomponazzi adopted a number of Stoic ideas. The first of these is the claim that virtue is its own reward (and not the ground for some other reward in an afterlife, which Pomponazzi rejected). The second is the Stoic attempt to reconcile freedom with determinism, which Pomponazzi thought was the most plausible of the many responses to this classic problem. He outlines the reasons why in his treatise *On Fate (De Fato)*, written in 1520 and inspired by his reading of Alexander's treatise of the same name. However, Pomponazzi rejected Alexander's position (and his criticisms of the Stoics), instead affirming the Stoic claims that contingency and chance are illusions, and that what appears to human beings as freedom is in fact subsumed within a larger wholly determined Nature. Consequently Pomponazzi's philosophy has been characterized as "a rather Stoic Aristotelianism" (Randall 1948: 279).

The wider diffusion of Stoic texts and ideas during the sixteenth century was inevitably closely tied with the continuing development of printing (invented in the middle of the previous century). Some of the most important engagements with Stoicism during this period were connected with the editing and printing of the works of Seneca. In this context stand Erasmus and Calvin.

Desiderius Erasmus of Rotterdam (1466–1536) produced two editions of the works of Seneca. The first, published in 1515, was the work of many hands, with a preface by Erasmus. When he saw the finished work published Erasmus was not happy with the edition, and considered it a source of embarrassment that his name was on the title page. In order to make amends for this poor edition he eventually produced another, published in 1529. His preface to the first edition suggests some admiration for his subject, but similar praise is nowhere to be found in the preface to the second edition. This suggests that Erasmus' interest in Seneca did not last throughout his career; he returned to Seneca not out of continuing interest in his subject but simply to put right the scholarly shortcomings of the first edition. Moreover, despite his editorial work on Seneca, Erasmus was sceptical of some of the central claims of Stoicism in his other works. In his *Praise of Folly* (*Moriae Encomium*, 1511), for instance, Erasmus criticizes the Stoic rejection of the emotions (the doctrine of *apatheia*) and questions the viability of the ideal of the sage. Although he certainly admired Seneca as a pagan moralist, Erasmus' sincere devotion to Christianity meant that any admiration would always be within strictly defined limits.

Towards the beginning of his intellectual career John Calvin (1509–64) wrote a commentary on Seneca's *On Mercy* (1532), which drew on the scholarly work of Erasmus. In the preface to his 1529 edition of Seneca's works, Erasmus encouraged others to expand on his notes to the text and to produce commentaries on Seneca; Calvin evidently took up the invitation. In his own preface, Calvin defends Seneca against both ancient and modern critics, proclaiming that "our Seneca was second only to Cicero, a veritable pillar of Roman philosophy" (Battles & Hugo 1969: 11). Having worked on the text so closely, Calvin was inevitably influenced by Seneca, whether positively or negatively, but the extent to which Seneca's Stoicism contributed to Calvin's later religious thought is much harder to determine. Some have suggested that Stoic notions of determinism and an internal moral law helped to shape his religious outlook (Beck 1969: 110), and others have gone so far as to suggest that "Calvinism is Stoicism baptized into Christianity" (see Battles & Hugo 1969: 46*), but no doubt the truth of the matter is somewhat more complex than this emphatic statement claims.

The publication of these and other editions of Seneca's works, along with the increasing availability of other ancient authors relevant to the study of Stoicism, led to a considerable interest in Stoicism in the latter part of the sixteenth century. Two figures in particular stand out: Montaigne and Lipsius.

Michel de Montaigne (1533–92) is best known as the author of the *Essais*, first published in 1580 and later expanded in 1588 and (posthumously) 1595. The *Essais* are permeated with Stoicism, although it would be a mistake to characterize Montaigne himself as a Stoic. His general admiration of Seneca can be seen in *Essai* 2.10, "On Books", and is repeated in *Essai* 2.32, "In Defence of Seneca and Plutarch". In *Essai* 1.33 he draws attention to a parallel between Seneca and early Christians with regard to their attitudes towards death, whereas *Essai* 1.14 is devoted to the explication of a saying by Epictetus – that men are upset not by things, but by their judgements about things (*Ench.* 5) – which he had inscribed in his library. However, Montaigne's mature view doubted the rational abilities of humankind and certainly would not have endorsed the ambitious Stoic ideal of the sage. Nevertheless he remained drawn to it, writing that, "if a man cannot attain to that noble Stoic impassibility, let him hide in the lap of this peasant insensitivity of mine. What Stoics did from virtue I teach myself to do from temperament" (*Essais* 3.10, in Screech 1991: 1153). It has been suggested that within the three chronological versions of the *Essais* it is possible to discern a development from a youthful interest in Stoicism, followed by a period of Scepticism, and finally a turn towards Epicureanism (Demonet 1985: 10). However, it is also possible to find Epicurean material in the earliest version and Stoic themes in the latest additions. Thus, Stoicism forms a key ingredient throughout the *Essais*.

One of the most important figures in the reception of Stoicism is Justus Lipsius (1547–1606), described by Montaigne as one of the most learned men then alive (*Essais* 2.12). Lipsius was an accomplished classical scholar, who produced editions of the works of Tacitus and Seneca. One of his most popular and influential works was a dialogue entitled *On Constancy* (*De Constantia*, 1584), which draws on Stoic sources in order to offer consolation in the face of public evils (in the form of civil war fuelled by religious controversies). Lipsius offers four arguments concerning such public evils: they are imposed by God; they are the product of necessity; they are in fact profitable to us; they are neither grievous nor particularly unusual. Three of these echo similar points made by Seneca in one of his letters (*Ep.* 107). Of Lipsius' four arguments, the most significant is the second, concerning fate or necessity. Lipsius distinguishes four different conceptions of fate, isolates the Stoic conception from his own and outlines four points at which the Stoic account of fate should be modified. His concerns are with the Stoic rejection of free will, contingency, miracles and the implication that God may himself be submitted to fate. Having negotiated these potentially dangerous stumbling blocks, Lipsius presents his readers with a version of Stoic ethics palatable to a Christian audience.

With *De Constantia* Lipsius laid the foundations for what has come to be known as Neostoicism, a philosophical movement that flourished in the last decades of the sixteenth century and the first half of the seventeenth century. In sum, a Neostoic is a Christian who draws on Stoic ethics, but rejects those aspects of Stoic materialism and determinism that contradict Christian teaching. After Lipsius, the most important Neostoic was Guillaume Du Vair (1556–1621), who translated Epictetus into French, and produced a number of works, including his own *Traité de la Constance* and *Philosophie morale des Stoïques*. Other Neostoics included Pierre Charron (1541–1603), who was a follower of Montaigne, and Francisco de Quevedo (1580–1645). Quevedo drew attention to Zeno of Citium's Semitic ancestry and attempted to discern the inspiration of the Old Testament, in particular Job's heroic endurance in the face of adversity, in the doctrines of the Stoa. Also worthy of note is Thomas Gataker (1574–1654), English churchman and editor of an important and impressive edition of Marcus Aurelius' *Meditations*, published in 1652, in which detailed parallels are adduced between the *Meditations* and the Bible. According to these Neostoics, the late Stoic authors Seneca, Epictetus and Marcus Aurelius could be read with profit by a Christian.

Another aspect of Lipsius' Stoic studies involved the compilation of Stoic material from ancient authors, and he published two collections of these fragments: the *Manuductio ad Philosophicam Stoicam* and the *Physiologia Stoicorum* (both 1604). These collections inaugurated the doxographical study of Stoicism (see Saunders 1955: chs 3–4) and were soon followed by Scioppius' *Elementa Philosophiae Stoicae Moralis* (1606). Another famous classical scholar of this period who greatly admired Stoicism was Daniel Heinsius (1580–1655), who wrote an oration entitled *De Stoica Philosophia* in which he praised the wisdom of the Stoa (see Bottin *et al.* 1993: 131).

Alongside the Neostoics that we have already mentioned, a wide range of philosophers in the seventeenth century drew on Stoic ideas. Hugo Grotius (1583–1645) drew on the Stoic theory of appropriation (*oikeiōsis*) in his political theory. René Descartes (1596–1650), although making little explicit engagement with the philosophies of antiquity in his published works, did engage in correspondence with Princess Elizabeth in August 1645, in which they discussed Seneca's essay *On the Happy Life*.

As the seventeenth century progressed, however, Stoicism came under increasing fire from a number of hostile critics (see Brooke 2004). These critics may be divided into two groups. On the one hand there were Catholics such as Pascal and Malebranche, who attacked Stoicism's arrogant claims concerning the happiness of the sage, produced solely by reason and without reference to God's grace. On the other hand there were Protestants such as Bramhall, Cudworth and Bayle, who attacked Stoicism for its determinism and its consequent denial of free will and miracles.

Blaise Pascal (1623–62) engaged critically with Stoicism in his *Pensées* and also in *L'Entretien de M. Pascal avec M. de Sacy* (1655), which is a discussion of Epictetus and Montaigne. Pascal's principal objection to the Stoicism of Epictetus is that it assumes too much power for the individual. For Epictetus, if we focus our attention on what is "up to us" then we can have complete control over our happiness. Pascal denounces this claim as "wickedly proud". For him, human happiness depends on the grace of God. Pascal suggests that although Epictetus does much to attack the vice of laziness, he does not offer a genuine path to virtue.

In a similar vein, Nicolas Malebranche (1638–1715) attacked Stoicism in his *Recherche de la vérité* (1674–75). Whereas Pascal focused his polemic against Epictetus, Malebranche's target was Seneca (see *Recherche* 2.3.4). What Malebranche found most objectionable in Seneca's Stoicism was the arrogance of the claim that it is possible to be happy in this life. For Malebranche the Christian, human life here on Earth is inherently miserable, for we are all sinners, and so we must wait for the next life before we can be truly happy. Stoicism's claim that one can indeed be happy here and now is, he argues, simply the product of human pride and arrogance.

Among the Protestant critics of Stoicism, Ralph Cudworth (1617–88) included Stoicism as one of the four types of atheism that must be refuted in his *True Intellectual System of the Universe* (1678). However, Cudworth qualified this by attributing Stoic atheism only to certain later Stoics, in particular Boethus of Sidon and Seneca, and acknowledging that the earlier Stoics, such as Zeno and Cleanthes, were indeed theists, if only imperfect theists. In his *Treatise of Free-will* (published posthumously in 1838) Cudworth argued against Stoic necessity and their doctrine of cyclical recurrence.

The Protestant theologian John Bramhall (1594–1663) also found Stoicism a disturbing philosophy. He was especially concerned with its doctrine of fate. In his famous debate with Thomas Hobbes (1588–1679) concerning liberty and necessity, Bramhall labelled Hobbes a Stoic for his determinism, and Hobbes did not reject the label, although he claimed that he was not copying the Stoics but had simply reached the same conclusion independently. Thus, Stoicism became associated with one of the most controversial philosophers of the seventeenth century. It was also about to be connected with the name of perhaps *the* most controversial philosopher of the age: Spinoza.

Around this time, the philosophy of Benedict de Spinoza (1632–77) came to public attention. His *Tractatus Theologico-Politicus* was published anonymously in 1670, and his *Ethica* and other works were published posthumously in 1677. Spinoza's philosophy identified God with Nature, supported a strict determinism, denied free will and miracles, and suggested that by the power of reason alone human beings may overcome their emotions and become happy. The resonances with ancient Stoicism are clear, and of all subsequent philosophers Spinoza is the one who comes closest to Stoicism, notwithstanding his explicit criticism of the Stoa for claiming that it is possible to overcome all emotions (in the *Ethica*) and his apparent admiration for ancient atomism (in his correspondence with Hugo Boxel). Indeed, G. W. Leibniz (1646–1716) described Spinoza as a member of "the sect of the new Stoics", along with Descartes, criticizing Stoicism as a philosophy of patience rather than hope (see Leibniz 1989: 282). What is especially interesting here, however, is the way in which the arrival of "Spinozism" affected the reception of Stoicism. A number of contemporaries, such as Giambattista Vico (1668–1744), soon noted the affinities between Spinozism and Stoicism. The Stoics were seen as the Spinozists of their day, and Spinoza was seen as a modern-day Stoic. But perhaps more importantly, Spinozism was quickly denounced as a form of atheism. It was not long before Stoicism was denounced as a form of proto-Spinozist atheism as well.

One of the first people to worry about the atheistic implications of Stoicism was Jakob Thomasius (1622–84), in his *Exercitatio de Stoica Mundi Exustione* (1676). In this work, Thomasius, one of whose students was Leibniz, attacked Lipsius and the Neostoic attempt to reconcile Stoicism with Christianity (see Bottin *et al.* 1993: 416–17). He was followed by Johann Franz Buddeus (1667–1729), the author of *De Erroribus Stoicorum* (1695) and *De Spinozismo ante Spinozam* (1701). Whereas Lipsius and Du Vair thought nothing wrong in a Christian reading and admiring the pagan ethics of Seneca or Epictetus, scholars such as Thomasius and Buddeus attempted to uncover the fundamental principles of Stoicism as a philosophical system, drawing on doxographical accounts of the early Stoics rather than the surviving texts of the late Stoics. And what they found was a philosophy of materialism and determinism that shared much in common with Spinozism and which, from an orthodox Christian perspective, was clearly atheistic. Whatever the Stoic God was, it was certainly not the God of the Holy Scriptures. Despite Lipsius' "emendations", ancient Stoicism remained a deterministic philosophy, denying both miracles and free will, making the ancient Stoics the Spinozists of antiquity.

Buddeus influenced his pupil the famous German historian of philosophy Johann Jakob Brucker (1696–1770), author of the *Historia Critica Philosophiae* (1742–44). Brucker gives a clear account of this new methodological approach to the study of Stoicism, and how it differs from Neostoicism:

> Great care should be taken, in the first place, not to judge
> of the doctrine of the Stoics from words and sentiments,

detached from the general system, but to consider them as they stand related to the whole train of premises and conclusions. For want of this caution, many moderns, dazzled by the splendid expressions which they have met with in the writings of the Stoics concerning God, the soul, and other subjects, have imagined that they have discovered an invaluable treasure: whereas, if they had taken the pains to restore these brilliants to their proper places in the general mass, it would soon have appeared, that a great part of their value was imaginary. (translated in Enfield 1819: 1,323)

Brucker's account of Stoicism, based on this methodological approach, formed the principal source for Denis Diderot's article on Stoicism in the *Encyclopédie* (published in 1765). In stark contrast to the Neostoics writing around a century and a half earlier, Diderot presented the Stoics in his *Encyclopédie* article as materialists, determinists and atheists. For Diderot, of course, this was no bad thing.

At the time that these controversies were taking place, others continued to be fascinated by the works of the later Stoics. Anthony Ashley Cooper, Third Earl of Shaftesbury (1671–1713), produced a series of notes inspired by Epictetus and Marcus Aurelius, posthumously published under the title *The Philosophical Regimen*, and his scholarly annotations on the text of Epictetus were included by John Upton in his 1739 edition of Epictetus' works. It has been suggested that Shaftesbury's own philosophy, presented in the *Characteristics of Men, Manners, Opinions, Times* (1711), is grounded upon his interest in Stoicism, and that he is "the greatest Stoic of modern times" (Rand 1900: xii). Like the Stoics, Shaftesbury presented philosophy as a task primarily concerned with transforming the self, of becoming a virtuoso of virtue rather than a pedant of learning.

Seneca, it has been suggested, was an important influence on Jean-Jacques Rousseau (1712–78), and one contemporary commentator went so far as to suggest that Rousseau was little more than a plagiarist of Seneca (Roche 1974: ix). Rousseau shared in common with the Stoics the thought that virtue would develop naturally in people who were left to their own devices; it is the unwanted influence of a corrupt society that interrupts this natural progression. Diderot, whom we have already met, was also fascinated by Seneca, writing an important study of him under the title *Essai sur les Règnes de Claude et de Néron* (1778), in which he attempted to defend Seneca against recent critics. In particular he was concerned to rebut the charges of hypocrisy and greed, charges that Diderot himself had levelled against Seneca in an earlier work. Rather than see Seneca's involvement at the court of Nero as a compromise of his Stoic principles, the mature Diderot suggested that we should instead see it as a heroic attempt to do one's duty in impossible circumstances. Seneca's failings were human failings, and it would be wrong to judge Seneca against the benchmark of the Stoic sage when he had never claimed to be one.

The continuing notoriety of Seneca in eighteenth-century France is further illustrated in the work of the pro-Epicurean philosopher Julien Offray De La Mettrie (1709–51) and in particular in his polemic *Anti-Senèque* (1750). By this time, the modern caricature of the Stoic as "sad, strict, and unyielding" had been firmly established:

> We shall be Anti-Stoics! Those philosophers are sad, strict, and unyielding; we shall be cheerful, sweet-natured, and indulgent. They are all soul and ignore their bodies; we shall be all body and ignore our souls. They appear impervious to pleasure or pain; we shall glory in feeling both.
>
> (La Mettrie 1996: 119)

The image of the strict and unyielding philosopher who is all soul and no body may bring to mind a German philosopher writing just a few decades later: Immanuel Kant (1724–1804). Despite the anti-Stoic polemics among German scholars such as Buddeus and Brucker, Stoicism continued to exert its influence on German philosophy. In Kant's case this was primarily via the works of Cicero. In particular Kant drew on Cicero's *On Duties* for his own *Grounding for the Metaphysics of Morals* (1785), in which he followed the Stoics in arguing among other things that externals have no inherent value, only the internal will has moral value and happiness is dependent upon this internal will. Kant's particular concern with the notion of duty reflects Cicero's discussion of duties, which, in turn, draws on Panaetius' now lost discussion of "appropriate actions". There is some distance between Kantian duty and early Stoic appropriate actions, but via Panaetius and Cicero it is possible to sketch a chain of influence from one to the other.

The nineteenth and twentieth centuries

As we have seen, from the Renaissance up to the eighteenth century Stoicism proved to be a vital influence on Western thought. The other Hellenistic schools of Epicureanism and Pyrrhonian scepticism also made their mark during this period. As their unofficial ancient reporter, Cicero was read widely. There was only limited interest in either Aristotle (still associated with medieval scholasticism) or Plato (whose popularity waned after the Italian Renaissance).

In the nineteenth century, especially in Germany, things began to change. The focus of attention shifted from the Hellenistic schools back to their Hellenic predecessors. The Hellenistic period was increasingly seen as an age of decline and corruption, whereas the Hellenic period was seen as a period of purity and creativity. Consequently there was renewed interest in the Hellenic philosophers Socrates, Plato and Aristotle, and a condescending dismissal of the later Hellenistic schools. This general shift in focus influenced German classical scholars of the period, who were often critical of Stoicism as a philosophical system (see Ierodiakonou 1999: 4). This shift was also mirrored by a dramatic decline in the reputation of Cicero, who was increasingly disparaged as a second-rate compiler of second-rate philosophy, most famously by the German scholar Theodor Mommsen (see MacKendrick 1989: 288–9).

Not surprisingly, Stoicism did not fare well in this new intellectual climate. In his *Lectures on the History of Philosophy*, for instance, G. W. F. Hegel (1770–1831) presented Stoicism as an unoriginal philosophy, merely drawing out a creative insight from Cynicism – "to live in accordance with Nature" – and refining it into a theoretical system, adding a dose of physics borrowed from Heraclitus. The later Stoics' concern with practical questions further damaged whatever speculative value there might have been in the early Stoa. By the standards of Hegel's own conception of what a philosophy should be, Stoicism did not score well. Stoicism reappears in Hegel's *Phenomenology of Spirit*, where it is presented as the product of a culture of bondage and fear. In such a climate the Stoic, according to Hegel, withdraws into the realm of pure thought, paying no attention to concrete master–slave distinctions. This is most graphically illustrated by the fact that both a slave and an emperor, Epictetus and Marcus Aurelius, could both adopt this philosophy. Stoicism, claims Hegel, is an inward-looking philosophy that mistakenly takes disengagement with the outside world to be a form of freedom.

This attitude towards Stoicism was by no means limited to Hegel. The "Left-Hegelian" Max Stirner (1806–56) summed up Stoicism in the following terms in his *The Ego and His Own*:

> The Stoics want to realize the *wise man*, the man with *practical philosophy*, the man who *knows how to live* – a wise life, therefore; they find him in contempt for the world, in a life without development, without spreading out, without friendly relations with the world, thus in the *isolated life*
> ...   (Stirner 1993: 22)

Perhaps unexpectedly, Stirner's famous adversaries Karl Marx (1818–83) and Friedrich Engels (1820–95) defended Stoicism against Stirner's caricature in *The German Ideology*: "The Stoical wise man by no means has in mind 'life without living development', but an *absolutely active* life, as is evident even from his outlook on nature, which is Heraclitian, dynamic, developing and living" (Marx & Engels 1964: 144).

These concerns about Stoicism – whether it is the product of a slave culture; whether it is disengaged from the world – are echoed in the work of Friedrich Nietzsche (1844–1900). Nietzsche's remarks about Stoicism appear in a wide range of passages that are scattered throughout his works, and they range from the highly critical and ironically dismissive to the respectful and admiring. On the one hand he famously attacks the ideal of living in accordance with Nature (Nietzsche 1990: §9), while on the other hand he cites Epictetus and Seneca as examples of great moralists (Nietzsche 1986: §282), acknowledging that Christianity has made it difficult for us to comprehend these great pagan thinkers directly (Nietzsche 1974: §122). Indeed, what is most striking in Nietzsche's explicit comments about Stoicism is the way in which it stands favourably when compared with Christian morality (Nietzsche 1982: §§131, 139, 546). For Nietzsche, the Stoic is a creature engaged in a process of self-domination (Nietzsche 1982: §251; 1990: §188), and self-domination is for him the highest form of "will to power".

There are also a number of striking resonances between Nietzsche's own philosophy and Stoicism, although almost all of them need to be qualified carefully. Nietzsche constructs what has been called a naturalistic ethic (Schatzki 1994), which shares much with Stoicism, although Nietzsche would not accept Stoic claims about the rational and providential ordering of the cosmos. Nietzsche also rejects what he takes to be harmful emotions such as pity (Nussbaum 1994), and yet argues elsewhere that the emotions are thoroughly natural and should not be rejected (Nietzsche 1990: §198). Nietzsche outlines a concept of eternal recurrence, although not necessarily as a cosmological doctrine. His image of the *Übermensch* and the thought that "man is something that should be overcome" echoes the Stoics' ideal sage and their equally harsh comments about the majority of humankind. In his *Schopenhauer as Educator* Nietzsche outlines a practical conception of philosophy as a way of life that draws an analogy between philosophy and the art of medicine, and yet elsewhere he is highly critical of the Socratic schools and their eudaimonism. In sum, although it would clearly be a mistake to suggest that Nietzsche was in any sense a modern Stoic, his works contain many interesting, if often ambiguous, resonances with Stoicism. One might say that the extent to which Nietzsche can follow the Stoics will be in direct proportion to how much he thinks they can offer a genuine philosophical alternative to the other-worldly philosophies of Platonism and Christianity.

Around the same time that Nietzsche was writing in Europe, in the English-speaking world a variety of literary authors became fascinated with the works of the later Stoics, in particular Marcus Aurelius. Thomas Arnold wrote an important essay on the Stoic Emperor (entitled "An Essay on Marcus Aurelius"), describing Epictetus and Marcus as "great masters of morals". This Victorian interest in Stoic authors, like many aspects of Victorian culture, ignored the developments of the Enlightenment and harked back to an earlier period. Marcus and Epictetus were read again as friends of Christianity, just as the Neostoics had read them some three hundred years earlier. Diderot's judgement in the *Encyclopédie* was seemingly forgotten. Within this context a number of books were written about the late Stoics, including F. W. Farrar's *Seekers After God* (1868), and Leonard Alston's *Stoic and Christian in the Second Century* (1906). These presentations of the late Stoics as quasi-religious thinkers no doubt did as much damage to the development of serious Stoic scholarship as the unfavourable judgements of the German classicists earlier in the century.

The philosophical influence of Stoicism in the twentieth century, as distinguished from the rise of academic scholarship devoted to Stoicism, becomes harder to trace. In English-speaking philosophy questions concerning language and logic came to dominate. Although some similarities have been noted between Stoic logic and some of the developments in modern logic, no one would suggest any direct influence. Interesting, though, is an essay by Bertrand Russell (1872–1970), entitled "Stoicism and Mental Health" (in his *In Praise of Idleness*). Here Russell advocates a return to "stoic self-command". In particular he suggests that reflecting on death can be both a healthy and helpful meditation, echoing the ancient consolations of Seneca and Epictetus. More recent English-speaking philosophers working in the field of ethics have benefited from the increase of scholarly work on ancient Stoicism and some have drawn on it for their own work, especially those working on the themes of the emotions, virtue ethics and moral perfectionism. One striking example of this is Lawrence Becker's bold attempt to resurrect a Stoical ethical tradition, imagining what Stoic ethics might look like today if it had persisted as a continuous philosophical tradition, adapted to the developments in our understanding of the physical world and confronted modern ethical theories (see Becker 1998). Also note-worthy is Martha Nussbaum's recent attempt to develop what she calls a "neo-Stoic" theory of the emotions. If, as the Stoics argue, our emotions reflect our value judgements, then they may well be "suffused with intelligence and discernment", Nussbaum suggests, forming a guide to the way in which we conceive, assess and value the world around us (see Nussbaum 2001).

On the continent, phenomenology dominated philosophy in the early twentieth century. In France this became intertwined with the existentialism associated with Jean-Paul Sartre (1905–80) and oth-ers. Via the influence of Hegel's discussion of master–slave dialectic in his *Phenomenology of Spirit*, Stoicism continued to exert its influ-ence. In Sartre's notebooks compiled during the Second World War he describes himself as a "Stoic", perhaps in the more popular sense of the word (Sartre 1984: 46). He goes on to characterize Stoicism as a philosophy directed towards a total existential transformation of the individual (*ibid.*: 82), a philosophy that might teach him how to live (*ibid.*: 185). However, he concludes that he cannot wholly endorse the Stoic conception of freedom as detachment from both external objects and other people (*ibid.*: 293).

In the 1960s the subject-centred philosophy of existentialism gave way to structuralism, a philosophical outlook that attempted to locate the subject as just one part within much larger structures and networks. It was within this context that two important French philosophers of the late twentieth century became fascinated with Stoicism.

The first of these was Michel Foucault (1926–84), who in his late works explored the theme of creating a "technology of the self" and whose discussions drew heavily on ancient philosophical authors. Stoics predominate among his sources and Foucault is reported to have said that his favourite philosophical author during this period of his life was Seneca (Eribon 1991: 331). Foucault's project, however, draws its principal inspiration from Socrates' injunction that one should "take care of oneself". But he draws extensively on the Stoics as the most important ancient philosophers who tried to develop techniques for doing so. Moreover, the fact that the Stoics developed such techniques within the context of a materialist ontology made their work highly amenable to Foucault's own wider philosophical outlook, although he does not comment on this affinity directly. However, despite Foucault's fascination with Stoic technologies of the self, in a number of places he proposes the pursuit of pleasure as the "goal" underpinning his later work, making him perhaps more of a modern Epicurean than a Stoic, notwithstanding his fascination with Stoic techniques and practices.

Alongside Foucault stands Gilles Deleuze (1925–95), who engaged explicitly with the Stoics in his 1969 book *Logique du sens*. There, his principal interest in the Stoics is twofold: they offer a theory of meaning or sense as a non-existing entity (i.e. the incorporeal sayables or *lekta*), and they offer a decidedly anti-Platonic image of the philosopher. For Deleuze, the Stoics stand at the beginning of a tradition of philosophy of immanence that opposes the transcendence of Platonism, a tradition that runs through Spinoza and Nietzsche and up to Deleuze himself. The Stoic theory of sense as a non-existing incorporeal highlights their rigorous materialism that claims that only bodies exist.

Beyond Deleuze's fairly brief explicit engagement with the Stoics in *Logique du sens*, there are a number of implicit resonances with Stoicism in his collaborative work with Félix Guattari, *Mille plateaux* (1980). This work reads like a vast manual or handbook and it follows on from their previous collaborative work *L'anti-Oedipe*, which Foucault characterized (in its preface) as a book of ethics proposing an art of living. In *Mille plateaux* we find a complex physics of flows and forces, combined with an ethic to dismantle the boundaries between self and cosmos, reminiscent of passages in Marcus Aurelius, along with a politics of cosmopolitanism. Although the differences from Stoicism are many, *Mille plateaux* nevertheless contains a number of unexpected echoes of some of the central themes of ancient Stoicism. Indeed, such echoes can be found throughout Deleuze's work, some coming directly from the Stoa, others mediated via Spinoza and Nietzsche (both important influences on Deleuze). Like Nietzsche before him, one of Deleuze's principal philosophical projects is to construct a philosophy of immanence that can stand as a genuine alternative to the Platonic tradition. The Stoics were the first, claims Deleuze, to offer any such alternative.

This recent presentation of Stoicism as a philosophy in opposition to Platonism captures the important ontological differences between these two philosophies, differences that we touched on in the discussion of Plato's *Sophist* in Chapter 4. Yet modern scholars are currently keen to stress the connections between Stoicism and Plato, drawing attention to points where the Stoics might have drawn on arguments or ideas in the Platonic dialogues. As with so much relating to the early Stoics, the explicit evidence for this remains limited.

Summary

I have offered only a cursory sketch of the later influence of Stoicism, but from what we have seen it is clear that there have been relatively few philosophers since antiquity who have been prepared explicitly to present themselves to their contemporaries as "Stoics". Lipsius and some of the subsequent Neostoics are perhaps the only people to have done so, and then only with important qualifications. By contrast, the Middle Ages and Renaissance saw many who were prepared openly to describe themselves as Aristotelians or Platonists. One of the reasons for this, of course, was a basic incompatibility between Stoic philosophy and Christian doctrine, notwithstanding the claims of Neostoic apologists. We have seen that the fortunes of Stoicism within the Christian West have varied depending on whether Stoicism was primarily associated with the often amenable ethics of the late Stoics or with the dangerous ideas about God and fate in the fragments of the early Stoics.

The scarcity of later figures prepared to present themselves as "Stoics" makes it difficult to talk of a "Stoic tradition" in the way in which one might legitimately talk of a Platonic or Aristotelian tradition. Moreover, the philosopher who comes closest to reviving a broadly Stoic worldview, Spinoza, explicitly distanced himself from the Stoics, for reasons that we shall probably never fully know.

Despite this somewhat negative conclusion, we can also see that Stoicism has nevertheless formed a pervasive, if sometimes diffuse, influence on Western thought. It formed an important element in the intellectual background for a wide range of key figures, from Augustine and Abelard to Erasmus and Montaigne, and infused the philosophical debates of the seventeenth century, contributing to the development of early modern philosophy. The Stoic authors Seneca and Epictetus continue to attract new readers and the details of Stoic ethical theory are being paid increasing attention in contemporary philosophical discussions.

Glossary of names

This list is selective. Further information about ancient figures may be found in the *Oxford Classical Dictionary*. Readers of French should also note the impressive multi-volume *Dictionnaire des Philosophes Antiques* (Paris: CNRS, 1989–), still in progress.

Aetius (1st–2nd cent. CE) doxographical source for Stoicism reconstructed from texts in Stobaeus and a text falsely attributed to Plutarch.

Alexander of Aphrodisias (2nd–3rd cent. CE) Aristotelian philosopher who argued against the Stoics.

Antipater of Tarsus (3rd–2nd cent. BCE) sixth head of the Stoa, succeeding Diogenes of Babylon.

Arcesilaus (4th–3rd cent. BCE) Academic Sceptic who attacked Stoicism.

Aristo of Chios (4th–3rd cent. BCE) pupil of Zeno and heterodox Stoic who rejected the doctrine of preferred and non-preferred indifferents.

Arius Didymus (1st cent. BCE) author of an important summary of Stoic ethics, preserved by Stobaeus.

Arrian (1st–2nd cent. CE) famous historian and pupil of Epictetus who recorded Epictetus' lectures now known as the *Discourses*.

Aulus Gellius (2nd cent. CE) literary author whose work *Attic Nights* includes a number of discussions of Stoicism.

Boethus of Sidon (2nd cent. BCE) Stoic philosopher, a pupil of Diogenes of Babylon, who deviated in physics by affirming the eternity of the world.

Calcidius (4th cent. CE) Christian Neoplatonic philosopher who discussed Stoic doctrine in his commentary on Plato's *Timaeus*.

Carneades (3rd-2nd cent. BCE) Academic Sceptic critical of Stoicism.

Cato the Younger (1st cent. BCE) Roman statesman and adherent of Stoicism famous for his noble suicide and often cited as a Roman example of a Stoic sage.

Chrysippus of Soli (3rd cent. BCE) third and most important head of the Stoa.

Cicero (1st cent. BCE) Roman statesman and philosophical author, a pupil of both Panaetius and Posidonius.

Cleanthes of Assos (4th–3rd cent. BCE) pupil of Zeno who became the second head of the Stoa.

Cleomedes (1st–2nd cent. CE) Stoic author of the cosmological text *The Heavens*.

Cornutus (1st cent. CE) Roman Stoic, with close connections to Seneca, who taught the poets Lucan and Persius.

Crates (4th–3rd cent. BCE) Cynic philosopher who, as one of Zeno's teachers, formed an important influence on the development of Stoicism.

Diogenes Laertius (3rd cent. CE) author of biographical and doxographical accounts of previous philosophers, including the Stoics.

Diogenes of Babylon (3rd–2nd cent. BCE) fifth head of the Stoa, succeeding Zeno of Tarsus.

Diogenes of Sinope (4th cent. BCE), Cynic philosopher often cited by Stoics as an example of a sage.

Epictetus (1st–2nd cent. CE) Stoic philosopher who taught in Rome and Nicopolis.

Galen of Pergamum (2nd cent. CE) Platonic philosopher and doctor whose works include important discussions of Stoicism.

Heraclitus (6th–5th cent. BCE) Presocratic philosopher often cited as an influence on Stoic physics.

Hierocles (1st–2nd cent. CE) Stoic author of the *Elements of Ethics* surviving only on papyrus.

Marcus Aurelius (2nd cent. CE) Roman Emperor and adherent of Stoicism.

Mnesarchus (2nd–1st cent. BCE) eighth head of the Stoa in Athens (possibly jointly with Dardanus), succeeding his teacher Panaetius.

Musonius Rufus (1st cent. CE) Roman Stoic of Etruscan origin who taught Epictetus.

Panaetius of Rhodes (2nd cent. BCE) seventh head of the Stoa.

Plutarch of Chaeronea (1st–2nd cent. CE) Platonic philosopher and literary biographer, famous for his *Parallel Lives*, who wrote polemics against Stoicism.

Polemo (4th–3rd cent. BCE) head of Plato's Academy whose lectures Zeno attended.

Posidonius (2nd–1st cent. BCE) studied with Panaetius and later taught philosophy at Rhodes.

Seneca (1st cent. CE) Stoic philosopher, dramatist and Roman statesman, one time tutor to the young Nero.

Sextus Empiricus (2nd–3rd cent. CE) Sceptical philosopher and doctor whose works include important discussions of Stoic philosophy.

Simplicius (5th–6th cent. CE) Neoplatonic philosopher who wrote a commentary on Epictetus' *Handbook* and discussed Stoic doctrines in his commentaries on Aristotle.

Socrates (5th cent. BCE) famous Athenian philosopher often cited by Stoics as an example of a sage.

Stilpo (4th cent. BCE) Megarian philosopher with whom Zeno studied.

Stobaeus (5th cent. CE) doxographical author whose *Anthology* preserves texts by Cleanthes, Arius Didymus, Musonius Rufus and a wide range of other Stoic fragments.

Zeno of Citium (4th–3rd cent. BCE) founder and first head of the Stoic school.

Zeno of Tarsus (3rd–2nd cent. BCE) fourth head of the Stoa, succeeding Chrysippus.

Glossary of terms

This list is selective. A wide range of Greek philosophical terms are discussed in J. O. Urmson, *The Greek Philosophical Vocabulary* (London: Duckworth, 1990), although the focus is on Platonic and Aristotelian vocabulary. Readers of French can also consult V. Laurand, *Le vocabulaire des Stoïciens* (Paris: Ellipses, 2002).

adequate impression (*phantasia kataleptikē*) an impression the truth of which is immediately obvious and beyond doubt.

all (*pan*) refers to the cosmos and the extra-cosmic void that surrounds it.

appropriate action (*kathēkon*) an action natural for a particular animal in a particular context.

appropriation (*oikeiōsis*) an animal's primary sense of concern for itself.

areas of study (*topoi*) three types of exercise or training outlined by Epictetus.

art (*technē*) a practical skill requiring expert knowledge.

assent (*sunkatathesis*) accepting an impression that has been presented to the soul.

assertible (*axiōma*) a proposition that can be brought together with others to form syllogistic arguments.

breath (*pneuma*) the active principle in Nature, sometimes identified with God, sometimes with the soul of God.

choice (*prohairesis*) Epictetus' name for the conscious decision-making part of the commanding faculty; what might now be called the "will" or "I".

cognition (*katalēpsis*) an assent to an adequate impression; a building block for knowledge.

cohesion (*hexis*) the level of tension of *pneuma* that generates physical unity in a body.

commanding faculty (*hēgemonikon*) the ruling part of the soul; what would now be called the mind.

common conceptions (*koinai ennoiai*) generalizations held by everyone based on shared impressions and preconceptions.

commonly qualified (*koinōs poion*) refers to the quality that a particular entity shares with other particular entities.

completely correct action (*katorthōma*) a perfected appropriate action arising from virtue.

conflagration (*ekpurōsis*) periodic moment of destruction of the cosmos in which it is transformed into pure creative fire.

creative fire (*pur technikon*) identified with both God and breath or *pneuma*; that to which the cosmos is reduced at the moment of conflagration.

emotion (*pathos*) a mental disturbance based on a rational judgement.

exercise (*askēsis*) the second stage in learning an art, coming after the study of the relevant theoretical principles.

existence (*einai*) ontological attribute reserved solely for bodies.

fate (*heimarmenē*) the continuous string of causes in Nature.

God (*theos*) a living being identified with Nature.

good emotion (*eupatheia*) a rational emotion, based on a correct assent; the three types are joy, caution and wishing.

happiness (*eudaimonia*) the ultimate goal of life, being that for the sake of which everything is done but which is not itself for the sake of anything else.

impression (*phantasia*) an imprint on the soul, usually the product of sensory experience but can also be the product of reasoning.

incorporeal (*asōmaton*) a non-bodily entity that is real but does not exist; the four types are void, time, place and sayable.

indifferent (*adiaphoron*) the class of items that are neither good nor bad, into which fall all externals.

knowledge (*epistēmē*) an organized and structured system of cognitions, akin to what would now be called scientific knowledge.

making progress (*prokopē*) category of those who are working towards the ideal of the sage.

mode (*tropos*) the structural form of a certain type of syllogistic argument.

nature (*phusis*) the level of tension of *pneuma* that generates biological life.

non-preferred (*apoproēgmenon*) sub-class of indifferents that one will try to avoid, although they are not strictly speaking bad.

peculiarly qualified (*idiōs poion*) refers to the unique quality that a particular entity has that makes it distinguishable from all other entities.

preconception (*prolēpsis*) naturally occurring conceptions that form the basis for consciously developed conceptions.

preferred (*proēgmenon*) sub-class of indifferents that one will choose, although they are not strictly speaking good.

principles (*archai*) the two corporeal aspects of the physical world.

sage (*sophos*) idealized image of the perfectly rational human being.

sayable (*lekton*) the meaning or sense conveyed by speech.

something (*ti*) anything that is real, whether a body or an incorporeal; the highest ontological class.

soul (*psuchē*) the level of tension of *pneuma* that generates the animal properties of perception, movement and reproduction.

speech (*lexis*) an articulate instance of voice that can convey meaning.

subsistence (*huphistasthai*) the ontological status of incorporeals; a sub-class of being something that stands in contrast to existence.

tension (*tonos*) a property of breath or *pneuma*, the level of which determines the *pneuma*'s characteristics.

total blending (*krasis di'holōn*) the complete mixture of two bodies in which both bodies are in every part of the mixture.

up to us (*eph' hēmin*) Epictetus' term for those things that are within one's control, principally one's assents to impressions that form the basis for one's opinions, desires and actions.

value (*axia*) the characteristic of preferred indifferents such as health, wealth and reputation, even though they are not strictly speaking good.

virtue (*aretē*) an excellent disposition of the soul, the only thing held to be good.

voice (*phōnē*) a physical movement of air by the mouth.

whole (*holon*) refers to the cosmos containing everything that exists, contrasted with the "all".

Guide to further reading

Ancient texts

Collections of fragments

The standard collection of fragments for the early Stoics is H. von Arnim, *Stoicorum Veterum Fragmenta*, 4 vols (Leipzig: Teubner, 1903–24). This contains the bulk of the surviving evidence for Zeno, Aristo, Cleanthes, Chrysippus, Diogenes of Babylon, Antipater and others in the original Greek and Latin. This collection is now slightly dated and for logic it has been superseded by K. Hülser, *Die Fragmente zur Dialektik der Stoiker*, 4 vols (Stuttgart: Frommann-Holzboog, 1987).

There are two very useful anthologies in English, both covering not only the Stoics but also the other Hellenistic schools: A. A. Long & D. N. Sedley, *The Hellenistic Philosophers*, 2 vols (Cambridge: Cambridge University Press, 1987) and B. Inwood & L. P. Gerson, *Hellenistic Philosophy: Introductory Readings*, 2nd edn (Indianapolis, IN: Hackett, 1997). I have relied on translations from both of these volumes for some of the quotations in this volume.

Older collections of fragments in English worth noting include G. H. Clark, *Selections from Hellenistic Philosophy* (New York: Appleton-Century-Crofts, 1940) and J. L. Saunders, *Greek and Roman Philosophy after Aristotle* (New York: Free Press, 1966). Also worth noting is a recent sourcebook for the philosophy of late antiquity: R. Sorabji, *The Philosophy of the Commentators 200–600 AD*, 3 vols (London: Duckworth, 2004). This collection translates many Stoic fragments preserved by authors of this period and has a very helpful commentary.

The fragments for the middle Stoics Panaetius and Posidonius can be found in M. van Straaten, *Panaetii Rhodii Fragmenta* (Leiden: Brill, 1952) and L. Edelstein & I. G. Kidd, *Posidonius: The Fragments* (Cambridge: Cambridge University Press, 1972). Kidd has supplemented the latter collection with a detailed commentary in *Posidonius: The Commentary*, 2 vols (Cambridge: Cambridge University Press, 1988), and with a translation of the fragments in *Posidonius: The Translation of the Fragments* (Cambridge: Cambridge University Press, 1999).

Stoic authors

The works of the three famous Stoic authors, Seneca, Epictetus (reported by Arrian) and Marcus Aurelius can all be found in Loeb Classical Library editions (Cambridge, MA: Harvard University Press), containing the original text with a facing English translation. I have often used these translations in this volume, occasionally modified.

For all three of these authors there are many other helpful editions and translations. The following is merely a selection:

Epictetus, *Discourses, Book I*, R. F. Dobbin (comm. and trans.) (Oxford: Clarendon Press, 1998).
Epictetus, *The Discourses of Epictetus*, introduction by C. Gill, R. Hard (trans.) (London: Everyman, 1995).
Epictetus, *The Encheiridion of Epictetus and its Three Christian Adaptations*, G. Boter (ed. and trans.) (Leiden: Brill, 1999).
Marcus Aurelius, *Ad Se Ipsum Libri XII*, J. Dalfen (ed.) (Leipzig: Teubner, 1987).
Marcus Aurelius, *Meditations*, M. Staniforth (trans.) (Harmondsworth: Penguin, 1964).
Marcus Aurelius, *Meditations*, introduction by C. Gill, R. Hard (trans.) (Ware: Wordsworth, 1997).
Marcus Aurelius, *Meditations*, G. Hays (trans.) (London: Weidenfeld & Nicolson, 2003).
Marcus Aurelius, *The Meditations of the Emperor Marcus Antoninus*, 2 vols, commentary by A. S. L. Farquharson (ed. and trans.) (Oxford: Clarendon Press, 1944). Translation reprinted with introduction by R. B. Rutherford (Oxford: Oxford University Press, 1989).
Seneca, *Dialogues and Letters*, C. D. N. Costa (trans.) (Harmondsworth: Penguin, 1997)
Seneca, *Letters from a Stoic*, R. Campbell (trans.) (Harmondsworth: Penguin, 1969).
Seneca, *Moral and Political Essays*, J. M. Cooper & J. F. Procopé (trans.) (Cambridge: Cambridge University Press, 1995).

We have also encountered a number of other Stoic authors. See the following editions and translations:

Cleomedes, *Caelestia*, R. B. Todd (ed.) (Leipzig: Teubner, 1990). Translated in A. C. Bowen & R. B. Todd, *Cleomedes' Lectures on Astronomy* (Berkeley, CA: University of California Press, 2004).
Cornutus, *Theologiae Graecae Compendium*, C. Lang (ed.) (Leipzig: Teubner, 1881). Translated in R. S. Hays, *Lucius Annaeus Cornutus' Epidrome (Introduction to the Traditions of Greek Theology): Introduction, Translation, and Notes*, PhD dissertation (Classics Department, University of Texas at Austin, 1983).
Hierocles, *Ethische Elementarlehre (Papyrus 9780)*, H. von Arnim (ed.), Berliner Klassikertexte 4 (Berlin: Weidmann, 1906). Edited with Italian translation in G. Bastianini & A. A. Long, "Hierocles, *Elementa moralia*", *Corpus dei Papiri Filosofici Greci e Latini* I 1**, 268–451 (Florence: Olschki, 1992).
Musonius Rufus, *Reliquiae*, O. Hense (ed.) (Leipzig: Teubner, 1905). Translated in C. E. Lutz, "Musonius Rufus: The Roman Socrates", *Yale Classical Studies* **10** (1947), 3–147.

Other authors

As we have seen, the study of Stoicism involves reading a wide range of ancient authors. The works of Cicero, Diogenes Laertius, Plutarch and Sextus Empiricus are all available in the Loeb Classical Library. Note also the following more recent translations of Cicero, the most important of the non-Stoic authors:

Cicero on the Emotions: Tusculan Disputations 3 and 4, M. Graver (trans.) (Chicago, IL: University of Chicago Press, 2002).
Cicero on Stoic Good and Evil: De Finibus Bonorum et Malorum Liber III and Paradoxa Stoicorum, M. R. Wright (ed. and trans.) (Warminster: Aris & Phillips, 1991).
On Duties, introduction by M. Griffin, E. M. Atkins (trans.) (Cambridge: Cambridge University Press, 1991).
On Moral Ends, introduction by J. Annas, R. Woolf (trans.) (Cambridge: Cambridge University Press, 2001).
The Nature of the Gods, P. G. Walsh (trans.) (Oxford: Oxford University Press, 1997).

Other authors relevant to the study of Stoicism, many of which have been cited in this volume, include:

Aetius, *De Placitis Reliquiae*, H. Diels (ed.), in *Doxographi Graeci* (Berlin: de Gruyter, 1879/1965). This text is partially reconstructed from a work attributed to Plutarch and so is partially translated in *Plutarch's Morals* [5 vols], vol. 3, W. W. Goodwin (ed.), 104–93 (Boston, MA: Little, Brown, 1888).

Alexander of Aphrodisias, *Alexander of Aphrodisias on Fate*, R. W. Sharples (ed. and trans.) (London: Duckworth, 1983).

Alexander of Aphrodisias, *Alexander of Aphrodisias on Stoic Physics: A Study of the De Mixtione*, R. B. Todd (ed. and trans.) (Leiden: Brill, 1976).

Arius Didymus, *Epitome of Stoic Ethics*, A. J. Pomeroy (ed. and trans.) (Atlanta, GA: Society of Biblical Literature, 1999).

Calcidius, *Timaeus a Calcidio Translatus Commentarioque Instructus*, J. H. Waszink (ed.) (Leiden: Brill, 1962).

Galen, *On the Doctrines of Hippocrates and Plato*, 3 vols, P. De Lacy (ed. and trans.) (Berlin: Akademie, 1978–84).

Lactantius, *Divine Institutes*, A. Bowen & P. Garnsey (trans.) (Liverpool: Liverpool University Press, 2003).

Philodemus, *De Stoicis*, in T. Dorandi, "Filodemo, Gli Stoici (*PHerc* 155 e 339)", *Cronache Ercolanesi* **12** (1982), 91–133.

Philodemus, *Filodemo, Storia dei filosofi: La stoà da Zenone a Panezio (PHerc. 1018)*, T. Dorandi (ed.) (Leiden: Brill, 1994).

Philodemus, *On Piety, Part 1*, D. Obbink (ed. and trans.) (Oxford: Clarendon Press, 1996).

Simplicius, *On Aristotle Categories*, 4 vols, M. Chase *et al.* (trans.) (London: Duckworth, 2000–2003).

Stobaeus, *Anthologium*, C. Wachsmuth & O. Hense (eds) (Berlin: Weidmann, 1884–1912).

Secondary literature

Hellenistic philosophy

For a short introduction to Hellenistic philosophy as a whole see R. W. Sharples, *Stoics, Epicureans, and Sceptics* (London: Routledge, 1996). For a more detailed survey see A. A. Long, *Hellenistic Philosophy* (London: Duckworth, 1974). For comprehensive coverage see K. Algra, J. Barnes, J. Mansfeld & M. Schofield (eds), *The Cambridge History of Hellenistic Philosophy* (Cambridge: Cambridge University Press, 1999). For an introduction to the Roman period see M. Morford, *The Roman Philosophers* (London: Routledge, 2002).

Stoicism

For another short introduction to Stoicism see F. H. Sandbach, *The Stoics* (London: Chatto & Windus, 1975). For general monographs and collections of papers devoted exclusively to Stoicism see:

Christensen, J. *An Essay on the Unity of Stoic Philosophy* (Munksgaard: Scandinavian University Books, 1962).

Edelstein, L. *The Meaning of Stoicism* (Cambridge, MA: Harvard University Press, 1966).

Epp, R. H. (ed.) "Spindel Conference: Recovering the Stoics", *Southern Journal of Philosophy* 23 (Suppl.) (1985).

Ierodiakonou, K. (ed.) *Topics in Stoic Philosophy* (Oxford: Clarendon Press, 1999).

Inwood, B. (ed.) *The Cambridge Companion to The Stoics* (Cambridge: Cambridge University Press, 2003).

Long, A. A. (ed.) *Problems in Stoicism* (London: Athlone, 1971).

Long, A. A. *Stoic Studies* (Cambridge: Cambridge University Press, 1996).

Reesor, M. E. *The Nature of Man in Early Stoic Philosophy* (London: Duckworth, 1989).

Rist, J. M. *Stoic Philosophy* (Cambridge: Cambridge University Press, 1969).

Rist, J. M. (ed.) *The Stoics* (Berkeley, CA: University of California Press, 1978).

Late Stoicism has been the subject of a number of studies:

Arnold, E. V. *Roman Stoicism* (Cambridge: Cambridge University Press, 1911).

Barnes, J. *Logic and the Imperial Stoa* (Leiden: Brill, 1997).

Reydams-Schils, G. *The Roman Stoics: Self, Responsibility, and Affection* (Chicago, IL: University of Chicago Press, 2005).

Todd, R. B. "The Stoics and their Cosmology in the First and Second Centuries AD", *ANRW* II.36.3 (1989), 1365–78.

Individual Stoics

Zeno

For Zeno see the recent collection of papers: T. Scaltsas & A. S. Mason (eds), *The Philosophy of Zeno: Zeno of Citium and his Legacy* (Larnaka: The Municipality of Larnaka, 2002). Note also:

Erskine, A. "Zeno and the Beginning of Stoicism", *Classics Ireland* 7 (2000), 51–60.

Hunt, H. A. K. *A Physical Interpretation of the Universe: The Doctrines of Zeno the Stoic* (Carlton: Melbourne University Press, 1976).

Rist, J. M. "Zeno and the Origins of Stoic Logic", in *Les Stoïciens et leur logique*, J. Brunschwig (ed.), 387–400 (Paris: Vrin, 1978).

Rist, J. M. "Zeno and Stoic Consistency", *Phronesis* 22 (1977), 161–74.

Schofield, M. "The Syllogisms of Zeno of Citium", *Phronesis* 33 (1983), 31–58.

Sparshott, F. E. "Zeno on Art: Anatomy of a Definition", in *The Stoics*, J. M. Rist (ed.), 273–90 (Berkeley, CA: University of California Press, 1978).

Chrysippus

For Chrysippus, in the first instance see J. B. Gould, *The Philosophy of Chrysippus* (Leiden: Brill, 1970). For some particular topics see:

Bobzien, S. "Chrysippus and the Epistemic Theory of Vagueness", *Proceedings of the Aristotelian Society* **102** (2002), 217–38.
Bobzien, S. "Chrysippus' Modal Logic and its Relation to Philo and Diodorus", in *Dialektiker und Stoiker*, K. Döring & T. Ebert (eds), 63–84 (Stuttgart: Franz Steiner, 1993).
Bobzien, S. "Chrysippus' Theory of Causes", in *Topics in Stoic Philosophy*, K. Ierodiakonou (ed.), 196–242 (Oxford: Clarendon Press, 1999).
Bowin, J. "Chrysippus' Puzzle about Identity", *Oxford Studies in Ancient Philosophy* **24** (2003), 239–51.
Tieleman, T. *Chrysippus' On Affections: Reconstruction and Interpretation* (Leiden: Brill, 2003).
Todd, R. B. "Chrysippus on Infinite Divisibility", *Apeiron* **7** (1973), 121–34.

Posidonius

Cooper, J. M. "Posidonius on Emotions", in his *Reason and Emotion*, 449–84 (Princeton, NJ: Princeton University Press, 1999).
Edelstein, L. "The Philosophical System of Posidonius", *American Journal of Philology* **57** (1936), 286–325.
Kidd, I. G. "Posidonius on Emotions", in *Problems in Stoicism*, A. A. Long (ed.), 200–215 (London: Athlone, 1971).
Kidd, I. G. "Posidonius and Logic", in *Les Stoïciens et leur logique*, J. Brunschwig (ed.), 273–83 (Paris: Vrin, 1978).
Kidd, I. G. "Posidonius as Philosopher-Historian", in *Philosophia Togata*, M. Griffin & J. Barnes (eds), 38–50 (Oxford: Clarendon Press, 1989).

Seneca

Seneca has received much attention. For a study of Seneca's thought in the context of his life see M. Griffin, *Seneca: A Philosopher in Politics* (Oxford: Clarendon Press, 1976). Brad Inwood has published a series of useful studies of Seneca, now gathered together in B. Inwood, *Reading Seneca: Stoic Philosophy at Rome* (Oxford: Clarendon Press, 2005). Note also the following very brief selection:

Asmis, E. "Seneca's 'On the Happy Life' and Stoic Individualism", *Apeiron* **23** (1990), 219–55.
Cooper, J. M. "Moral Theory and Moral Improvement: Seneca", in his *Knowledge, Nature, and the Good*, 309–34 (Princeton, NJ: Princeton University Press, 2004).
Costa, C. D. N. (ed.) *Seneca* (London: Routledge & Kegan Paul, 1974).

172

Mitsis, P. "Seneca on Reason, Rules and Moral Development", in *Passions and Perceptions*, J. Brunschwig & M. Nussbaum (eds), 285–312 (Cambridge: Cambridge University Press, 1993).

Rist, J. M. "Seneca and Stoic Orthodoxy", *ANRW* II.36.3 (1989), 1993–2012.

Rosenmeyer, T. G. *Senecan Drama and Stoic Cosmology* (Berkeley, CA: University of California Press, 1989).

Veyne, P. *Seneca: The Life of a Stoic*, D. Sullivan (trans.) (New York: Routledge, 2003).

Cornutus

Cornutus has been discussed in G. W. Most, "Cornutus and Stoic Allegoresis: A Preliminary Report", *ANRW* II.36.3 (1989), 2014–65, and G. R. Boys-Stones, *Post-Hellenistic Philosophy* (Oxford: Oxford University Press, 2001), ch. 3.

Musonius Rufus

Musonius Rufus is treated well in C. E. Lutz, "Musonius Rufus: The Roman Socrates", *Yale Classical Studies* **10** (1947), 3–147, which also includes a text and translation. See also:

Charlesworth, M. P. "The Philosopher (Musonius Rufus)", in his *Five Men: Character Studies from the Roman Empire*, 31–62 (Cambridge, MA: Harvard University Press, 1936).

Engel, D. M. "The Gender Egalitarianism of Musonius Rufus", *Ancient Philosophy* **20** (2000), 377–91.

Parker, C. P. "Musonius the Etruscan", *Harvard Studies in Classical Philology* **7** (1896), 123–37.

Van Geytenbeek, A. C. *Musonius Rufus and Greek Diatribe* (Assen: Van Gorcum, 1963).

Epictetus

For an expert introduction to Epictetus see A. A. Long, *Epictetus: A Stoic and Socratic Guide to Life* (Oxford: Clarendon Press, 2002). Note also:

Bonhöffer, A. *The Ethics of the Stoic Epictetus*, W. O. Stephens (trans.) (New York: Peter Lang, 1996).

De Lacy, P. "The Logical Structure of the Ethics of Epictetus", *Classical Philology* **38** (1943), 112–25.

Hershbell, J. "The Stoicism of Epictetus: Twentieth Century Perspectives", *ANRW* II.36.3 (1989), 2148–63.

Hijmans, B. L. *Askēsis: Notes on Epictetus' Educational System* (Assen: Van Gorcum, 1959).

Long, A. A. "Epictetus, Marcus Aurelius", in *Ancient Writers: Greece and Rome*, T. J. Luce (ed.), 985–1002 (New York: Scribner's, 1982).

Long, A. A. "Epictetus as Socratic Mentor", *Proceedings of the Cambridge Philological Society* **46** (2000), 79–98.

Long, A. A. "The Socratic Imprint on Epictetus' Philosophy", in *Stoicism: Traditions and Transformations*, S. K. Strange & J. Zupko (eds), 10–31 (Cambridge: Cambridge University Press, 2004).

Stanton, G. R. "The Cosmopolitan Ideas of Epictetus and Marcus Aurelius", *Phronesis* **13** (1968), 183–95.

Stephens, W. O. "Epictetus on How the Stoic Sage Loves", *Oxford Studies in Ancient Philosophy* **14** (1996), 193–210.

Stockdale, J. B. "Testing Epictetus's Doctrines in a Laboratory of Human Behaviour", *Bulletin of the Institute of Classical Studies* **50** (1995), 1–13.

Xenakis, J. *Epictetus: Philosopher-Therapist* (The Hague: Martinus Nijhoff, 1969).

Marcus Aurelius

For a philosophical study of Marcus Aurelius see P. Hadot, *The Inner Citadel: The Meditations of Marcus Aurelius*, M. Chase (trans.) (Cambridge, MA: Harvard University Press, 1998). For a more literary approach see R. B. Rutherford, *The Meditations of Marcus Aurelius: A Study* (Oxford: Clarendon Press, 1989). Note also:

Asmis, E. "The Stoicism of Marcus Aurelius", *ANRW* II.36.3 (1989), 2228–52.

Brunt, P. A. "Marcus Aurelius in his *Meditations*", *Journal of Roman Studies* **64** (1974), 1–20.

Cooper, J. M. "Moral Theory and Moral Improvement: Marcus Aurelius", in his *Knowledge, Nature, and the Good*, 335–68 (Princeton, NJ: Princeton University Press, 2004).

Rist, J. M. "Are You a Stoic? The Case of Marcus Aurelius", in *Jewish and Christian Self-Definition 3*, B. F. Meyers & E. P. Sanders (eds), 23–45 (London: SCM Press, 1982).

Hierocles

Hierocles has been discussed in two important papers:

Inwood, B. "Hierocles: Theory and Argument in the Second Century AD", *Oxford Studies in Ancient Philosophy* **2** (1984), 151–84.

Long, A. A. "Hierocles on *Oikeiōsis* and Self-Perception", in *Hellenistic Philosophy: Vol. I*, K. J. Boudouris (ed.), 93–104 (Athens: International Center for Greek Philosophy and Culture, 1993). Reprinted in his *Stoic Studies*, 250–63 (Cambridge: Cambridge University Press, 1996).

Cleomedes

Cleomedes is examined in R. Goulet, *Cléomède, Théorie Élémentaire* (Paris: Vrin, 1980), which includes a French translation of *The Heavens*. For studies in English see:

Algra, K. "The Treatise of Cleomedes and its Critique of Epicurean Cosmology", in *Epikureismus in der späten Republik und der Kaiserzeit*, M. Erler & R. Bees (eds), 164–89 (Stuttgart: Steiner, 2000).

Todd, R. B. "Cleomedes and the Problems of Stoic Astrophysics", *Hermes* **129** (2001), 75–8.

Todd, R. B. "Cleomedes and the Stoic Concept of Void", *Apeiron* **16** (1982), 129–36.

Formative influences

For the influence of earlier philosophers on the development of Stoicism see:

Goulet-Cazé, M.-O. *Les Kynica du stoïcisme* (Stuttgart: Franz Steiner Verlag, 2003).

Long, A. A. "Heraclitus and Stoicism", *Philosophia* **5/6** (1975–76), 133–56. Reprinted in his *Stoic Studies*, 35–57 (Cambridge: Cambridge University Press, 1996).

Long, A. A. "Socrates in Hellenistic Philosophy", *Classical Quarterly* **38** (1988), 150–71. Reprinted in his *Stoic Studies*, 1–34 (Cambridge: Cambridge University Press, 1996).

Sandbach, F. H. *Aristotle and the Stoics*, Cambridge Philological Society suppl. vol. 10 (Cambridge: Cambridge Philological Society, 1985).

Striker, G. "Plato's Socrates and the Stoics", in *The Socratic Movement*, P. A. Vander Waerdt (ed.), 241–51 (Ithaca, NY: Cornell University Press, 1994).

Nature of philosophy

For Stoic ideas about the nature of philosophy see J. Sellars, *The Art of Living: The Stoics on the Nature and Function of Philosophy* (Aldershot: Ashgate, 2003). Note also:

Hadot, P. "Philosophie, discours philosophique, et divisions de la philosophie chez les Stoïciens", *Revue Internationale de Philosophie* **45** (1991), 205–19.

Ierodiakonou, K. "The Stoic Division of Philosophy", *Phronesis* **38** (1993), 57–74.

Newman, R. J. "*Cotidie meditare*: Theory and Practice of the *meditatio* in Imperial Stoicism", *ANRW* II.36.3 (1989), 1473–1517.

Logic and language

For Stoic logic, in the first instance see:

Bobzien, S. "Stoic Syllogistic", *Oxford Studies in Ancient Philosophy* **14** (1996), 133–92.

Bobzien, S. "Logic", in *The Cambridge Companion to The Stoics*, B. Inwood (ed.), 85–123 (Cambridge: Cambridge University Press, 2003).

Kneale, W. & M. Kneale, *The Development of Logic* (Oxford: Clarendon Press, 1962), ch. 3.

Mates, B. *Stoic Logic* (Berkeley, CA: University of California Press, 1953).

Mueller, I. "An Introduction to Stoic Logic", in *The Stoics*, J. M. Rist (ed.), 1–26 (Berkeley, CA: University of California Press, 1978).

For Stoic discussions of language in general, including topics not directly addressed in this volume, see:

Atherton, C. "Hand over Fist: The Failure of Stoic Rhetoric", *Classical Quarterly* **38** (1988), 392–427.

Atherton, C. *The Stoics on Ambiguity* (Cambridge: Cambridge University Press, 1993).

Blank, D. & C. Atherton, "The Stoic Contribution to Traditional Grammar", in *The Cambridge Companion to The Stoics*, B. Inwood (ed.), 310–27 (Cambridge: Cambridge University Press, 2003).

Frede, M. "Principles of Stoic Grammar", in *The Stoics*, J. M. Rist (ed.), 27–75 (Berkeley, CA: University of California Press, 1978). Reprinted in his *Essays in Ancient Philosophy*, 301–37 (Minneapolis, MN: University of Minnesota Press, 1987).

Frede, M. "The Stoic Notion of a *Lekton*", in *Language*, S. Everson (ed.), 109–28 (Cambridge: Cambridge University Press, 1994).

Lloyd, A. C. "Grammar and Metaphysics in the Stoa", in *Problems in Stoicism*, A. A. Long (ed.), 58–74 (London: Athlone, 1971).

Long, A. A. "Language and Thought in Stoicism", in *Problems in Stoicism*, A. A. Long (ed.), 75–113 (London: Athlone, 1971).

Epistemology

Arthur, E. P. "The Stoic Analysis of the Mind's Reactions to Presentations", *Hermes* **111** (1983), 69–78.

Annas, J. "Stoic Epistemology", in *Epistemology*, S. Everson (ed.), 184–203 (Cambridge: Cambridge University Press, 1990).

Frede, M. "Stoics and Skeptics on Clear and Distinct Impressions", in *The Sceptical Tradition*, M. Burnyeat (ed.), 65–93 (Berkeley, CA: University of California Press, 1983). Reprinted in his *Essays in Ancient Philosophy*, 151–76 (Minneapolis, MN: University of Minnesota Press, 1987).

Hankinson, R. J. "Stoic Epistemology", in *The Cambridge Companion to The Stoics*, B. Inwood (ed.), 59–84 (Cambridge: Cambridge University Press, 2003).

Ioppolo, A.-M. "Presentation and Assent: A Physical and Cognitive Problem in Early Stoicism", *Classical Quarterly* **40** (1990), 433–49.

Jackson-McCabe, M. "The Stoic Theory of Implanted Preconceptions", *Phronesis* **49** (2004), 323–47.

Reed, B. "The Stoics' Account of the Cognitive Impression", *Oxford Studies in Ancient Philosophy* **23** (2002), 147–80.

Sandbach, F. H. "*Ennoia* and *Prolēpsis* in the Stoic Theory of Knowledge", *Classical Quarterly* **24** (1930), 44–51. Reprinted in *Problems in Stoicism*, A. A. Long (ed.), 22–37 (London: Athlone, 1971).

Sandbach, F. H. "Phantasia Katalēptikē", in *Problems in Stoicism*, A. A. Long (ed.), 9–21 (London: Athlone, 1971).

Scott, D. "Innatism and the Stoa", *Proceedings of the Cambridge Philological Society* **34** (1988), 123–53.

Todd, R. B. "The Stoic Common Notions: A Re-examination and Reinterpretation", *Symbolae Osloenses* **48** (1973), 47–75.

Watson, G. *The Stoic Theory of Knowledge* (Belfast: Queen's University, 1966).

Ontology

For ontology, in the first instance see J. Brunschwig, "Stoic Metaphysics", in *The Cambridge Companion to The Stoics*, B. Inwood (ed.), 206–32 (Cambridge: Cambridge University Press, 2003). For more detailed treatments see:

Brunschwig, J. "La théorie stoïcienne du genre suprême et l'ontologie platonicienne", in *Matter and Metaphysics*, J. Barnes & M. Mignucci (eds), 19–127 (Naples: Bibliopolis, 1988). Published in English as "The Stoic Theory of the Supreme Genus and Platonic Ontology", in his *Papers in Hellenistic Philosophy*, 92–157 (Cambridge: Cambridge University Press, 1994).

Caston, V. "Something and Nothing: The Stoics on Concepts and Universals", *Oxford Studies in Ancient Philosophy* **17** (1999), 145–213.

Menn, S. "The Stoic Theory of Categories", *Oxford Studies in Ancient Philosophy* **17** (1999), 215–47.

Rist, J. M. "Categories and their Uses", in *Problems in Stoicism*, A. A. Long (ed.), 38–57 (London: Athlone, 1971).

Sedley, D. "The Stoic Theory of Universals", *Southern Journal of Philosophy* **23** suppl. ("Spindel Conference: Recovering the Stoics", R. H. Epp (ed.)) (1985), 87–92.

Physics and cosmology

For general studies of Stoic physics see:

Hahm, D. E. *The Origins of Stoic Cosmology* (Columbus, OH: Ohio State University Press, 1977).

Lapidge, M. "*Archai* and *Stoicheia*: A Problem in Stoic Cosmology", *Phronesis* **18** (1973), 240–78.
Lapidge, M. "Stoic Cosmology", in *The Stoics*, J. M. Rist (ed.), 161–85 (Berkeley, CA: University of California Press, 1978).
Sambursky, S. *Physics of the Stoics* (London: Routledge & Kegan Paul, 1959).
Solmsen, F. "Cleanthes or Posidonius? The Basis of Stoic Physics", in his *Kleine Schriften 1*, 436–60 (Hildesheim: Olms, 1968).
Todd, R. B. "Monism and Immanence: The Foundations of Stoic Physics", in *The Stoics*, J. M. Rist (ed.), 137–60 (Berkeley, CA: University of California Press, 1978).
White, M. J. "Stoic Natural Philosophy", in *The Cambridge Companion to The Stoics*, B. Inwood (ed.), 124–52 (Cambridge: Cambridge University Press, 2003).

For some specific topics in physics see:

Lewis, E. "Diogenes Laertius and the Stoic Theory of Mixture", *Bulletin of the Institute of Classical Studies* **35** (1988), 84–90.
Lewis, E. "The Stoics on Identity and Individuation", *Phronesis* **40** (1995), 89–108.
Long, A. A. "The Stoics on World-Conflagration and Everlasting Recurrence", in *Southern Journal of Philosophy* **23** suppl. ("Spindel Conference: Recovering the Stoics", R. H. Epp (ed.)) (1985), 13–37.
Mansfeld, J. "Providence and the Destruction of the Universe in Early Stoic Thought", in *Studies in Hellenistic Religions*, M. J. Vermaseren (ed.), 129–88 (Leiden: Brill, 1979). Reprinted in his *Studies in Later Greek Philosophy and Gnosticism* (Aldershot: Ashgate, 1989).
Sedley, D. "The Origins of Stoic God", in *Traditions of Theology*, D. Frede & A. Laks (eds), 41–83 (Leiden: Brill, 2002).

Fate and determinism

For issues surrounding freedom and determinism see S. Bobzien's impressive *Determinism and Freedom in Stoic Philosophy* (Oxford: Clarendon Press, 1998), but note also:

Botros, S. "Freedom, Causality, Fatalism, and Early Stoic Philosophy", *Phronesis* **30** (1985), 274–304.
Frede, D. "Stoic Determinism", in *The Cambridge Companion to The Stoics*, B. Inwood (ed.), 179–205 (Cambridge: Cambridge University Press, 2003).
Gould, J. B. "The Stoic Conception of Fate", *Journal of the History of Ideas* **35** (1974), 17–32.
Long, A. A. "Freedom and Determinism in the Stoic Theory of Human Action", in *Problems in Stoicism*, A. A. Long (ed.), 173–99 (London: Athlone, 1971).

Long, A. A. "The Stoic Conception of Fate", *Journal of the History of Ideas* **35** (1974), 17–32.
Long, A. A. "Stoic Determinism and Alexander of Aphrodisias *De Fato* (i-xiv)", *Archiv für Geschichte der Philosophie* **52** (1970), 247–68.
Reesor, M. "Necessity and Fate in Stoic Philosophy", in *The Stoics*, J. M. Rist (ed.), 187–202 (Berkeley, CA: University of California Press, 1978).
Salles, R. "Compatibilism: Stoic and Modern", *Archiv für Geschichte der Philosophie* **83** (2001), 1–23.
Salles, R. "Determinism and Recurrence in Early Stoic Thought", *Oxford Studies in Ancient Philosophy* **24** (2003), 253–72.

Psychology

Annas, J. *Hellenistic Philosophy of Mind* (Berkeley, CA: University of California Press, 1992), chs 2–5.
Gill, C. "Did Chrysippus understand Medea?", *Phronesis* **28** (1983), 136–49.
Long, A. A. "Soul and Body in Stoicism", *Phronesis* **27** (1982), 34–57.
Sedley, D. "Chrysippus on Psychophysical Causality", in *Passions and Perceptions*, J. Brunschwig & M. C. Nussbaum (eds), 313–31 (Cambridge: Cambridge University Press, 1993).

Ethics

For good general studies of Stoic ethics see B. Inwood, *Ethics and Human Action in Early Stoicism* (Oxford: Clarendon Press, 1985) and T. Brennan, *The Stoic Life: Emotions, Duties, and Fate* (Oxford: Oxford University Press, 2005). Note also:

Barney, R. "A Puzzle in Stoic Ethics", *Oxford Studies in Ancient Philosophy* **24** (2003), 303–40.
Betegh, G. "Cosmological Ethics in the *Timaeus* and Early Stoicism", *Oxford Studies in Ancient Philosophy* **24** (2003), 273–302.
Blundell, M. W. "Parental Nature and Stoic *Oikeiōsis*", *Ancient Philosophy* **10** (1990), 221–42.
Bobzien, S. "Stoic Conceptions of Freedom and their Relation to Ethics", in *Bulletin of the Institute of Classical Studies* suppl. 68 ("Aristotle and After", R. Sorabji (ed.)) (1997), 71–89.
Brennan, T. "Reservation in Stoic Ethics", *Archiv für Geschichte der Philosophie* **82** (2000), 149–77.
Brouwer, R. "Sagehood and the Stoics", *Oxford Studies in Ancient Philosophy* **23** (2002), 181–224.

Engberg-Pedersen, T. *The Stoic Theory of Oikeiosis* (Aarhus: Aarhus University Press, 1990).

Frede, M. "The Stoic Doctrine of the Affectations of the Soul", in *The Norms of Nature: Studies in Hellenistic Ethics*, M. Schofield & G. Striker (eds), 93–110 (Cambridge: Cambridge University Press, 1986).

Inwood, B. "Goal and Target in Stoicism", *Journal of Philosophy* **83** (1986), 547–56.

Kerferd, G. B. "What Does the Wise Man Know?", in *The Stoics*, J. M. Rist (ed.), 125–36 (Berkeley, CA: University of California Press, 1978).

Kidd, I. G. "Stoic Intermediates and the End for Man", in *Problems in Stoicism*, A. A. Long (ed.), 150–72 (London: Athlone, 1971).

Long, A. A. "Carneades and the Stoic *telos*", *Phronesis* **12** (1967), 59–90.

Long, A. A. "The Logical Basis of Stoic Ethics", *Proceedings of the Aristotelian Society* (1970–71), 85–104.

Long, A. A. "Representation and the Self in Stoicism", in *Psychology*, S. Everson (ed.), 102–20 (Cambridge: Cambridge University Press, 1991).

Long, A. A. "The Stoic Concept of Evil", *Philosophical Quarterly* **18** (1968), 329–43.

Long, A. A. "Stoic Eudaimonism", *Proceedings of the Boston Colloquium in Ancient Philosophy* **4** (1988), 77–101.

Sorabji, R. *Emotion and Peace of Mind: From Stoic Agitation to Christian Temptation* (Oxford: Oxford University Press, 2000).

Sorabji, R. "Is Stoic Philosophy Helpful as Psychotherapy?", *Bulletin of the Institute of Classical Studies* suppl. 68 ("Aristotle and After", R. Sorabji (ed.)) (1997), 197–209.

Strange, S. K. "The Stoics on the Voluntariness of the Passions", in *Stoicism: Traditions and Transformations*, S. K. Strange & J. Zupko (eds), 32–51 (Cambridge: Cambridge University Press, 2004).

Striker, G. "Antipater, or The Art of Living", in *The Norms of Nature: Studies in Hellenistic Ethics*, M. Schofield & G. Striker (eds), 185–204 (Cambridge: Cambridge University Press, 1986).

Striker, G. "Following Nature: A Study in Stoic Ethics", *Oxford Studies in Ancient Philosophy* **9** (1991), 1–73.

Tsekourakis, D. *Studies in the Terminology of Early Stoic Ethics*, Hermes Einzelschriften 32 (Wiesbaden: Steiner, 1974).

Williams, B. "Stoic Philosophy and the Emotions: Reply to Richard Sorabji", *Bulletin of the Institute of Classical Studies* suppl. 68 ("Aristotle and After", R. Sorabji (ed.)) (1997), 211–13.

Politics

For Stoic politics see the important study by M. Schofield, *The Stoic Idea of the City* (Cambridge: Cambridge University Press, 1991), plus:

Baldry, H. C. "Zeno's Ideal State", *Journal of Hellenic Studies* **79** (1959), 3–15.

Devine, F. E. "Stoicism on the Best Regime", *Journal of the History of Ideas* **31** (1970), 323–36.

Obbink, D. & P. A. Vander Waerdt, "Diogenes of Babylon: The Stoic Sage in the City of Fools", *Greek, Roman, and Byzantine Studies* **32** (1991), 355–96.

Reydams-Schils, G. "Human Bonding and *Oikeiosis* in Roman Stoicism", *Oxford Studies in Ancient Philosophy* **22** (2002), 221–51.

Vander Waerdt, P. A. "Zeno's *Republic* and the Origins of Natural Law", in *The Socratic Movement*, P. A. Vander Waerdt (ed.), 272–308 (Ithaca, NY: Cornell University Press, 1994).

Later influence

The only single volume study of the Stoic legacy from antiquity to the present day is M. Spanneut, *Permanence du Stoïcisme: De Zénon à Malraux* (Gembloux: Duculot, 1973). For Seneca's later impact see G. M. Ross, "Seneca's Philosophical Influence", in *Seneca*, C. D. N. Costa (ed.), 116–65 (London: Routledge & Kegan Paul, 1974). Note also a recent collection of essays: S. K. Strange & J. Zupko (eds), *Stoicism: Traditions and Transformations* (Cambridge: Cambridge University Press, 2004).

For Stoicism in late antiquity see:

Colish, M. L. *The Stoic Tradition from Antiquity to the Early Middle Ages*, 2 vols (Leiden: Brill, 1985).

Graeser, A. *Plotinus and the Stoics: A Preliminary Study* (Leiden: Brill, 1972).

Sorabji, R. "Stoic First Movements in Christianity", in *Stoicism: Traditions and Transformations*, S. K. Strange & J. Zupko (eds), 95–107 (Cambridge: Cambridge University Press, 2004).

Spanneut, M. *Le Stoicisme des pères de l'Eglise: De Clément de Rome à Clément d'Alexandrie* (Paris: Seuil, 1957).

Witt, R. E. "The Plotinian Logos and its Stoic Basis", *Classical Quarterly* **25** (1931), 103–11.

For Simplicius' commentary on Epictetus see Simplicius, *Commentaire sur le Manuel d'Épictète*, I. Hadot (ed.) (Leiden: Brill, 1996) and Simplicius, *On Epictetus Handbook*, 2 vols, T. Brennan & C. Brittain (trans.) (London: Duckworth, 2002).

The question of the extent to which Stoicism influenced Arabic philosophy is contentious. For a study claiming a wide influence see F. Jadaane, *L'influence du Stoïcisme sur la pensée musulmane* (Beirut: El-Machreq, 1968). For a more cautious view see D. Gutas, "Pre-Plotinian Philosophy in Arabic (Other than Platonism and Aristotelianism): A Review of the Sources", *ANRW* II.36.7 (1993), 4939–73. The text by al-Kindi that is said to draw upon Epictetus is translated in G. Jayyusi-Lehn, "The Epistle of Ya'qub ibn Ishaq al-Kindi on the Device for Dispelling Sorrows", *British Journal of Middle Eastern Studies* **29** (2002), 121–35.

For a survey of Stoicism in the Middle Ages see G. Verbeke, *The Presence of Stoicism in Medieval Thought* (Washington, DC: The Catholic University of America Press, 1983). Note also:

Ebbesen, S. "Where Were the Stoics in the Late Middle Ages?", in *Stoicism: Traditions and Transformations*, S. K. Strange & J. Zupko (eds), 108–31 (Cambridge: Cambridge University Press, 2004).

Lapidge, M. "The Stoic Inheritance", in *A History of Twelfth-Century Western Philosophy*, P. Dronke (ed.), 81–112 (Cambridge: Cambridge University Press, 1988).

Reynolds, L. D. "The Medieval Tradition of Seneca's *Dialogues*", *Classical Quarterly* **18** (1968), 355–72.

Reynolds, L. D. *The Medieval Tradition of Seneca's Letters* (Oxford: Oxford University Press, 1965).

Peter Abelard's dialogue is in J. Marenbon & G. Orlandi, *Peter Abelard, Collationes* (Oxford: Clarendon Press, 2001), and his relation to Stoicism is discussed in C. Normore, "Abelard's Stoicism and Its Consequences", in *Stoicism: Traditions and Transformations*, S. K. Strange and J. Zupko (eds), 132–47 (Cambridge: Cambridge University Press, 2004).

For a survey of Stoicism in the Renaissance see J. Kraye, "Stoicism in the Renaissance from Petrarch to Lipsius", in *Grotius and the Stoa*, H. W. Blom & L. C. Winkel (eds), 21–45 (Assen: Royal Van Gorcum, 2004). Note also W. J. Bouwsma, "The Two Faces of Humanism: Stoicism and Augustinianism in Renaissance Thought", in *Itinerarium Italicum*, H. A. Oberman & T. A. Brady (eds), 3–60 (Leiden: Brill, 1975), plus the following specific studies and texts:

Battles, F. L. & A. M. Hugo, *Calvin's Commentary on Seneca's De Clementia* (Leiden: Brill, 1969).

Kraye, J. "Angelo Poliziano", in *Cambridge Translations of Renaissance Philosophical Texts, Volume I: Moral Philosophy*, J. Kraye (ed.), 192–9 (Cambridge: Cambridge University Press, 1997).

Moreau, P.-F. "Calvin: fascination et critique du stoïcisme", in *Le stoïcisme au XVIe et au XVIIe siècle*, P.-F. Moreau (ed.), 51–64 (Paris: Albin Michel, 1999).

Oliver, R. P. *Niccolo Perotti's Version of The Enchiridion of Epictetus* (Urbana, IL: University of Illinois Press, 1954).

Panizza, L. A. "Stoic Psychotherapy in the Middle Ages and Renaissance: Petrarch's *De Remediis*", in *Atoms, Pneuma, and Tranquillity: Epicurean and Stoic Themes in European Thought*, M. J. Osler (ed.), 39–65 (Cambridge: Cambridge University Press, 1991).

Partee, C. *Calvin and Classical Philosophy* (Leiden: Brill, 1977), ch. 8.
Randall, J. H. "Pietro Pomponazzi", in *The Renaissance Philosophy of Man*, E. Cassirer, P. O. Kristeller & J. H. Randall (eds), 257–79 (Chicago, IL: University of Chicago Press, 1948).

Justus Lipsius' *De Constantia* is forthcoming in English in Justus Lipsius, *On Constancy*, introduction by J. Sellars, J. Stradling (trans.) (Bristol: Bristol Phoenix Press, 2006). For studies of Lipsius and Neostoicism see:

Anderton, B. "A Stoic of Louvain: Justus Lipsius", in his *Sketches from a Library Window*, 10–30 (Cambridge: Heffer, 1922).
Cooper, J. M. "Justus Lipsius and the Revival of Stoicism in Late Sixteenth-Century Europe", in *New Essays on the History of Autonomy*, N. Brender & L. Krasnoff (eds), 7–29 (Cambridge: Cambridge University Press, 2004).
Deitz, L. & A. Wiehe-Deitz, "Francisco de Quevedo", in *Cambridge Translations of Renaissance Philosophical Texts, Volume 1: Moral Philosophy*, J. Kraye (ed.), 210–25 (Cambridge: Cambridge University Press, 1997).
Du Vair, G. *The Moral Philosophie of the Stoicks*, introduction by R. Kirk, T. James (trans.) (New Brunswick, NJ: Rutgers University Press, 1951).
Ettinghausen, H. *Francisco de Quevedo and the Neostoic Movement* (Oxford: Oxford University Press, 1972).
Lagrée, J. "Constancy and Coherence", in *Stoicism: Traditions and Transformations*, S. K. Strange & J. Zupko (eds), 148–76 (Cambridge: Cambridge University Press, 2004).
Lagrée, J. "Juste Lipse: destins et Providence", in *Le stoïcisme au XVIe et au XVIIe siècle*, P.-F. Moreau (ed.), 77–93 (Paris: Albin Michel, 1999).
Lagrée, J. *Juste Lipse et la restauration du stoïcisme* (Paris: Vrin, 1994).
Lagrée, J. "La vertu stoïcienne de constance", in *Le stoïcisme au XVIe et au XVIIe siècle*, P.-F. Moreau (ed.), 94–116 (Paris: Albin Michel, 1999).
Levi, A. H. T. "The Relationship of Stoicism and Scepticism: Justus Lipsius", in *Humanism and Early Modern Philosophy*, J. Kraye & M. W. F. Stone (eds), 91–106 (London: Routledge, 2000).
Marin, M. "L'influence de Sénèque sur Juste Lipse", in *Juste Lipse: 1547–1606*, A. Gerlo (ed.), 119–26 (Brussels: University Press, 1988).
Méchoulan, H. "Quevedo stoïcien?", in *Le stoïcisme au XVIe et au XVIIe siècle*, P.-F. Moreau (ed.), 189–203 (Paris: Albin Michel, 1999).
Morford, M. *Stoics and Neostoics: Rubens and the Circle of Lipsius* (Princeton, NJ: Princeton University Press, 1991).
Morford, M. "Towards an Intellectual Biography of Justus Lipsius – Pieter Paul Rubens", in *Bulletin de l'Institut Historique Belge de Rome* **68** ("The World of Justus Lipsius: A Contribution Towards his Intellectual Biography", M. Laureys (ed.)) (1998), 387–403.
Oestreich, G. *Neostoicism and the Early Modern State*, D. McLintock (trans.) (Cambridge: Cambridge University Press, 1982).

Papy, J. "Lipsius' (Neo-)Stoicism: Constancy between Christian Faith and Stoic Virtue", in *Grotius and the Stoa*, H. W. Blom & L. C. Winkel (eds), 47–71 (Assen: Royal Van Gorcum, 2004).

Saunders, J. L. *Justus Lipsius: The Philosophy of Renaissance Stoicism* (New York: The Liberal Arts Press, 1955).

Young, R. V. "Justus Lipsius", in *Cambridge Translations of Renaissance Philosophical Texts, Volume 1: Moral Philosophy*, J. Kraye (ed.), 200–209 (Cambridge: Cambridge University Press, 1997).

Zanta, L. *La renaissance du stoïcisme au XVIe siècle* (Paris: Champion, 1914).

For the impact of Stoicism on the literature of this period see:

Barbour, R. *English Epicures and Stoics: Ancient Legacies in Early Stuart Culture* (Amherst, MA: University of Massachusetts Press, 1998).

Monsarrat, G. D. *Light from the Porch: Stoicism and English Renaissance Literature* (Paris: Didier-Érudition, 1984).

Shifflett, A. *Stoicism, Politics, and Literature in the Age of Milton: War and Peace Reconciled* (Cambridge: Cambridge University Press, 1998).

For Stoicism and seventeenth-century philosophy see:

Brooke, C. "Stoicism and Anti-Stoicism in the Seventeenth Century", in *Grotius and the Stoa*, H. W. Blom & L. C. Winkel (eds), 93–115 (Assen: Royal Van Gorcum, 2004).

Debrabander, F. "Psychotherapy and Moral Perfection: Spinoza and the Stoics on the Prospect of Happiness", in *Stoicism: Traditions and Transformations*, S. K. Strange & J. Zupko (eds), 198–213 (Cambridge: Cambridge University Press, 2004).

James, S. "Spinoza the Stoic", in *The Rise of Modern Philosophy*, T. Sorell (ed.), 289–316 (Oxford: Clarendon Press, 1993).

Kristeller, P. O. "Stoic and Neoplatonic Sources of Spinoza's *Ethics*", *History of European Ideas* 5 (1984), 1–15.

Rutherford, D. "Leibniz and the Stoics: The Consolations of Theodicy", in *The Problem of Evil in Early Modern Philosophy*, E. J. Kremer & M. J. Latzer (eds), 138–64 (Toronto: University of Toronto Press, 2001).

Rutherford, D. "*Patience sans Espérance*: Leibniz's Critique of Stoicism", in *Hellenistic and Early Modern Philosophy*, J. Miller & B. Inwood (eds), 62–89 (Cambridge: Cambridge University Press, 2003).

Rutherford, D. "On the Happy Life: Descartes vis-à-vis Seneca", in *Stoicism: Traditions and Transformations*, S. K. Strange & J. Zupko (eds), 177–97 (Cambridge: Cambridge University Press, 2004).

For Stoicism in the eighteenth century see:

Rand, B. *The Life, Unpublished Letters, and Philosophical Regimen of Anthony, Earl of Shaftesbury* (London: Sawn Sonnenschein, 1900).

Reich, K. "Kant and Greek Ethics II: Kant and Panaetius", *Mind* **48** (1939), 446–63.
Roche, K. F. *Rousseau: Stoic and Romantic* (London: Methuen, 1974).
Schneewind, J. B. "Kant and Stoic Ethics", in *Aristotle, Kant, and the Stoics*, S. Engstrom & J. Whiting (eds), 285–301 (Cambridge: Cambridge University Press, 1996).
Stewart, M. A. "The Stoic Legacy in the Early Scottish Enlightenment", in *Atoms, Pneuma, and Tranquillity*, M. J. Osler (ed.), 273–96 (Cambridge: Cambridge University Press, 1991).
Tiffany, E. A. "Shaftesbury as Stoic", *Publications of the Modern Language Association of America* **38** (1923), 642–84.

Further material can be found on Stoicism in the early modern period in J. Miller & B. Inwood (eds), *Hellenistic and Early Modern Philosophy* (Cambridge: Cambridge University Press, 2003).

For a discussion of Hegel's attitude towards Stoicism see:

Gourinat, M. "Hegel et le stoïcisme", in *Les Stoïciens*, G. Romeyer Dherbey & J.-B. Gourinat (eds), 523–44 (Paris: Vrin, 2005).

Nietzsche's complex relationship with the Stoa is considered in:

Elveton, R. O. "Nietzsche's Stoicism: The Depths are Inside", in *Nietzsche and Antiquity*, P. Bishop (ed.), 192–203 (Rochester, NY: Camden House, 2004).
Nussbaum, M. C. "Pity and Mercy: Nietzsche's Stoicism", in *Nietzsche, Genealogy, Morality: Essays on Nietzsche's Genealogy of Morals*, R. Schacht (ed.), 139–67 (Berkeley, CA: University of California Press, 1994).
Schatzki, T. R. "Ancient and Naturalistic Themes in Nietzsche's Ethics", *Nietzsche Studien* **23** (1994), 146–67.

For Stoicism in twentieth-century French thought see:

Bénatouïl, T. "Deux usages du stoïcisme: Deleuze, Foucault", in *Foucault et la philosophie antique*, F. Gros & C. Lévy (eds), 17–49 (Paris: Kimé, 2003).
Bowden, S. "Deleuze et les Stoïciens: une logique de l'événement", *Bulletin de la Société Américaine de Philosophie de Langue Française* **15** (2005), 72–97.
Davidson, A. "Ethics as Ascetics: Foucault, the History of Ethics, and Ancient Thought", in *The Cambridge Companion to Foucault*, G. Gutting (ed.), 115–40 (Cambridge: Cambridge University Press, 1994).
Eribon, D. *Michel Foucault*, B. Wing (trans.) (Cambridge, MA: Harvard University Press, 1991), ch. 22.
Hadot, P. "Reflections on the Idea of the 'Cultivation of the Self'", in his *Philosophy as a Way of Life*, 206–13 (Oxford: Blackwell, 1995).
Jaffro, L. "Foucault et le stoïcisme", in *Foucault et la philosophie antique*, F. Gros & C. Lévy (eds), 51–83 (Paris: Kimé, 2003).

Simont, J. "Se vaincre soi-même plutôt que la fortune (Le stoïcisme chez Sartre et Deleuze)", in *Sartre en sa maturité*, 'Études sartriennes' VI, G. Idt (ed.), 175–91 (Paris: Université Paris X, 1995).

References

Annas, J. 1992. *Hellenistic Philosophy of Mind*. Berkeley, CA: University of California Press.

Arnold, E. V. 1911. *Roman Stoicism*. Cambridge: Cambridge University Press.

Baldry, H. C. 1959. "Zeno's Ideal State". *Journal of Hellenic Studies* **79**, 3–15.

Barnes, J. 1997. *Logic and the Imperial Stoa*. Leiden: Brill.

Battles, F. L. & Hugo, A. M. 1969. *Calvin's Commentary on Seneca's De Clementia*. Leiden: Brill.

Beck, L. W. 1969. *Early German Philosophy: Kant and his Predecessors*. Cambridge, MA: Harvard University Press.

Becker, L. C. 1998. *A New Stoicism*. Princeton, NJ: Princeton University Press.

Bocheński, I. M. 1951. *Ancient Formal Logic*. Amsterdam: North-Holland.

Boter, G. 1999. *The Encheiridion of Epictetus and its Three Christian Adaptations*. Leiden: Brill.

Bottin, F. *et al.* 1993. *Models of the History of Philosophy: From its Origins in the Renaissance to the "Historia Philosophica"*. Dordrecht: Kluwer.

Brooke, C. 2004. "Stoicism and Anti-Stoicism in the Seventeenth Century". In *Grotius and the Stoa*, H. W. Blom & L. C. Winkel (eds), 93–115. Assen: Royal Van Gorcum.

Brouwer, R. 2002. "Sagehood and the Stoics". *Oxford Studies in Ancient Philosophy* **23**, 181–224.

Brunschwig, J. 1988. "La théorie stoïcienne du genre suprême et l'ontologie platonicienne". In *Matter and Metaphysics*, J. Barnes & M. Mignucci (eds), 19–27. Naples: Bibliopolis. Published in English as "The Stoic Theory of the Supreme Genus and Platonic Ontology", in Brunschwig's *Papers in Hellenistic Philosophy*, 92–157 (Cambridge: Cambridge University Press, 1994).

Brunschwig, J. 2003. "Stoic Metaphysics". See Inwood (2003), 206–32.

Caston, V. 1999. "Something and Nothing: The Stoics on Concepts and Universals". *Oxford Studies in Ancient Philosophy* **17**, 145–213.

Cooper, J. M. 1999. "Posidonius on Emotions". In *Reason and Emotion*, 449–84. Princeton, NJ: Princeton University Press.

Demonet, M.-L. 1985. *Michel de Montaigne, Les Essais*. Paris: Presses Universitaires de France.

Dobbin, R. F. 1998. *Epictetus, Discourses, Book I*. Oxford: Clarendon Press.

Ebbesen, S. 2004. "Where Were the Stoics in the Late Middle Ages?". In *Stoicism: Traditions and Transformations*, S. K. Strange & J. Zupko (eds), 108–31. Cambridge: Cambridge University Press.

Enfield, W. 1819. *The History of Philosophy, from the Earliest Times to the Beginnings of the Present Century, Drawn up from Brucker's Historia Critica Philosophiae*, 2 vols. London: William Baynes.

Eribon, D. 1991. *Michel Foucault*, B. Wing (trans.). Cambridge, MA: Harvard University Press.

Fakhry, M. 1994. *Ethical Theories in Islam*, 2nd edn. Leiden: Brill.

Frede, M. 1983. "Stoics and Skeptics on Clear and Distinct Impressions". In *The Skeptical Tradition*, M. Burnyeat (ed.), 65–93. Berkeley, CA: University of California Press.

Frede, M. 1999. "Stoic Epistemology". In *The Cambridge History of Hellenistic Philosophy*, K. Algra, J. Barnes, J. Mansfeld & M. Schofield (eds), 295–322. Cambridge: Cambridge University Press.

Gigante, M. 1995. *Philodemus in Italy: The Books from Herculaneum*. Ann Arbor, MI: University of Michigan Press.

Gould, J. B. 1970. *The Philosophy of Chrysippus*. Leiden: Brill.

Goulet-Cazé, M.-O. 2003. *Les Kynica du stoïcisme*. Stuttgart: Franz Steiner Verlag.

Graeser, A. 1972. *Plotinus and the Stoics*. Leiden: Brill.

Gutas, D. 1993. "Pre-Plotinian Philosophy in Arabic (Other than Platonism and Aristotelianism): A Review of the Sources". *ANRW* II.36.7, 4939–73.

Hadot, P. 1998. *The Inner Citadel: The Meditations of Marcus Aurelius*, M. Chase (trans.). Cambridge, MA: Harvard University Press.

Hahm, D. E. 1977. *The Origins of Stoic Cosmology*. Columbus, OH: Ohio State University Press.

Hankinson, R. J. 2003. "Stoic Epistemology". See Inwood (2003), 59–84.

Ierodiakonou, K. 1999. "The Study of Stoicism: Its Decline and Revival". In *Topics in Stoic Philosophy*, K. Ierodiakonou (ed.), 1–22. Oxford: Clarendon Press.

Inwood, B. (ed.) 2003. *The Cambridge Companion to The Stoics*. Cambridge: Cambridge University Press.

Jadaane, F. 1968. *L'influence du Stoïcisme sur la pensée musulmane*. Beirut: El-Machreq.

Kneale, W. & M. Kneale 1962. *The Development of Logic*. Oxford: Clarendon Press.

Kraye, J. 1997. *Cambridge Translations of Renaissance Philosophical Texts, Volume I: Moral Philosophy*. Cambridge: Cambridge University Press.

La Mettrie, J. O. 1996. *Machine Man and Other Writings*, A. Thomson (trans.). Cambridge: Cambridge University Press.

Lapidge, M. 1973. "*Archai* and *Stoicheia*: A Problem in Stoic Cosmology". *Phronesis* **18**, 240–78.

Leibniz, G. W. 1989. *Philosophical Essays*, R. Ariew & D. Garber (trans.). Indianapolis, IN: Hackett.

Locke, J. 1975. *An Essay Concerning Human Understanding*. Oxford: Clarendon Press.

Long, A. A. 1970–71. "The Logical Basis of Stoic Ethics". *Proceedings of the Aristotelian Society* **71**, 85–104. Reprinted in his *Stoic Studies*, 134–55 (Cambridge: Cambridge University Press, 1996).

Long, A. A. 1988. "Socrates in Hellenistic Philosophy". *Classical Quarterly* **38**, 150–71. Reprinted in his *Stoic Studies*, 1–34 (Cambridge: Cambridge University Press, 1996).

Long, A. A. 1989. "Stoic Eudaimonism". *Proceedings of the Boston Area Colloquium in Ancient Philosophy* **4**, 77–101. Reprinted in his *Stoic Studies*, 179–201 (Cambridge: Cambridge University Press, 1996).

Long, A. A. 1993. "Hierocles on *Oikeiôsis* and Self-Perception", in *Hellenistic Philosophy: Vol. I*, K. J. Boudouris (ed.), 93–104 (Athens: International Center for Greek Philosophy and Culture, 1993). Reprinted in his *Stoic Studies*, 250–63 (Cambridge: Cambridge University Press, 1996).

MacKendrick, P. 1989. *The Philosophical Books of Cicero*. London: Duckworth.

Marenbon, J. & G. Orlandi 2001. *Peter Abelard, Collationes*. Oxford: Clarendon Press.

Marx, K. & F. Engels 1964. *The German Ideology*, C. Dutt (trans.). Moscow: Progress Publishers.

Nietzsche, F. 1974. *The Gay Science*, W. Kaufmann (trans.). New York: Vintage.

Nietzsche, F. 1982. *Daybreak*, R. J. Hollingdale (trans.). Cambridge: Cambridge University Press.

Nietzsche, F. 1986. *Human, All Too Human*, R. J. Hollingdale (trans.). Cambridge: Cambridge University Press.

Nietzsche, F. 1990. *Beyond Good and Evil*, R. J. Hollingdale (trans.). Harmondsworth: Penguin.

Nussbaum, M. C. 1994. "Pity and Mercy: Nietzsche's Stoicism". In *Nietzsche, Genealogy, Morality: Essays on Nietzsche's Genealogy of Morals*, R. Schacht (ed.), 139–67. Berkeley, CA: University of California Press.

Nussbaum, M. C. 2001. *Upheavals of Thought: The Intelligence of the Emotions*. Cambridge: Cambridge University Press, 2001.

Obbink, D. 1996. *Philodemus, On Piety, Part 1*. Oxford: Clarendon Press.

Obbink, D. & P. A. Vander Waerdt 1991. "Diogenes of Babylon: The Stoic Sage in the City of Fools". *Greek, Roman, and Byzantine Studies* **32**, 355–96.

Oliver, R. P. 1954. *Niccolo Perotti's Version of The Enchiridion of Epictetus*. Urbana, IL: University of Illinois Press, 1954.

Panizza, L. A. 1991. "Stoic Psychotherapy in the Middle Ages and Renaissance: Petrarch's *De Remediis*". In *Atoms, Pneuma, and Tranquillity: Epicurean and Stoic Themes in European Thought*, M. J. Osler (ed.), 39–65. Cambridge: Cambridge University Press.

Rand, B. 1900. *The Life, Unpublished Letters, and Philosophical Regimen of Anthony, Earl of Shaftesbury*. London: Sawn Sonnenschein.

Randall, J. H. 1948. "Pietro Pomponazzi". In *The Renaissance Philosophy of Man*, E. Cassirer, P. O. Kristeller & J. H. Randall (eds), 257–79. Chicago, IL: University of Chicago Press.

Rist, J. M. 1969. *Stoic Philosophy*. Cambridge: Cambridge University Press.

Rist, J. M. 1989. "Seneca and Stoic Orthodoxy". *ANRW* II.36.3, 1993–2012.

Roche, K. F. 1974. *Rousseau: Stoic and Romantic*. London: Methuen.

Rosenmeyer, T. G. 1989. *Senecan Drama and Stoic Cosmology*. Berkeley, CA: University of California Press.

Ross, G. M. 1974. "Seneca's Philosophical Influence". In *Seneca*, C. D. N. Costa (ed.), 116–65. London: Routledge & Kegan Paul.

Sambursky, S. 1959. *Physics of the Stoics*. London: Routledge & Kegan Paul.

Sandbach, F. H. 1930. "*Ennoia* and *Prolēpsis* in the Stoic Theory of Knowledge". *Classical Quarterly* **24**, 44–51. Reprinted in *Problems in Stoicism*, A. A. Long (ed.), 22–37 (London: Athlone, 1971).

Sartre, J.-P. 1984. *War Diaries: Notebooks from a Phoney War*, Q. Hoare (trans.). London: Verso.

Saunders, J. L. 1955. *Justus Lipsius: The Philosophy of Renaissance Stoicism*. New York: Liberal Arts Press.

Schatzki, T. R. 1994. "Ancient and Naturalistic Themes in Nietzsche's Ethics". *Nietzsche Studien* **23**, 146–67.

Schofield, M. 1991. *The Stoic Idea of the City*. Cambridge: Cambridge University Press.

Schofield, M. 2003. "Stoic Ethics". See Inwood (2003), 233–56.

Scott, D. 1988. "Innatism and the Stoa". *Proceedings of the Cambridge Philological Society* **34**, 123–53.

Screech, M. A. 1991. *Michel de Montaigne: The Complete Essays*. Harmondsworth: Penguin.

Sedley, D. 2002. "The Origins of Stoic God". In *Traditions of Theology*, D. Frede & A. Laks (eds), 41–83. Leiden: Brill.

Sedley, D. 2003. "The School, from Zeno to Arius Didymus". See Inwood (2003), 7–32.

Sellars, J. 2003. *The Art of Living: The Stoics on the Nature and Function of Philosophy*. Aldershot: Ashgate.

Sorabji, R. 1988. *Matter, Space, and Motion*. London: Duckworth.

Sorabji, R. 2000. *Emotion and Peace of Mind: From Stoic Agitation to Christian Temptation*. Oxford: Oxford University Press.

Sorabji, R. 2004. *The Philosophy of the Commentators, 200–600 AD: 2. Physics*. London: Duckworth.

Stirner, M. 1993. *The Ego and Its Own*, S. Byington (trans.). London: Rebel Press.

Todd, R. B. 1973. "The Stoic Common Notions: A Re-examination and Reinterpretation". *Symbolae Osloenses* **48**, 47–75.

Todd, R. B. 1978. "Monism and Immanence: The Foundations of Stoic Physics". In *The Stoics*, J. M. Rist (ed.), 137–60. Berkeley, CA: University of California Press.

Index of passages

Fin. 3.20 (= LS 59 D = IG II-102) 120, 128
Fin. 3.21 (= LS 59 D = IG II-102) 109
Fin. 3.31 (= LS 64 A = IG II-102) 128
Fin. 3.33 (= LS 60 D = IG II-102) 77–8
Fin. 3.41 113
Fin. 3.44 112
Fin. 3.45–8 112
Fin. 3.62 (= LS 57 F = IG II-103) 131
Fin. 3.63 (= LS 57 F = IG II-103) 131
Fin. 3.74 53
Fin. 3.75 36
ND 1.41 64
ND 2.21 (= IG II-23) 93
ND 2.22 (= LS 54 G = IG II-23) 94
ND 2.35 (= IG II-23) 126
ND 3.35 87
Parad. 2 39
Parad. 35 37
Pro Murena 62 39
Tusc. 1.79 9
Tusc. 3.1–21 34
Tusc. 3.6 35
Tusc. 3.10–21 36
Tusc. 3.10 37
Tusc. 4.14 117

Cleanthes
Hymn (= LS 54 I = IG II-21) 7, 91–2

Clement of Alexandria
Stromata 4.26 132

Cleomedes
Cael. 1.1 96
Cael. 1.1.43–54 (= LS 49 G) 97
Cael. 1.1.104–11 97
Cael. 1.5 96

Damascius
Philosophical History 46d 135

Diogenes Laertius
6.63 129

7.2–3 (= IG II-1) 4
7.4 (= IG II-1) 6
7.28 (= IG II-1) 109
7.39 (= LS 26 B = IG II-2) 42, 44
7.40 (= LS 26 B = IG II-2) 42–3, 43
7.41 (= LS 26 B = IG II-2) 43
7.41–3 (= LS 31 A = IG II-3) 42, 55
7.45 (= IG II-3) 65
7.50 (= LS 39 A = IG II-3) 65, 68
7.51 (= LS 39 A = IG II-3) 65
7.53 (= LS 39 D = IG II-3) 77, 78
7.54 (= LS 40 A = IG II-3) 71, 76
7.55–6 (= LS 33 H = IG II-3) 61
7.61 (= LS 30 C = IG II-3) 86
7.63 (= LS 33 F = IG II-3) 62
7.65 (= LS 34 A = IG II-3) 58
7.69–74 (= LS 34 K, 35 A = IG II-3) 58
7.85 (= LS 57 A = IG II-94) 107, 107–8
7.87 (= IG II-94) 125
7.87–8 (= IG II-94) 125
7.89 (= IG II-94) 77, 122, 124
7.108 (= IG II-94) 120
7.111 (= IG II-94) 115
7.116 (= IG II-94) 118
7.128 (= IG II-94) 9
7.134 (= LS 44 B = IG II-20) 86, 88
7.138 (= LS 47 O = IG II-20) 100
7.140 (= IG II-20) 96
7.142 (= IG II-20) 9, 93, 94, 97, 98, 99
7.143 (= IG II-20) 94
7.149 (= IG II-20) 100
7.151 (= LS 48 A = IG II-20) 89
7.157 (= IG II-20) 105
7.159 (= IG II-20) 105
7.160 (= LS 31 N = IG II-1) 6, 113
7.161 6
7.170 7
7.174 29
7.176 109
7.183 (= IG II-1) 7
7.187 (= IG II-1) 85
7.200 (= LS 32 I) 64

Index

on theory and practice 33, 45–6

Nature 91–5, 126–8; *see also* living
according to Nature
Neoplatonists, Neoplatonism 24–5,
25–6, 100, 135–6
Neostoics, Neostoicism 144–5, 147,
148, 153, 156
Nero (the emperor) 12, 14, 15, 109,
149
Nicopolis 15–16
Nietzsche, F. 151–2, 155
nominalism 84
no one argument 85
Nussbaum, M. 154

Olympiodorus 136, 138
ontology 2, 3, 61, 62–3, 81–6

Painted Stoa 1, 2, 5
Panaetius of Rhodes 9–10, 11, 25,
150
rejected conflagration 9, 99
on the Stoic sage 41
pantheism 91, 99
papyrus (texts surviving on) 8, 18
Pascal, B. 3, 145
Paul (St) 13, 138
peculiarly qualified 86
periodic destruction of the world *see*
eternal recurrence
Peripatetics *see* Aristotle, Aristotelianism
Perotti, N. 140
Persaeus 6
Persius 2, 13
Petrarch (Francesco Petrarca) 139–40
Philo (pupil of Stilpo) 56
Philodemus 40
philosophy
analogy with medicine 34–5, 48,
124, 140, 152
and philosophical discourse 44–52
Stoic conception of 26–9, 31–6, 48

three areas of study (*topoi*) 50–52
three parts of 42–4, 50, 52–4
Philostratus 14
physics 51, 91–5
place 83
Plato, Platonism 5, 9, 11, 12, 21, 23,
26, 29, 122, 130, 132, 136, 140,
150, 152, 155, 156
his Demiurge 91
on expertise versus knack 121–2
on ontology 81–3, 85
on the soul 10, 22, 120
Platonic Ideas, Forms 84–6
Plotinus 26, 93, 95, 136
Plutarch 1, 8, 19, 21, 30, 39, 43, 44,
129–30
pneuma
as active principle 87, 88, 90, 91, 92,
97, 98, 103
degrees of tension 91, 104–5
as human soul 104–6
Polemo 5, 87
Politian (Angelo Poliziano) 140
politics 129–33
Pomponazzi, P. 140–41
Porphyry 25, 135, 136, 137, 138
Posidonius 10–11, 19, 20, 25, 94
on emotions 119–20
on the parts of philosophy 43, 53
on the soul 10, 22, 119–20
Praxagoras 105–6
preconception 76–8
principles 86–90, 99, 104
providence 92, 99–104, 152
psychology 104–6; *see also* soul
Pyrrho, Pyrrhonism 22, 73, 150

Quevedo, F. de 144

rationality 108–9, 110–11
Renaissance 3, 18, 139–41, 156
Rhodes 10, 20
Rome, Roman 2, 8, 9, 13, 14, 15, 37–8,
39, 109, 132, 133